THE
NARROW
SEA

THE
NARROW
SEA

Barrier, bridge and gateway
to the world – the history
of the English Channel

Peter Unwin

review

First published in 2003 by REVIEW
a division of Headline Book Publishing

10 9 8 7 6 5 4 3 2 1

Cataloguing in Publication Data is available from the British Library

ISBN 0 7472 4436 7

Typeset in Bell MT by Avon DataSet Ltd,
Bidford-on-Avon, Warwickshire

Designed by Ben Cracknell

Printed and bound in Great Britain by
Mackays of Chatham plc, Chatham, Kent

HEADLINE BOOK PUBLISHING
A division of Hodder Headline
338 Euston Road
London NW1 3BH

www.reviewbooks.co.uk
www.hodderheadline.com

For my daughter Jo

CONTENTS

TEXT PERMISSIONS

WHY THE CHANNEL MATTERS

Beside its European neighbours – the Mediterranean and the Black Sea, the North Sea and the Baltic – the English Channel seems an insignificant piece of water. It is famously 21 miles wide at its narrowest: on a good day Frenchmen can see the cliffs of Dover, and Englishmen can see Cap Gris Nez. Even at its widest, the Channel is a mere 100 miles across; it stretches 300 miles from end to end and it is less than 30,000 square miles in extent. Its very names suggest the domestically diminutive, for 'Channel' derives from the Dutch 'canal' and the French 'Manche' from its sleeve-like shape. Yet the Channel tells a historical tale as complicated as the Mediterranean or Baltic, or indeed the Atlantic Ocean, and it has as great a psychological significance. From every point of view, the English Channel matters.

To start with, it is something far greater than the greatest of rivers. To cross it was a major enterprise for early and medieval man. It has frustrated many invaders. Even today it can inflict nasty surprises on anyone who embarks improvidently on its waters. No one has yet come near to throwing a bridge across the English Channel, and it was 200 years before the eighteenth-century conception of a tunnel under it came to fulfilment. The prevailing winds blow into it from the west, out of the wide Atlantic. Throughout history they have complicated navigation and dictated naval strategy, and when they brew up into hurricanes they bring destruction to Channel shipping and the Channel coasts. Tides too are powerful and their patterns complicate everything from navigation to the efforts of cross-Channel swimmers. They play tricks, and in places bestow benefits, as for example in the way a flood tide in the western Channel is counterbalanced by an ebb in the eastern, so that a fortunate port in the middle like Southampton, tucked away behind the Isle of Wight, enjoys unusually prolonged high tides.

Like its winds, the Channel's currents come from the west. Over the centuries they have scoured the coasts, bringing fine sand to the French beaches and pebbles to the English, and piling up great barriers such as Dorset's Chesil Bank along the shore. Many of these coasts have advanced seawards over the centuries. Others are still yielding to the steady battering of the sea. But ever since the ancient ice cap receded, the land sank, the sea level rose and seas first broke through to create the Straits of Dover and make Britain an island, the broader structure of the coasts has remained constant. The cliffs of Dover face Blanc Nez and Gris Nez across the straits, carved from the same chalk. The wilder cliffs of Devon and Cornwall face those of Brittany. Elsewhere the coasts are gentler, with lower-lying country punctuated by the occasional drowned lagoon and the mouths of little rivers.

These low-lying coasts and gaps in the cliffs provide the essential conditions for the establishment of ports, more numerous on the English side. The first people to use them were the Channel's fishermen, but traders came to some of them before the beginnings of recorded history. Little ships have always slipped across between Britain and France, for even the early ones were capable of making a Channel crossing. Now Dover and Calais have most of the cross-Channel traffic, handling more business than any other ports in Britain or France. In the same way, Southampton and Le Havre grew to become the termini of the great transatlantic liners. Plymouth, Portsmouth and Cherbourg became naval bases. Falmouth, Plymouth, Dunkirk, Boulogne and St Malo made names for themselves as the home ports of explorers and privateers. And from every creek and half-sheltered beach the fishermen put to sea.

The Seine is the only river of any note that empties into the Channel. The Loire and the Severn reach the sea away around the capes of Brittany and Cornwall; and the Rhine and Scheldt, like the Thames, empty into the North Sea beyond the North Foreland and Ostend. Yet the importance of these river mouths to our story is so great that there is a historical argument for redefining the Channel more expansively than a geographer would, so as to embrace all of them. In the same way, there is a case for seeing the Channel extending out beyond Brittany and the Scilly Isles into the Western Approaches, where homecoming ships felt their way towards the Channel and where so many battles for control of the narrow seas have been fought. But on the map the geographical limits of the Channel are clear. To square this particular circle, I have abandoned the search for consistency. The very title of this book permits a modest ambiguity, and in its pages you will find the expression 'the Channel' used in a geographer's sense or a historian's as circumstances require.

Geographers and historians, like strategists, geologists, businessmen and mariners, have been thinking and writing about the Channel for centuries, each of them in search of what is its true essence for their particular discipline. In the process, the simple words 'the English Channel' have been burdened with significance and symbolic baggage that have become material reality. Some of these particular inter-pretations are worth isolating, before we turn to the chronicle of the Channel.

In the mood that is most familiar to the British reader, the English Channel stands for the sea as defence and demarcation. This mood sees the Channel above everything else as the obstacle that kept invaders out of Britain and made island and islanders different from the continent and fellow Europeans. Repeatedly in history this has seemed the very essence of the Channel, giving it an existential significance for Britain and the British. Englishmen from Shakespeare to Winston Churchill and Englishwomen from Elizabeth I to Vera Lynn have celebrated this face of the Channel. It is an interpretation to which a certain kind of Briton still clings when he finds himself faced with such continental challenges as illegal immigrants, the Channel Tunnel, the euro or the European sausage.

In another mood the Channel symbolises something quite as significant as this, and yet its polar opposite. This view sees the waters between Britain and France not as an obstacle but as a link between mainland and island, a saltwater highway that has borne shiploads of settlers, missionaries, merchants, refugees and conquerors back and forth throughout history. This is the highway that brought the forebears of nearly all today's Britons to Britain and, after millennia of to-ings and fro-ings by Celts, Romans, Angles and Saxons, Vikings and Normans, Dutchmen, Huguenots, Jews and east European refugees, carried the Allied armada to the Normandy invasion beaches in 1944. On this view the Channel, far from dividing, binds Britain and the continent together, in a European whole united by historical experience and present-day advantage, made richer by the diversity of its constituent parts.

The saltwater highway runs not just north–south but east–west as well. From the sixteenth century onwards, Channel seafaring became as much a blue water affair as the business of the narrow seas. French and English Channel ports got into the business of global exploration and gave the Channel its third significance. So French adventurers sailed away from Dieppe and St Malo, as English buccaneers sailed from Plymouth and Falmouth. The Lizard was the last the Pilgrim Fathers saw of Old England on their way to the New. Drake went round the world from Plymouth Hoe and sallied out from it to raid the Spanish Main. For two centuries Portsmouth Dockyard fitted out the ships of the Royal Navy, and merchantmen waited in the Downs for a rare easterly wind to take them down-Channel to the Atlantic on their way to the harbours of New England, China or the Coromandel coast of India.

These first three interpretations of the Channel come easily to Englishmen and Frenchmen who turn their minds to the subject. But the Channel has also a wider importance. To all the peoples of northern Europe, from the Dutch on the North Sea past the Danes at the mouth of the Baltic to the Russians at the far end of the Gulf of Finland, the English Channel is the gateway to the oceans of the world. They can, if they must, travel otherwise, past the Faeroes and Orkneys on their way to the Atlantic, but for most purposes the Channel route serves them better. For northern Europeans, the Straits of Dover are a gateway to the world. They have always been as significant for them as the Straits of Gibraltar are for the peoples of the Mediterranean.

The next meaning of the English Channel is different again. It concerns power. Throughout much of history, sovereignty over these waters has bestowed power and control not just over them and in the lands beside them, but throughout the known world. Here Julius Caesar nearly lost the reputation for god-like omnipotence which, preserved, carried him to the imperial purple. Here William the Conqueror united his new power in England with his old continental strength, building in the process an empire which, under later kings, extended from the Scottish border to the Pyrenees. Here the Armada failed to give the King of Spain the power to remake a Europe bound together by the universal Church. In the narrow seas England claimed the sovereignty of its Courts of Admiralty long before the Royal Navy made Britain the one power that ruled the waves. From the Channel, wrote one eighteenth-century First Lord of the Admiralty, 'all our exterior efforts are derived'.[1] On these coasts Napoleon and Hitler challenged British supremacy, and here in 1944 Britain, Canada and the United States set out to bring freedom to the continent on Anglo-Saxon terms. These are waters in which over the centuries world power has been nurtured.

The Channel has had a final broader significance for Europeans, and for people of European stock settled overseas. Here, as at the Pillars of Hercules, the Atlantic world has met the European. The process has been going on ever since Phoenician traders from the Mediterranean came out into the Atlantic and into the jaws of the Channel in search of Celtic tin. It has brought benefits to both Europe and the Atlantic, but history has never quite seen the end of the rivalry between the two.

The choice between Europe and the Atlantic has consumed much of British history. It has still not been unequivocally decided. Now the wider issue of the transatlantic relationship between Europe and the

United States comes to join it. Here let me plunge boldly into the forecasting business. Britons and other Europeans scarcely know it yet, but as they get deeper into the new century they will face a fundamental choice. Confronted with the American assumption of global hegemony, should they accept it and make the best of it? Or should they challenge it, seek to rival it? The choice is going to provide much of the stuff of the history of the twenty-first century. It flows directly from the age-old interaction, played out in large part in the Channel, between the Atlantic and Europe.

After the theory, a few facts. In their memorable spoof of English history, *1066 and All That*, Sellar and Yeatman announced that the ancient Britons whom the Romans conquered were 'only natives at that time'.[2] There was more to the Celts of northern France and southern Britain than that. They built Channel-side societies and explored the Channel's waters long before the coming of the Romans. Iron Age tribes of common Celtic origin occupied both shores of the Channel, trading, marrying, plotting and sometimes fighting together, making perhaps a single Celtic community of interrelated tribes at home beside the sea and comfortable upon it. When, on the other hand, Julius Caesar came to the French coast, his men thought it the edge of the world, and his two cross-Channel expeditions were for the Romans rare ventures into the realms of tides and tempests, which nearly came unstuck. But 100 years later came the Roman invasion under Claudius, and his settlement planted in Britain the Roman way of life long familiar on the other side of the Channel. In doing so, it made the Channel an internal sea of the Roman Empire, with Romans and Romanised Celtic noblemen leading similar civilised lives on the British side and the French.

In the fifth century, Rome departed and heathen Angles, Saxons and Jutes poured into the country just as the Franks were storming into Gaul. The first invaders famously arrived in that corner of Britain, Kent, to which the Romans had come first; and it was there that in the end, after long struggle between the invaders and the Britons whom Rome had deserted, St Augustine landed, bringing Roman Christianity to the country and so binding the island to the mainland once again.

Four hundred years later came a challenge to that unity from the heathen Norsemen. They came raiding in their separate war parties, as much along the Channel coast as the eastern shores of England. But then they settled, married and eventually converted to Christianity in both England and northern France. Their descendants established themselves in England and Normandy, separated by the Channel yet linked by cross-Channel connections. When Duke William defeated King Harold at Hastings, one heir of the Vikings overcame another, binding Normandy and England together in a cross-Channel kingdom that endured for a hundred years, producing laws, administrative systems and Norman cathedrals in common.

In the end, Normandy reverted to the French Crown, but the English kings held on to great areas of France for much of the Middle Ages. So down the years Englishman fought Frenchman in France and at sea and, when the French raided the Cinque Ports, in England itself, creating powerful myths about themselves, their enemies and the relationship between the two. Gradually, the English were driven from France, until in the end Mary Tudor, who has gone down in history as the most un-English of English queens, surrendered Calais, England's last stronghold in France.

The challenge of the Armada – Catholic Europe's 'Enterprise of England' – brought more symbolism, more national epic with it; and in the wake of its defeat Shakespeare took the lead in linking the idea of England's precious isolation behind the Channel with the very idea of Englishness. Those Channel defences faced new assaults. As the Spanish threat faded, there came a short challenge from the Dutch, fulfilled when Dutch William drove Catholic James from the throne of England. Then the ancient struggle with France resumed, with the Channel once again seen as the sure protection behind which England sheltered. One Louis succeeded another as the personification of the French threat to Britain, and after them came the revolutionary French and Napoleon himself – and even after a century of entente cordiale there are those who believe that the menace is not done with yet. But all these Frenchmen were held at bay by the Channel and by English sea power, which shut the French fleet up in its Channel and Atlantic ports, challenging Napoleon to embark the soldiers of the Army of the Coasts of the Ocean and attempt the invasion of England.

It is battles and heroism that have created the most vivid memories of history lessons, but the Channel has always had about it a peaceful everyday reality as well, a reality that did quite as much to shape England as memories of war. Contact between England and the continent has rarely been broken, and one side of the Channel has never failed to influence the other. The flow of ideas back and forth has been a fact of life for six millennia. So has cross-Channel trade, in everything from local fish and English wool to wine brought all the way from the Mediterranean to comfort Roman soldiers. Today the commodities may be different, but three times more British trade crosses the Channel and the North Sea than the Atlantic. Even war was rarely an absolute barrier to cross-Channel contact. Throughout the Napoleonic Wars, for example, both governments maintained a discreet but official ferry service to take influential individuals, sensitive messages, indispensable luxuries and released prisoners of war back and forth between Paris and London. The white cliffs of Dover have looked like teeth bared in defiance of invaders from before the time of Christ to the twentieth century, but more often they have extended a smiling welcome to more peaceable visitors.

For another century after Waterloo, therefore, while the English and the French went on watching each other edgily across the Channel, spasmodically throwing up fortifications against imagined dangers of invasion, they welcomed each other's products and ideas and found refreshment in each other's company. The nineteenth century saw the development of cross-Channel communications: boat trains that ever more reliably linked London and Paris, the cross-Channel telegraph, Captain Webb the swimmer, Louis Blériot the flyer, even attempts at tunnel-building. Gradually the two countries edged towards political as well as personal friendship.

Finally, the twentieth century saw the apogee of two Channel stories: as the stretch of water that linked friendly neighbours and at the same time as the ultimate guarantor of British identity and security. In 1904

Britain and France committed themselves to the entente cordiale which, ten years later, brought a British Expeditionary Force to France. For four years and three months, until Germany sued for an armistice, British troops held their sector of the Western Front, a line running south from the North Sea coast just inside Belgium, some 50 miles inland from the Channel ports. In those years the Channel, like all that corner of northern France, passed into British folk memory, engrained deep in the consciousness of the troops on their way to the front and coming back across the Channel in their leave ships and hospital ships. The Dover Patrol kept them safe, securing the Channel against a German intrusion that would have cut the British army off from home. From his headquarters in Montreuil-sur-Mer, Douglas Haig conducted his last bloody battles, and in the training camp at Étaples beside the sea his sergeants tried to give their raw recruits some idea of the horrors that awaited them in the trenches.

On the English side of the water the war was simultaneously remote and ever-present. When the winds were right, the great bombardments that preceded the offensives could be heard in Kent and Sussex; and when in March 1918 Ludendorff committed the German armies in the West to a last desperate push, he aimed first not at Paris but towards the Channel ports, hoping that if he could break through there he would cut off the British army from the French, drive it into the sea and end the war before the Americans arrived in force. When he failed, when the Channel ports were safe, there was nothing left for the German armies except retreat all the way to the Rhine and to national defeat.

Between the wars, the Channel told a story of day trips and seaside holidays and semi-detached estates beside the sea, of Golden Arrow journeys to gay Paree and of sad expeditions to the war graves of Flanders. But in twenty years, in June 1940, the Germans were back, their armoured divisions ripping through the Ardennes and across the plains of northern France; and this time in a matter of weeks they reached those places on the Channel coast – Dunkirk, Calais, Boulogne, St Valéry and Dieppe – which in the earlier war had been resolutely denied them. To get most of the men of the Allied armies away required military sacrifice at Calais and a vast naval evacuation from Dunkirk. The rest of the British army was rescued from ports further down the coast – from Cherbourg, St Malo, Brest and Nantes – and by high summer, German forces lined the whole southern shore of the Channel, ready for the decisive onslaught on England.

Throughout the late summer of 1940 the German air force fought for supremacy over the Channel and south-east England. Radar saw the air fleets coming in across the sea, and the famous Few went up to intercept and destroy them. The story of the Channel, for centuries already locked away in the British psyche, became one of raw survival. For if the Luftwaffe had driven the air force out of the skies it could have shut the navy out of the Straits of Dover, leaving the seas clear for the German navy to put an army ashore on the coast of Kent and Sussex.

Instead, the Royal Air Force drove the Luftwaffe into retreat and the threat of invasion was lifted. History swung the other way, and within months the British were improvising cross-Channel sorties of their own – gallant little commando raids on lonely Channel beaches and radar stations. The Canadians attempted their doomed attack upon Dieppe, learning lessons for the future at a terrible price. Meanwhile the British and Canadian armies trained and prepared. The Americans came to join them. German aircraft were driven out of the skies above the Channel, and German intelligence was bamboozled with false information fed to it across the sea through the electronic airwaves.

All this led slowly but inexorably to D-Day, 6 June 1944. The story of the Normandy landings, of the ingenuity that made them possible and of the gallantry on both sides in the vicious battles that followed, added yet another chapter to the Channel's history. This one was shared with Americans and Canadians, Poles, Czechs and Free Frenchmen, and not least with the indomitable Germans. For the British it was the final gallant episode in their story of the Channel, after which everything that followed seemed anti-climax.

So much for the Channel's meaning for British history. For 2,000 years the Channel played a central role in that history, helping to make Britain what it is, and helping to shape the stories the British told about themselves. But it has also shaped a wider European story. For from the sixteenth century onwards it was the Channel that denied successive European rulers continental pre-eminence, and so barred the way to any single hegemony and therefore to a united Europe. Philip of Spain, successive kings of France, Napoleon, Kaiser Bill and Adolf Hitler all failed to get across it and destroy their British enemies. So the Channel kept Europe safe for the development of the nation state.

In the sixteenth century, Europe turned its back on the single, continent-wide community that medieval Christendom had represented. It put its faith instead in *raison d'état*, national interest and balance of power – all of them concepts which, for better or for worse, dominated the political history of the continent for 500 years.

In the end, Europe said goodbye to all that. The continent's twentieth-century wars wrote *finis* to the European nations as world powers. They left them relatively weak, dependent on Moscow or Washington. For half a century the two superpowers, neither of them truly European, divided Europe along the line of the Iron Curtain. Now, with the collapse of the Soviet empire, that divide is gone, and people talk of a Europe at last made whole. But still there are rival formulations in play. On the one hand, Treaty of Rome loyalists still seek the uncertain destination of 'an ever closer union of the peoples of Europe'. On the other, their opponents reassert the claims of a looser kind of association based on Europe's historic nation states.

And again, as so often in its history, the Channel divides the proponents of the rival formulations. Instinctively, most Britons still align themselves with the advocates of a Europe of nations. Across the Channel, most of their neighbours want a Europe drawing ever more closely together. Each side caricatures the other and exaggerates the differences between them. But something real is at stake: the nature of the European Union, the last best hope of the continent. It is going to be a protracted argument. We shall see no more sea battles in the Channel or dogfights over the cliffs of Dover, no more generals setting out to destroy their enemies. Yet the great European argument continues. Every Monday morning British statesmen, parliamentarians

and officials go off through the Channel Tunnel to meet their continental partners and take the argument further in Luxembourg,
Strasbourg and Brussels. The Channel has always been an essential
element of the European map, playing a persistent role in European
history, uniting and dividing in turn. Often it has marked a divide
between two different ideas of Europe. Today, in these early years of
the twenty-first century, it still does.

CHAPTER 1

FROM THE LAND BRIDGE TO THE LEGIONS

I magine yourself 9,000 years back in time and 200 miles out in space, somewhere above the English Channel. Western Europe is spread below you, newly free from its ice cap, green now, scarcely touched by man. Far to the north the retreating ice still obscures the underlying land forms. But the western face that the continent presents to the Atlantic is something you would recognise if you went into space today. In the south lies the Iberian promontory, followed by the long scoop of the Bay of Biscay. Closer to home, Finistère, Land's End and the western capes of Ireland stab out into the ocean.

Today, outline maps of the prehistoric European land-mass are readily available, and experts are confident they are more or less accurate.[1]

They provide a starting point for any exploration of the English Channel. They show that nine millennia ago, much of the basic shape of today's Channel was there to be seen by the man in the moon. The sea thrusts in from the west between the capes of Cornwall and Brittany. The Normandy peninsula juts northwards and pinches the waters more narrowly. The familiar taper continues towards the east. But the essential feature of the Channel throughout historical times is missing. For between Picardy and Kent a land bridge links Britain to the continent. It extends northwards over most of today's North Sea, as far as the level of Yorkshire and Heligoland. The arm of the sea thrusting into the body of the continent between Britain and France is not a channel but a fjord. Nine thousand years ago Britain was not an island and the continent was not isolated.

Yet the story of the Channel's coasts and waters does not start 9,000 years ago. A walk on the beach anywhere between Exmouth and Swanage reveals how the land lay in earlier, scarcely imaginable times, with traces of the creatures that then inhabited it. UNESCO has designated these 95 miles of coastline a World Heritage Site, for they constitute one of the richest sources of prehistorical evidence in the world. 'Because the rocks are sloping downwards,' says the local expert in a newspaper article, 'if you walk horizontally along the beach you can walk through time for 180 million years.'[2] The fossils found in these rocks range from the age when fishes predominated, through the age of the reptiles, of the dinosaurs, of the birds and on into the age of the mammals. The story of their discovery is in a way as astonishing as the relics themselves, for in 1811 a carpenter's daughter, Mary Anning, an untrained amateur in matters archaeological, unearthed the skeleton of an ichthyosaurus in the cliff-face near Lyme Regis, and went on to find the first nearly complete plesiosaurus and the first British pterodactyl. Predictably, the marketing departments of Devon and Dorset councils have branded this the 'Jurassic Coast'.

The last true ice age came gradually to its end. As the ice retreated, sea levels rose, land masses surged, sank and tilted. The seas advanced, marshes were formed, the land withdrew. Something like eight millennia ago the land bridge gradually sank below sea level. There came a time when the first trickles of salt water from east and west met. Gradually the trickles became creeks, the creeks channels, the channels open waters. In the Straits of Dover the waters of the North Sea and the Channel met. The new divide left the same kinds of flora and fauna on mainland and islands, and human beings of the same stock, living by hunting, gathering and fishing. Channel coastlines receded and Britain, Ireland, the Isle of Man and the Western Isles, Anglesey and the Isle of Wight became islands. The Channel assumed its historical significance, providing a passage from the North Sea to the Atlantic and separating Britain physically from the continent.

Perhaps 8,000 years ago, agriculture made its first marginal appearances in western Europe. Settled life began to put its mark on both sides of the Channel. Soon afterwards, early man turned his hand to creating astonishingly ambitious mounds, stone circles and avenues of standing stones in all their mystery. Such things are found on Mediterranean islands, but the greatest concentration lies along the Atlantic face of Europe from Iberia to the Scottish islands. Most relevant to our Channel purposes are the megaliths of Brittany. These mysterious monuments were erected by communities that clung to the edge of the land and faced out into the Atlantic, and the archaeological evidence shows that they had more in common with other coastal peoples than with Europe's inland worlds. Cautious but nevertheless perilous coastal navigation bound them together, and from their time probably date the first cross-Channel voyages.

There is unquestionable archaeological evidence of cross-Channel contact by the time of the early Bronze Age, 4,000 years ago. A millennium and a half later comes literary evidence from an eyewitness. In 325 BC a traveller from the Mediterranean named Pytheas embarked on an Atlantic voyage. He travelled overland from his home in Marseilles to the mouth of the Gironde and thence by sea to the jaws of the Channel, visited Britain and sailed right round it, and went on northwards, perhaps to the mouth of the Elbe, perhaps to Iceland. On his return he wrote an account of his travels called *On the Ocean*. His original text was lost, but the accounts of eighteen classical writers based on it have survived, each of them crediting Pytheas by name. Taken together, voyage and narrative make Pytheas the Greek of Marseilles a Captain Cook of the ancient world and the founding father of the history of north-west Europe. From others' use of Pytheas's lost account, we get our first glimpse of the Channel through the eyes of a named man.

Pytheas probably travelled in local ships, following established trading routes. From the captains with whom he sailed he learned that Ushant was called Uxisame, Land's End Belerion, and Britain the Pretannic Isles. He described it as triangular in shape, and recorded its northern and eastern corners as Orcas (Orkney) and Kantion (Kent). He gave an account of the island's products, most notably tin, and claimed to have found tin-traders on an islet off the Channel coast that he called Ictis. Archaeologists believe Ictis is St Michael's Mount or Mount Batten in Plymouth Sound.

Out of Pytheas's story grew curiosity in the classical world about Britain and in particular about British tin. Tin was an essential raw material in the manufacture of bronze, itself used in everything from weapons to drinking vessels and ceremonial vases. Tin was rare within the classical world, but widespread along Europe's Atlantic coast. The search for it sent Mediterranean seamen and traders following in Pytheas's wake, willing to risk the ocean's vagaries in their concern to swap the luxuries of the classical world for tin. One of the places at which they traded was a little port on the Hampshire coast which Victorian antiquarians christened Hengistbury Head.

Today's archaeological trail at Hengistbury Head, at the easternmost end of the Bournemouth–Christchurch waterfront, gives a Channel-side review of all this prehistory and early history. The site stretches for a mile and a half, the Channel waters of Poole Bay on one side, the shallows of Christchurch Harbour on the other: a tranquil world of wind, sea, grass and sand, holding faint traces of early man. Channel waves bang on one shore, the harbour's ripples lap on the other, and a final spit of sand curls round till it almost closes the harbour entrance.

There are traces of human occupation at Hengistbury Head going back 12,500 years, to times when Britain was still firmly linked to the continent, and the Isle of Wight to Britain. Then this coastal parkland lay far inland. Stone Age hunter-gatherers occupied a hill top that is today Hengistbury's knuckle above the sea. Their usual relics have been found here – scrapers and weapon-heads and traces of their camp fires. Now the sea is gradually washing away the hill top on which they settled. About 500 yards eastwards along the coast there is a later Stone Age camp site, dated to 9,500 years ago, where archaeologists have found evidence of the use of bow and arrow. Four thousand years later, it is still the Stone Age but the land bridge to the continent has gone. By now the inhabitants wield axes, herd animals, grow wheat and barley, make pottery, erect huts and shut themselves in with fences.

Two thousand years later it is the Bronze Age – say 1500 BC. By now, man has abandoned his settlements on Hengistbury Head. He uses it instead as an elaborate cemetery, reserved, to judge by what has so far been uncovered, for persons of importance. By the Iron Age, however, live residents are back, and by the time Pytheas comes to the Channel there is a sophisticated community here. It had a trading reputation and a primitive industrial capacity. It protected itself from landward attack by digging dykes and defensive banks across the isthmus that links it to the mainland, and looked out not on to the sea but on to the sheltered waters of Christchurch Harbour.

A few traces of an old port have been found in those sheltered waters at Hengistbury. More substantial evidence is now coming to light at a site inside Poole Harbour in Dorset, a few miles to the west of Hengistbury. Archaeologists are exploring traces of stone and timber jetties, and looking for evidence that traders from the Mediterranean came here, as they came to Hengistbury, over 2,000 years ago. They wanted to buy tin in particular, as well as copper, silver, gold and perhaps iron, and skins, slaves and hunting dogs. In return they offered wine, pottery and other Mediterranean luxuries.

There is an eyewitness description of the kind of ships that served Hengistbury's cross-Channel trade. In *The Civil War* Julius Caesar describes having ships built during his Spanish campaign. He 'ordered his men to build boats of the type his experience in Britain had taught him to make. The keels and ribs were made of light wood; the rest of the hull was made of woven withies and covered with hides'.[3] We know such ships as currachs, and centuries later they were still in service, carrying saints of the early church such as Brendan on his mysterious journeys. And in another of his chronicles, *The Conquest of Gaul*, Caesar describes the more powerful and heavily built ships of a seagoing tribe based in southern Brittany, a description to be recounted later in this chapter. Caesar was writing 300 years after Pytheas's time, but ships such as he described had probably served Atlantic coastal travellers for centuries. With favourable weather, they could make the crossing from Hengistbury to the tip of Normandy in a long summer's day or carry a traveller like Pytheas to Britain from the Gironde in a week.

When he travelled beyond the bounds of the Roman Empire, Pytheas was describing a Celtic world. Around his time, 2,300 years ago, the Celts, whom we think of today as fragmentary little nations clinging to the western edge of Europe in Galicia and Brittany, Wales, Ireland, Scotland and Cornwall, were the predominant people of central Europe, occupying a swathe of territory that ran from the Carpathians to the tip of Brittany and into Britain and Ireland. Prehistorians still dispute the way their influence travelled, whether by conquest, migration, inter-marriage, trade or all of these and more. But travel it did, across the Channel as much as overland.

So by 600 BC Celtic tribes were fully established on both sides of the English Channel. The Celts dominated life in Britain and Gaul and maintained cross-Channel contact. Contact took the usual form of most human interaction, an admixture of trade, warlike raids, cross-Channel migrations, social and even family connections, and the flight of the occasional refugee from military or political trouble at home.

These pre-Roman Celtic societies achieved many of the ideals of civilisation. They cleared the forests for agriculture and forestry. Tribal structures delivered security, and the tribes' members delivered collective labour. Archaeology shows that the arts flourished. To this day Brittany and Cornwall can give a sense of the character of this Celtic world. Among the historical and archaeological relics are Celtic crosses. Both places are suffused with Celtic legends reflecting Celtic fact. From the

Celts' day almost to our own, Cornwall and Brittany have been separated for most practical purposes from the land masses to which they are attached. Hence the persistence of Celtic ways; hence too the fact that, even today, they seem subtly un-English and un-French, and the persistence of cross-Channel similarities between the two.

For a long time the Roman Republic lived in uneasy co-existence with its Celtic neighbours but eventually, in Gaul, it committed itself to a policy of conquest. First the Romans occupied southern France from the Alps to the Garonne and made a Roman province of it. Three generations later came Julius Caesar's conquest of the rest of Gaul, which carried the legions to the Rhine and the Channel coast. But in the north-west of Gaul, the commander of the Seventh Legion, Publius Crassus, got at cross-purposes with a tribe, the Veneti, who occupied southern Brittany, and before long Caesar had a general uprising on his hands. His story of how in 56 BC he dealt with it gives us the first account in history of amphibious warfare in the narrow northern seas.

'The Veneti,' says Caesar, 'are much the most powerful tribe on this coast. They have the largest fleet of ships, in which they traffic with Britain; they excel other tribes in knowledge and experience of navigation; and as the coast lies exposed to the violence of the open sea and has but few harbours, which the Veneti control, they compel nearly all who sail those waters to pay toll.'[4] They also had ships which in these waters were more serviceable than those of the Romans, being 'built and rigged in a different manner from ours':

They were made with much flatter bottoms, to help them ride shallow water caused by shoals or ebb-tides. Exceptionally high bows and sterns fitted them for use in heavy seas and violent gales, and the hulls were made entirely of oak, to enable them to stand any amount of shocks and rough usage . . . They used sails made of raw hides or thin leather . . . probably because they thought that ordinary sails would not stand the violent storms and squalls of the Atlantic . . .[5]

Against these amphibious Veneti, the Romans were out of their element: 'the enemy's [ships] were much better adapted for sailing such treacherous and stormy waters. We could not injure them by ramming because they were so solidly built, and their height made it difficult to reach them with missiles or board them with grappling-irons.'[6] When Caesar laid siege to the Venetis' coastal forts, the defenders could easily sail away to another. 'After taking several strongholds,' Caesar says, he 'saw that all this labour was being wasted'. He decided that he must wait for the ships he was having built further down the Atlantic coast of Gaul. But directly his smart new fleet hove in sight, 'two hundred and twenty enemy ships, perfectly equipped and ready for immediate action, sailed out of harbour and took up stations facing it'.[7]

Battle was joined, some say in the Gulf of Morbihan, others in Quiberon Bay, both in southern Brittany. At first the Roman commanders were nonplussed, unable to find a way to get at the taller and more manoeuvrable enemy ships. Eventually they went to work with hooks on poles with which, going alongside the Veneti ships, they pulled down their rigging. At that, the advantage at last shifted to the Romans, for their ships carried oarsmen while the Venetis 'depended wholly on their sails and rigging; when stripped of these they were at once immobilised'.[8] After that it was a soldiers' battle, and the Romans butchered their enemies. Nature too played a hand; when the Veneti tried to flee, a dead calm prevented their escaping. Caesar took self-righteous revenge on this troublesome tribe that had fought him so effectively, and soon Brittany, like the rest of the French Channel coast, went under the Roman yoke. Caesar had conquered all Gaul, and in the process almost doubled the extent of Roman possessions in the west.

He might have stopped at the French Channel coast, yet he still found reasons to go on. His hold on office was secure as long as there was fighting to be done, but he had enemies in Rome. If he declared his campaign in Gaul complete, the Senate might relieve him of his command. His officers wanted fame, and further conquest would win it. Britain sounded seductive: there were the minerals, pearls, silver, hunting dogs and slaves that had for so long been imported from places across the Channel such as Hengistbury Head. Caesar could also claim defensive reasons for expansion, or at least for attempting a reconnaissance across the water. The northern Gauls, especially the Veneti, moved freely across the Channel, he argued, and it was easy for rebels among them to flee there from Roman retribution. Order in Gaul, Caesar could assert with some slight plausibility, demanded an expedition into Britain. So after a brief but bloody campaign against the Germans he committed himself, in the late summer of 55 BC, to a cross-Channel invasion.

Caesar's account of his expeditions to Britain in 55 BC and the following year is as self-serving as his story of the defeat of the Veneti. But he gives the facts as well as his often tendentious interpretation of them. His account makes this the first documented invasion of Britain in history.

The tribes of Gaul and Britain had done business together for centuries, but the invasion was for Caesar a step into the unknown: 'he interviewed traders from all parts', he writes, but 'he could not ascertain anything about the size of the island, the character and strength of the tribes which inhabited it, their manner of fighting and customs, or the harbours capable of accommodating a large fleet of ships'.[9] So he sent an officer, one Gaius Volusenus, to explore the British coastline, while he himself moved his army up to the Channel coast. At Boulogne he assembled a fleet of eighty transports, and eighteen more, destined to carry cavalry, were sent to a place that is probably the little fishing port of Ambleteuse. The Britons despatched envoys to parley with him, and he sent a Gallic chieftain, one Commius, home with them on the first diplomatic mission to Britain of which there is a record. Commius was 'to visit as many tribes as possible, to urge them to entrust themselves to the protection of Rome, and to announce his impending arrival'.[10]

Volusenus returned, having spent four days examining the British coast from the sea. His report encouraged Caesar to launch his expedition. Finally, at about midnight on a September night, he put to sea with a force of two Roman legions plus auxiliaries. After a delay in mid-Channel while he waited in vain for his cavalry transports to join him, he approached the coast. Arriving at nine in the morning beneath what sound like the cliffs of Dover, Caesar found the Britons ready to defend themselves. He writes that warriors were drawn up on the heights, where the 'lie of the land was such that javelins could be hurled from the cliffs right on to the narrow beach enclosed between them and the sea'. He told his officers they must land further up the coast, found that 'both wind and tidal current were in his favour . . . and after proceeding about seven miles ran his ships aground on an evenly sloping beach, free from obstacles'.[11]

Caesar was going ashore somewhere between Walmer and Deal. The Britons were there before him, and he faced all the difficulties of an opposed landing. 'The size of the ships made it impossible to run them aground except in fairly deep water,' he writes; 'and soldiers, unfamiliar with the ground, with their hands full, had at the same time to jump down from the ships, get a footing in the waves, and fight the enemy.' The Britons, 'standing on dry land or advancing only a short way into the water, fought with all their limbs unencumbered and on perfectly familiar ground, boldly hurling javelins and galloping their horses, which were trained to this kind of work'.[12]

Not unnaturally, the legionaries hung back. They were finally stirred to action, Caesar tells us, by the words of the standard-bearer of the Tenth Legion. 'Jump down, comrades,' Caesar has him saying, 'unless you want to surrender our eagle to the enemy; I, at any rate, mean to do my duty to my country and my general.'[13] Into the surf he went, and his comrades followed him ashore, but at first they were unable to form up in proper Roman order. There was a danger that they would be cut down in small groups where they stood, here on the wrong side of the Channel on the coast of Kent.

Eventually, however, they drove off the Britons. Caesar had made the first of the very few opposed cross-Channel landings that history has recorded. Once his legionaries were safely ashore it looked as if the south-east of Britain was open to him, but the Channel weather took its turn, as it does so often in this story. 'It happened to be full moon that night, at which time the Atlantic tides are particularly high,' Caesar writes. This was 'a fact unknown to the Romans. The result was that the warships used in the crossing which had been beached, were water-logged, and the transports, which were riding at anchor, were knocked about by the storm.' The whole army fell into consternation, 'for they had no other vessels in which they could return, nor any materials for repairing the fleet, and, since it had been generally understood that they were to return to Gaul for the winter, they had not provided themselves with a stock of grain for wintering in Britain'.[14] The Channel's winds and tides had asserted themselves, and Caesar was trapped on a hostile shore with a small force of infantry and no cavalry, unprepared for a winter campaign and with no immediate communication with the continent.

The British chiefs saw their opportunity to resume hostilities. But before they could mount a new attack, Caesar set about restoring the situation. Somehow he repaired his ships and sent for more. A small cavalry unit at last reached him from Ambleteuse. The men of the Seventh Legion were sent out to forage for food. The Britons attacked them as they did so and it took a rescue party led by Caesar himself to save them. The Britons pressed harder, driving Caesar back to his camp beside the sea. Again the Romans drove them off, but by now Caesar had had enough. Eager to be out of this first cross-Channel operation before the winter, he withdrew his whole force, taking hostages with him. It had been an inglorious venture. Only Roman discipline saved it from becoming the first of many military disasters recorded in the Channel's history.

Caesar came back to Britain in the following year, 54 BC. Throughout the winter he had had men at work building ships: 600 transports and twenty-eight ships of war. He says that he had them designed specifically for the job, built wider than the Roman norm, able to carry a heavy cargo including animals, easy to manoeuvre inshore and to run up on the landing beaches, and capable of being both sailed and rowed. By now Caesar seems to have fancied himself as an expert on Channel conditions, and he committed himself to a scientifically doubtful and potentially catastrophic supposition: the ships could be built to lie low in the water, he says, because 'he had found that owing to the frequent ebb and flow of the tides the waves in the Channel were comparatively small'.[15]

This expedition was to be a serious invasion. Caesar was committing his personal credit to the waves. He was bringing five legions and 2,000 horsemen to Britain, leaving only three legions and a further 2,000 cavalry to garrison all Gaul. Eventually he set sail from Boulogne at sunset, and once again the Channel weather soon faced him with difficulties: 'about midnight the wind dropped, with the result that he was driven far out of his course by the tidal current and at daybreak saw Britain left behind on the port side'.[16] The fleet and army were, in short, adrift in the North Sea, and neither the parties of his friends whom Caesar had brought along, nor his hostages from Gaul to answer for its good behaviour, would be much help in extracting him from his predicament. Only heroic rowing by soldiers and the ships' crews brought the heavily laden transports back to the chosen landing place near Deal.

This time the invaders found the shoreline undefended. Caesar at once struck boldly inland, finding the Britons entrenched in a woodland stronghold, probably near Canterbury. The Seventh Legion cleared the wood by storm and the army set off to pursue the enemy. But yet again the Channel weather played a hand: 'dispatch riders brought news from Atrius of a great storm in the night, by which nearly all the ships had been damaged or cast ashore: the anchors and cables had not held, and the sailors and their captains could not cope with such a violent gale, so that many ships were disabled by running foul of one another'.[17] Caesar called off the pursuit, returned to the coast and set about building a fort within which his ships could be beached and protected from raiding Britons and Channel weather alike.

By the time he was able to turn his attention inland once again, he found a strong force gathered to challenge him. Strenuous fighting ensued, in which, to read between the lines of Caesar's account, the Britons gave as good as they got. But they were up against disciplined legionaries in substantial numbers. An attack penetrated the Roman lines but was broken. The Britons fled, and their tribal coalition broke up. The way was clear for Caesar to advance to the Thames. He forced a crossing at a defended ford and advanced northwards, harassed only by guerrilla fighters, towards the heart of the British resistance. Some tribes turned traitor and told Caesar where he could find his main opponent, near St Albans. Here he attacked and destroyed the main British resistance.

Caesar had now defeated or subjugated most of the south-eastern British tribes. But still he was challenged, first by a sudden attack on his coastal base by a coalition of Kentish rulers, which would have been fatal if his men had not been able to beat it off; then by fear of a rising against the Romans in a restive Gaul; and throughout by the ever-present danger that a Channel gale would destroy his ships and cut him off on a hostile coast. Whether he had intended this second expedition to Britain as another reconnaissance or an attempt at permanent conquest is not known, but in the event he withdrew to Gaul before the winter, taking hostages, promises and perhaps some booty with him. Of course Caesar does not say so, but it looks as if this second, more ambitious cross-Channel venture came at times as close to disaster as his first.

It was to be a century before the Romans next sent an army across the Channel. Their interest in the island persisted, however. They still wanted its tin and its silver, its slaves and hunting dogs. They now knew something about its affairs at first hand but they wanted continuing political information, about its tribes and their doings and, in particular, about their relationships with their fellow Celts in northern Gaul. For their part, the Celts wanted to pursue the cross-Channel contacts that had flourished long before the Romans set foot on Channel beaches. The British tribal leaders in particular were eager for Mediterranean luxuries and Roman sophistication. All this encouraged cross-Channel travel, contact and trade. The focus of contact seems to have moved eastwards, however, with the old links between Normandy and Hengistbury Head yielding before the attractions of the short sea-crossing to Kent. There was certainly no question of Britain relapsing into isolation after Caesar's visits.

Yet the Channel could have continued indefinitely to mark the political limit of the Roman world. The legions still had their hands full on the mainland. In the year AD 9 the German tribes annihilated two Roman legions in the Teutoberg forest. For Romans who suspected that Caesar had twice come close to disaster on the coast of Kent, their fate must have been a salutary warning to stay safely within Roman territory.

But other factors drove the Romans to expand the bounds of empire. Manifest destiny was at work. So were less noble motives. There were goods to be traded, booty to be won. Expansion gave soldiers and administrators the chance of promotion. The Emperors themselves needed success abroad to reinforce their positions at home. So when in AD 40 a group of British tribal leaders fled to Gaul for Roman protection from the vengeance of their enemies at home, the Emperor Gaius (better known to history as Caligula who made his horse a consul) seized the opportunity. 'The Emperor Gaius unquestionably planned an invasion of Britain,' Tacitus tells us, 'but his impulsive ideas shifted like a weathercock.'[18] He marched an army to the French coast but his preparations to get them to Britain, half-baked at best, came to nothing. Assassins struck him down; and once he was safely dead Roman writers had a field day, accusing him of taking the legions to the Channel coast for no better purpose than to gather seashells by the seashore.

Caligula's assassins put his uncle Claudius on the imperial throne. The new emperor was terrified of the job. He was a 'club-foot stammerer, on the face of it the most unlikely conqueror of all',[19] but he yearned for glory and he turned a willing ear to the advocates of an expedition across the Channel. The scepticism of such men as Strabo, who argued that an expedition was unnecessary since Rome's relations with British chieftains had already made 'virtually the whole island a Roman possession', was swept aside. Plans were made for an invasion and four legions were earmarked for the task. With auxiliaries, the force numbered about 40,000 men. The Romans were committing perhaps 15 per cent of their military strength in Europe to a cross-Channel invasion. This time they were in deadly earnest.

The invasion force was led by one of Rome's finest, Aulus Plautius, but he had difficulty in keeping his army in hand. His men feared this strange element, the ocean, and many refused to embark; this time it needed more than a bold eagle-bearer to move them. Finally Claudius himself sent Plautius a letter of encouragement. He read it to his men, got them at last into his ships, and in the late summer of AD 43 led the whole force to the coast of Kent. The fleet found an anchorage in the sheltered waters that at the time separated the mainland from the Isle of Thanet. Here, in what later came to be known as the Wantsum Channel, were landing places far safer than Caesar's beaches. The Wantsum has long since vanished under fields and marshes, but two miles inland from the little Channel port of Sandwich, next to the remains of the Roman fort at Richborough, can be seen the place where the army went ashore and where it first encamped. The walls visible today, built centuries after the first landings, rear up against the pale English sky with all the assurance of ancient Rome. Behind them stretch the marshes, and a long flat horizon between sky and sea.

Plautius's vanguard built a ten-acre camp at Richborough. Nearby, on a larger site which archaeology has not yet identified, he encamped his reinforcements. From here the legions set out to march towards London, as Julius Caesar had done a century earlier. The road they took was a direct projection of Richborough's main axis. It became Watling Street, the main link between London and the Channel coast, and an essential part of the Empire's communications system.

At the Medway the Romans encountered the army of a tribe that had declared itself their enemies, the Catuvellaunians. They forced a crossing and moved on to the Thames. They captured London; and from here the main force marched towards Colchester. A pause followed, while Claudius hurried to Britain to join his troops. He stayed for only sixteen days, but it was long enough for him to claim the glory that had eluded Julius Caesar and impose a Roman conquest on the Britons.

While Plautius was landing in Kent, a second force of legionaries crossed the Channel further west, perhaps to Chichester Harbour. At some stage of Plautius's advance, one legion, II Augusta, was sent away overland to the south-west. At its head was a soldier who was to become the Emperor Vespasian. It advanced into the land of the Romans' clients, the Atrebates. The legionaries marched into Chichester (and may have joined hands with the men of the separate invasion force there). They took the Isle of Wight, naming it Vectis – a name that now adorns boarding houses in Shanklin and Ryde. Then they advanced westwards, past Hengistbury, captured the largest hill-fort in Europe, Maiden Castle (where the skeleton of a British warrior has been uncovered, with the death-dealing Roman ballista bolt still embedded in his backbone), and fought their way to the Exe. All the north coast of the Channel except Devon and Cornwall was now firmly in Roman hands. A Roman presence was to remain there for the best part of four centuries.

The story of the Roman settlement of most of Britain is complex and sometimes bloody, but we are concerned only with the south of the island. Here, Roman authority was quickly established and, until the end of the Roman period, not seriously questioned. Celtic civilisation flourished under Roman protection. To it were added Roman wealth, skills, taste and sophistication. Along the British Channel coast, therefore, there gradually grew up a settled Celto-Roman world, expressed in a patchwork of old British towns, Roman settlements, the occasional fort, and spacious villas.[20] This civilisation, to which the Britons gave most of the weight and the Romans most of the form, raised population densities and living standards to higher levels than were to be attained again for a thousand years. Simon Schama calls Roman Britain 'a hybrid, polyglot, rather easy-going province'.[21] It mirrored a similar Celto-Roman civilisation along the Channel coast of France. The sea between remained an essential everyday thoroughfare between them. Its users, like all who went down to the sea in ships, could encounter unpredictable hazards, but it marked no other difference between these two provinces of the Empire.

Richborough was developed into a major imperial port, and archaeologists have found traces of a triumphal arch there through which newcomers entered the province of Britain. The Romans recovered the fertile fields of today's Romney Marsh from marshland and the Channel's waters. Dover became a Roman port, and on a high point within its medieval castle the stump of a Roman lighthouse can still be seen. In the town itself is 'the painted house', which probably served as an hotel for important travellers where they could prepare themselves for the perils of the deep or put their seasickness behind them. There too, between the west cliffs and the east, the remains of the old Roman harbour have been uncovered, the base for cross-Channel ferries and naval operations alike. Pevensey has the remains of a Roman fort and so does Portchester behind Portsmouth. Chichester, carefully rectilinear, has all the marks of Roman order superimposed on an older British settlement. Further west, the Romans quarried stone at Portland and based a garrison at Exeter, a frontier city to keep the unconquered Celts at bay.

The most extensive impression of the good life that the Romans brought to the British aristocracy, however, is to be found at Fishbourne, on the water's edge just outside Chichester. Here is one of the finest of all civilian Roman sites in Britain. In his villa and gardens at Fishbourne, a British ruler under Roman protection enjoyed all the pleasures that Rome could offer to its reliable allies. At first, it had served a military purpose, as a supply base for Roman forces operating in the south-west, but as the conquest moved forward, administrative and then residential considerations came to the fore. A Roman client-king, Tiberius Claudius Cogidubnus, may (or, depending on the point reached in the continuing archaeological argument, may not) have used Fishbourne as office and home from which he ran this part of Britain for his Roman masters. But whatever the historical facts that underlie it, Fishbourne today offers splendid buildings around a splendid garden, learned archaeological argument, expanses of delicate mosaics and a sense of historical peace.

Roman rule in Britain lasted for almost exactly 400 years. But eventually, as Edward Gibbon tells us in *The Decline and Fall of the Roman Empire*, events began to press in upon the Romans. Barbarians assailed the Empire's borders. Rome was threatened by the corruption of its leaders and the sloth of its citizens. Tax revenues were inadequate, Roman manpower insufficient – and when barbarian auxiliaries were enrolled, there was friction and worse between them and the Roman citizens. Rival Caesars began to compete with one another, until the Empire was split into western and eastern. Like Assyria and Egypt, like Spain and France after them, like Britain yesterday, Russia today and the United States tomorrow, the Romans learned that no empire lasts for ever.

Nor did the idyll of peaceful Roman rule on the shores of the English Channel. By the end of the third century the Empire in the north-west was under pressure. In Gaul the threat came from across the Rhine; in

Britain at first from the Picts from Scotland and the Scots from Ireland. Soon sea-borne raiders joined in, attacking the North Sea coasts of Britain and Gaul and pressing on into the Channel. In response the Romans reinforced their fleet and established a line of coastal forts extending from Norfolk to Hampshire. At Richborough, where the Romans first arrived, they now built the four-square fortress with strong defensive bastions that still dominates this part of the coast of Kent. Similar forts were built at Reculver, on the north coast of Kent, at Dover and Pevensey, Lympne and Portchester, places that later would be fortified against Vikings, Spaniards, Frenchmen and Germans in turn. The fleet, the Classis Britanniae based at Dover, was devoted to the same purpose. Similar defences were built on the other side of the Channel and a Roman commander, the Count of the Saxon Shore, was put in charge of the whole defensive system, with his headquarters at Boulogne.

The external threat was matched by internal difficulties. There was dissension among the remaining defenders of the Roman world in the west. British princes declared themselves independent kings. An ambitious sailor of the Classis Britanniae, Carausius, proclaimed himself Emperor. Romans and their allies in the British and Gallic provinces grew uneasy, demoralised. One of the Empire's last stalwarts, the barbarian chief turned Roman general Flavius Stilicho, was sent to Britain to restore order. He was initially successful but then he was called away, and he took garrison troops with him. Roman Britain 'was dying very slowly, with neither a bang nor a whimper but with rather a long-drawn-out sigh'.[22]

In 406, the last Roman soldiers were pulled out of Britain to help hold the Empire's frontier on the Rhine. In 408 the British themselves sent away the remaining Roman administrators, who were probably glad to take themselves off while they could. Yet some Britons still looked to Rome for help. They got short shrift: 'Then the Romans told the Britons plain,' wrote the chronicler Bede long afterwards, 'that it was not for their ease to take such travailous journeys for their defence: and bid them rather to snatch up their weapons themselves, and undertake to learn to withstand their enemy, whom nothing else did make stronger than they but their own faint and cowardous hearts.'[23] The Britons appealed to the Emperor Honorius himself to save them, but by now the Visigoths were sacking the very city of Rome. A group of upper-class Britons – aristocrats, administrators and merchants – fled to Brittany, where Rome's protection still had value. Their compatriots who remained in Britain faced new invaders and new conquerors.

CHAPTER 2

SAXONS, FRANKS AND VIKINGS

T he Roman garrisons left Britain early in the fifth century. Gradually the country, like the continent, descended into what used to be called the 'Dark Ages', 'a long period', wrote Sir Frank Stenton, one of the greatest historians of the Anglo-Saxon period, 'of which the history cannot be written'.[1] But over the period of 600 years that separates the departure of the Romans from the arrival of the Normans, England and Europe slowly returned to civilisation, re-entered the realms of history and re-established cross-Channel contacts. Those centuries saw the coming of the Anglo-Saxons and the Franks, storming across the North Sea and the Rhine and subjugating the Celto-Roman societies that the legions left behind them. They saw these Anglo-Saxon sea-rovers and Frankish conquerors develop a softer side, with the conversion of England and France to Christianity and the establishment of cross-Channel links under the mantle of the universal Church. Then this rebirth of civility in western Europe was threatened by new barbarians, the Vikings. But eventually the Vikings were contained, and their descendants holding the dukedom of Normandy embraced Christianity. In the early eleventh century the

Danes made a last convulsive effort at conquest that created a transient Danish–English empire centred on the North Sea, but they too were tamed. And finally came William of Normandy's victory at Hastings and with it a cross-Channel Norman empire.

First, the assault of the Franks and Saxons, and the defeat of Romanised Celtic societies on both sides of the Channel. In Britain the story is best built around three shadowy but nevertheless real human beings, Vortigern, Hengist and Horsa.

Vortigern or 'the Vortigern', a title that historians render as 'sublime leader', was an ambitious British warlord determined to defend his country's Celto-Roman society. Here *The Anglo-Saxon Chronicle*, the primary source of information about these centuries, comes into the picture. In 443, it tells us, 'the Britons sent to Rome and asked them for help against the Picts, but they had none there because they were campaigning against Attila, king of Huns . . . and then they . . . made the same request to the princes of the Angle race'.[2]

The 'princes' who responded were Hengist and Horsa, who set out from the Friesland coast in northern Germany to support the Britons. They came in three ships, 'three keels', which must have been open boats, clinker-built, perhaps 40 feet long, the size of a modern lifeboat, each rowed by around forty oarsmen. The great Anglo-Saxon poem *Beowulf* describes a very similar errand of bloodthirsty mercy, and in its pounding verse comes as close as anything ever will to conveying the spirit of such a voyage:

> On time went; on their waves was their ship,
> A boat under bergs. The boys all ready
> Stepped on the stem; the stream was washing
> The sound on the sand; those seamen bare
> Into the breast of the bark bright adornments,
> Wondrous war-armour; well out they shoved her,
> (Wights willing to journey) with wooden beams bounden,
> Went then over the waves, as the wind drave her,
> The foamy-necked floater, to a fowl best likened,

Till about the same time on the second day
Her winding stem had waded so far
That the sailors land could see,
Shore-cliffs shining, mountains sheer,
Spreading sea-nesses; then was the sound crossed
At the end of the ocean.[3]

Hengist and Horsa 'sought out Britain in the landing place which is named Ebba's Creek, at first to help the Britons, but later they fought against them'. Thus *The Anglo-Saxon Chronicle* summarises their landing at Pegwell Bay in the Isle of Thanet, at the mouth of the Wantsum Channel in which Plautius's Roman ships had anchored 400 years earlier. The deal was, says Bede, that 'They then who came were allowed by the Britons a place to dwell among them, with that condition that the one should war for the peace and safety of the country against the enemy, the other should pay them due wages for their warfare.'[4] Legend has it that the newcomers had been promised as much land as an ox-hide would cover, but cut it into a strip that encompassed half the county. So cheated, Vortigern stopped paying his bills to his allies when once they had driven off the Picts. It was, in Simon Schama's words, 'one of the most spectacular misjudgements in British history... The Saxon warriors expressed their displeasure at being double-crossed by going on a rampage.'[5]

The newcomers sent for reinforcements and *The Anglo-Saxon Chronicle* lists some of their incursions as they stormed ashore on the Channel coast. In 477 'Aelle and his three sons ... came to the land of Britain with three ships at the place which is named Cymen's Shore and there killed many Welsh [Britons, trying to defend land that is now the Owers sandbanks off Selsey in Sussex] ...' In 491 'Aelle and Cissa besieged Anderitum [Pevensey], and killed all who lived there.' In 495 'two chieftains, Cerdic and Cynric his son, came to Britain with five ships at the place which is called Cerdic's Shore [probably again Selsey]'. And in 501 'Port and his two sons, Bieda and Maegla, came with two ships to Britain at the place which is called Portsmouth, and killed a certain young British man − a very noble man.'[6] Over the years such raiders came in their hundreds, and gradually they came to dominate the English coast of the Channel.

The first impact of their arrival on a quiet shore must have been as horrific as that of any invader. Imagine a couple of boats sweeping onto a deserted Channel beach. Fifty-odd warriors leap into the surf. A child from a nearby British village peers at them from behind a tuft of grass on the bank of earth at the top of the beach. The raiders move inland, towards the village. They find it deserted but for an old man too lame to flee. They cut him down, take what bits and pieces of movable property they can find and put a torch to the huts.

Fairly or unfairly, the Anglo-Saxons have gone down in folk memory, if not in history, as less savage than the Vikings who came 400 years after them and who did to them what they had done to the Britons. But the Saxon invaders wanted what the British property-owning classes held and conflict was inevitable. The Britons fought back, often successfully. Overall, however, the tide ran with the invaders. Faced with such onslaughts, the Britons appealed for help to Rome: 'The barbarians push us to the sea; the sea pushes us back on the barbarians. Between these two kinds of death, we are either drowned or slaughtered.'[7] But it was too late to look for help from within what was left of the Roman Empire.

The invaders did not have things all their own way. Stenton describes British victories that sometimes set back the tide of invasion for decades. Out of obscure raiding, warfare and mayhem emerge the half-documented stories of Ambrosius Aurelianus, a valiant and often successful British warlord; the legends, reflecting unknown facts, of King Arthur; and the memory of a Welsh resistance fighter, Coel Hen, whom British children used to celebrate as Old King Cole.[8] Gradually, however, the Britons were driven into the hills of Wales and the north, and into the south-west peninsula. Eventually the Saxons held the Channel coast from the North Foreland to the Tamar, leaving Celts still holding it in Cornwall, where Cornish patriots would say they hold it still.

Matters developed rather differently on the other side of the Channel. If anything, the barbarian onslaught was even more devastating on the continent than in Britain. The story of the Vandals, for example, is one of a tidal wave that swept across the Rhine, across Gaul and on into Spain, North Africa and the final destruction of the Roman Empire in the West. But in northern Gaul, Romanised society for a time succeeded in turning the Vandal influx aside and in holding the sea-borne raiders at bay. While much of Britain fell to the Anglo-Saxons, on the other side of the Channel Romanised communities maintained a tenuous order and some relics of Roman life.

In this Celtic society in France, and in what remained of Celtic society in Britain, Christianity endured. We know that before the Roman Empire became officially Christian, Britain and Gaul had had their Christian martyrs. Traces of a few Christian churches have been found even in Britain, one of them within the Roman fortifications at Richborough. The faith persisted after the departure of the Romans and through the Dark Ages.

The story of St Patrick, for example, tells us something about this persistence, as well as the possibilities of travel, including cross-Channel travel. He was born somewhere in the west of Scotland, about the time of the Roman withdrawal. His father was a Romanised upper-class Briton and in settled times Patrick could have looked forward to a career as a leading British churchman. But at the age of sixteen he was seized by Irish pirates and sold to a chieftain in Antrim, where he worked in captivity as a herdsman. Somehow he escaped to the continent, returned to Britain, and lived for a time as a monk on an island off the Channel coast, which may have been St Michael's Mount. He went back to the continent, was ordained, probably at Auxerre, and lived there for years. Finally he returned to Britain, and from there went back to Ireland, to become the patron saint of the land of his servitude.

So the Channel and the Irish Sea presented no insuperable obstacle to St Patrick, and he sets a pattern for the movement of other Christian leaders. Bede, for example, credits Bishop Germanus of Auxerre with what looks like the first miracle ever to be performed on Channel waters. He was on his way to Britain to help root out heresy and 'half-way over the passage from the shore of Gaul to Britain . . . suddenly, as they were sailing, the might of evil spirits cometh to withstand them . . . they raiseth tempests, they take away the day from heaven with a night of clouds . . . the mariners in despair gave over their office . . .' His companions wake Germanus and 'taking in the name of the Holy Trinity a few sprinkles of water, he breaketh the raging of the waves . . .'[9]

A more famous saint, Columba, settled in Iona in 563 and started to convert the Picts. St Cuthbert preached the gospel in Northumbria. And in the late seventh century St Wilfrid, on the run from enemies in his native Northumbria, came south, based himself at Selsey in Sussex opposite the Isle of Wight, and set about converting the South Saxons. On their behalf he performed another Channel miracle, and the account of it introduces us for the first time to fishing in the English Channel. 'He not only delivered them from the misery of eternal damnation,' says Bede, 'but also from a horrible murrain of temporal death.' No rain had fallen for three years, and famine stalked the South Saxons. 'It is reported that ofttimes 40 or 50 men being famished for hunger would go together to some cliff . . . and there joining hand in miserable sort would cast themselves all down together, either to be killed with the fall or drowned in the waves.' Wilfrid baptises them, and at once the rain falls. He brings them worldly advice as well as miracles and teaches them to fish; on his advice they 'gat whencesoever they might eel nets together and cast them into the sea, and by the help of grace divine soon took 300 fishes of divers kinds . . .'[10] Wessex fishermen learned from Wilfrid's example, and an eleventh-century schoolmaster has them catching 'herrings and salmon, porpoises and sturgeon, oysters and crabs, mussels, winkles, cockles, plaice and flounders and lobsters, and many similar things'.[11]

In 590 the great Pope Gregory succeeded to the throne of St Peter. Six years later he sent Augustine and his monks to Britain to convert the English. It was a mission intended to bring Roman authority as much as the faith to England. Like so many invaders before him, Augustine landed on a Kentish beach. He came ashore in Pegwell Bay, where Hengist and Horsa had landed, and went to the court of a Kentish king, Aethelbert. The king had a Christian wife, a Frank from across the Channel, and he soon converted to the faith himself. He set Augustine up, first in the Isle of Thanet and then in Canterbury. There he was consecrated Archbishop of the English, and established subordinate bishoprics at London and Rochester.

For another century, the conversion of England continued, but with many setbacks. *The Anglo-Saxon Chronicle* describes one of them. Augustine was succeeded by one of his monks, Laurence, as bishop in Kent. When Aethelbert's son turned against the Christians, Laurence's heart at first failed him and he planned to flee to France. 'But St Peter the apostle scourged him fiercely one night, because he wanted to abandon God's flock thus, and ordered him boldly to instruct the king in the true faith.'[12]

There were cross-purposes and worse between Irish influences and the Roman ones that came in across the Channel, between the Northumbrian bishops and the followers of St Augustine. But by the middle of the seventh century, Augustine's Roman school of doctrine had prevailed. By the end of it, England was Christian and linked, through Canterbury, to the continent. By establishing his archbishopric there, Augustine had reinforced the axis that ran along the old Roman Watling Street from London, through Rochester and Canterbury, to the Kentish coast. Old King Cole had gone down fighting to preserve what was left of Britain's fading contacts with Rome. Now the Old Kent Road linked Britain to a new Rome, ecclesiastical rather than imperial. 'Kent,' Caesar had written, 'is the landing-place for nearly all the ships from Gaul,'[13] and so it had remained throughout the Roman occupation. Now it was re-established as Britain's gateway to Gaul, and the continent's gateway to Britain.

While Augustine and his successors were creating an ecclesiastical England linked to Rome and centred on Canterbury, the kings of Wessex were slowly building a politically united, Christian England centred on Winchester. They fought other regional rulers, kings of Mercia, Northumbria and East Anglia, and later the invading Vikings. Wessex suffered as many defeats as it won victories, and only in 802, some 200 years after Augustine came to England, did Egbert of Wessex succeed in establishing a claim to call himself king of the English.

In the ninth century Alfred tried to build on the basis that Egbert had provided. He did much to unite England politically, and history has also recognised his more peaceful, domestic achievements, as the king who spread civility, culture and the love of learning throughout England. He valued knowledge and invention. 'The saddest thing about any man,' he said, 'is that he be ignorant, and the most exciting thing is that he *knows*.'[14] He learned Latin and arranged the translation of Latin texts into English, 'so that all the youth of free men now among the English people . . . are able to read English writing as well'. He made his capital, Winchester, a centre of civilisation and strengthened its links with the rest of the Christian world. For just as Augustine's decision to base himself in Canterbury had increased the importance of Kent in cross-Channel contacts, so the emergence of Wessex created another axis to the continent. Southampton became Winchester's Channel port. Directly opposite the mouth of the Seine, it was well placed as a terminus of cross-Channel trade. When Alfred died in 899, 'the Saxon kings had come', in Simon Schama's words, 'a long way from the ferocious pagan axemen of the *adventum* to the makers of libraries'.[15] But there was a clear limit to his achievement. He was, says *The Anglo-Saxon Chronicle*, 'king over all the English race except that part which was under Danish control . . .'[16] That qualification takes us back over a hundred years to the beginning of the story of the Vikings.

The Viking challenge afflicted England, the Low Countries, Ireland and northern France. It came with furious energy out of heathen lands in the distant north, yet it first showed itself to history's recording angel on a beach half-way up the English Channel. One day in the year 789 a royal official called Beaduheard, the king's reeve at Dorchester in Wessex, was told that men from strange ships had landed at Portland. He set off to investigate, perhaps taking them for smugglers and determined to ensure that they paid a toll on any goods they sold here. Instead he encountered raw violence: 'and then the reeve rode there and wanted to compel them to go to the king's town, because he did not know what they were; and they killed him. Those were the first ships of the Danish men which sought out the land of the English race.'[17]

They were indeed the first of a new wave of sea-rovers, raiders and pirates, setting out from lonely fiords in Denmark and Norway to make violent fortunes on the coasts of England and France. More came quickly, and in 793 a raiding party descended on the monastery at Lindisfarne on the coast of Northumbria, looting and destroying. They went on to raid Jarrow and Iona. By 832 they were in Kent, and 'heathen men raided across Sheppey'.[18] In 835, 'a great raiding ship-army came to Cornwall'. In 837, Wulfheard fought and defeated thirty-three ship-loads of the raiders, but another band of freebooters fought and killed Aethelhelm at Portland. In 860, 'a great raiding ship-army' – this one setting out from across the Channel, probably from the Somme estuary, rather than Scandinavia – attacked and destroyed Winchester. In 877, 120 ship-loads of invaders landed at Swanage, and in 893 yet another gang of raiders, this time coming from Boulogne, raided Lympne on the Kent coast. The Danes were doing to English towns and villages all along the Channel coast what centuries earlier the Angles, Saxons and Jutes had done to the Britons.

Word of the Vikings' ferocity rang round western Christendom. 'Ruthless, wrathful, foreign, purely pagan people',[19] an Irish monk called them. The churchmen prayed daily: 'From the fury of the Norsemen, deliver us, O Lord.' At first murder, destruction, rape and loot were their objectives; but soon they wanted land as well, or a payment in gold in return for taking their fury elsewhere. The Isle of Thanet comes back into the story. There, close to where the Romans had landed, where Hengist and Horsa had spread their ox-hide and Augustine had converted Aethelbert, the Vikings staked their claim for a first corner of England. In 851, 'the heathen men stayed in Thanet over the winter'[20] and in 865, the inhabitants bribed them to take their mayhem elsewhere. Every year more invaders came, and soon they demanded not just money or a landholding or an estate but kingdoms. By the 870s they ruled Northumbria and disputed Mercia and East Anglia. A tenth-century bishop wrote, 'the pirates are so strong with God's consent that in battle one will often put flight to ten ... And often ten or twelve, one after another, will disgracefully insult the thane's wife ... while he who considered himself proud and powerful and brave enough before that happened, looks on.'[21] In the end they brought the battle to dominate England to Wessex. *The Anglo-Saxon Chronicle* shows Alfred sheltering from them in Athelney, fighting them all over Wessex, and eventually building a fleet to engage them at sea.

The Vikings' ships were beautifully effective instruments of war. They were fast, open boats, propelled by perhaps thirty oars, with a square sail on a stumpy mast that was highly effective before the wind. They could cope with heavy seas, yet their shallow draft enabled them to penetrate quiet estuaries or land on a shoaling beach. Alfred hoped that if he had a fleet of his own he could intercept the Vikings before they got ashore. *The Anglo-Saxon Chronicle* records that his ships were almost twice as long as the Danes', some with sixty oars, some with more. They were swifter, steadier and more responsive than the enemy's, built 'neither of Friesian design nor of Danish, but as it seemed to himself that they might be most useful'. [22]

Alfred used this new weapon of war to engage the attackers before they went ashore, or cut them off after they had landed. So he is recorded as trapping three Danish ships in the mouth of a Devon river, sinking two of them and killing their crews. In 882, 'King Alfred went out to sea with ships and fought against 4 ship-loads of Danish men, and took two of the ships, and killed the men; and two [ship-loads] surrendered to him, and the men were badly knocked about and wounded before they surrendered.'[23] He brought captured raiders to Winchester and hanged them. In the end, Alfred fought the Danes to a standstill. England was in effect divided along the line of the Danelaw. The Danes took the north and east of England, and the mouth of the Thames. The English held London and Wessex, which now embraced the whole south coast of England.

The Norsemen made as great an impact in France. Their raids along the Channel and Atlantic coasts brought the same kind of paralysis they brought to England. Then, just as they had advanced against Wessex, they advanced up the Seine into the heart of the country of the Franks. By 885 they were besieging Paris. As in England, their onslaughts produced counter-blows and they lacked the men to hold the broad areas they had seized. The time was ripe for a deal, and in 911 the Franks and the Normans came to terms. The Normans committed themselves to serve the Frankish kings as mercenaries. In return they were assured of the lands they held around the mouth of the Seine. They were to hold Normandy as tenants of the king of France.

Established around the Bay of the Seine and in the Cotentin peninsula, the Normans became a formidable Channel power. They committed themselves to their new homeland, but their subordination to the Frankish kings had its limits. They made other alliances, went empire-building in Sicily and Calabria, and at times helped Viking raiders. By the middle of the tenth century, therefore, a southern England consolidated around the Anglo-Saxon house of Wessex looked across the water at a powerful and thrusting Norman duchy centred on Bayeux and controlling, directly or through allies, all of the western Channel coast of France. Attention no longer focused on Kent, the Straits of Dover and Calais but on the middle Channel, directly between Normandy and Wessex. The Channel and its coastlines were once again coming into the focus of history. It was a process that culminated at Hastings in 1066.

But before that dénouement comes this chapter's penultimate development. All over Christendom men feared the coming of the millennium. Would it mark the end of the world, or would it bring new temporal horrors? In England, it brought the hostile attentions of a new generation of Danes seeking to complete the work the Vikings had begun, conquer all England and build an English–Danish empire around the North Sea.

We have seen that over 200 years the isolated little groups of Vikings who set out as sea-rovers grew into forces capable of taking and holding Normandy and northern England. Meanwhile, the areas from which they came had developed politically into formal, centralised kingdoms. Denmark had become a serious power with serious ambitions and now it turned its attention to England. Between 1003 and 1014 it despatched armies and fleets across the North Sea in annual invasions.

In 1001, for example, *The Anglo-Saxon Chronicle* tells us, a Danish 'ship-army' rampaged along the English Channel coast and 'raided and burned almost everywhere'.[24] It moved westwards down the coast, probably fighting both on land and at sea. It advanced from Sussex into Hampshire, where it fought and killed men with good Anglo-Saxon names such as Aethelward, Leofric, Leofwine, Wulfhere and Godwine. It went on into Dorset and Devon, burning manors and putting more Anglo-Saxon bands to flight. Finally it turned back to the Isle of Wight in search of yet more opportunities for mayhem. The English used every means they knew to counter the Danes: they fought them, plotted against them, bribed them with Danegeld, fled before them. King Ethelred, damned by history as the Unready, took refuge from his enemies at the court of their distant Norse relations in Normandy. Then he went back to fight them; and finally he submitted to them. In April 1016, he died. The restlessly ferocious Cnut, King of Denmark, married his widow. He ruthlessly destroyed rivals and made himself King Canute of England.

He did not succeed in making England Danish. Indeed he probably did not even try. In the north, to be sure, the Danish kingdom centred on York was old-established and strong. But Denmark itself was far from southern England, and very different. So in the south, and in Wessex in particular, Cnut adapted himself to English influences. The influence on the Danes of the English aristocracy and churchmen there was as great as that of the Danish newcomers on the English. Cnut preserved English institutions, made use of English advisers. He mellowed and built himself a manor at Bosham, the little Channel port on Chichester Harbour. He has gone down in English history not as the ferocious, all-conquering Cnut but as the wise Canute who stood upon the beach there and demonstrated to his courtiers that not even a king could turn back the tide. His daughter was buried beneath the chancel of Bosham Church.

Cnut became a Christian and went on pilgrimage to Rome, and as soon as he got back to England turned to settling the profits of a Channel harbour on the cathedral of the Christian church that Augustine had founded. *The Anglo-Saxon Chronicle* gives a very good impression of an eleventh-century harbour when it records that in 1031 Cnut 'gave into Christ Church in Canterbury the harbour of Sandwich, and all the rights that arise there from either side of the harbour, so that whenever the tide is at its very highest and the very fullest [and] a ship is floating as close to the land as it might closest be, and man stands on that ship and has a "tapor-axe" in his hand . . .' [25] Canute, who in his prime had made a habit of mutilating his prisoners, adopted in his maturity some of the civilised and civilising characteristics of Alfred's Wessex.

In any case, the Anglo-Danish Empire lasted only twenty years. Danish and English interests were very different and they pulled in different directions. When Canute died in 1035 and was buried in Winchester, the empire died with him. His three sons divided his inheritance and became bitter rivals. The stage was set for the thirty-year struggle for the English throne that was to be waged between Saxon, Danish and Norman claimants and which culminated, on 14 October 1066, in battle on a hillside beside the Channel coast of Sussex.

The political and dynastic details of that struggle need not concern us. The essence of the story is that decades of war, negotiation, chicanery and political intermarriage had produced rulers and would-be rulers in Denmark, England and Normandy whose families were inextricably entangled with one another. The old absolute, almost racial distinction between Vikings and Anglo-Saxons was long gone. The descendants of Anglo-Saxon and Viking raiders had merged into an interrelated, international ruling class. They saw each other more as rivals than as relatives, and they pursued their rivalries by methods as lethal as the old confrontations between Anglo-Saxon and Viking armies. Yet they formed almost a single extended family whose members were constantly at odds, often at feud, sometimes at war with one another. The prize they fought for was the throne of England.

On 5 January 1066 the abscess fed by these bitter rivalries burst. On that day, Edward the Confessor died, sending 'a righteous soul to Christ, a holy spirit into God's keeping'. Three men had claims to succeed him. They were Harald Hardrada, King of Norway; Harold Godwineson, Edward's brother-in-law; and William the Bastard, Duke of Normandy. 'Every single one of them,' Norman Davies writes, 'was a Viking, or a client of Vikings, or a descendant of Vikings . . . In effect, 1066 saw a complicated scramble for the final Viking spoils in England.'[26]

Harold was with Edward at Westminster when the old king died. Edward may or may not have given him a final blessing: his dying gesture was ambiguous and variously interpreted. But Harold was on the spot and moved quickly to get the approval of the members of the old Anglo-Saxon Council, the Witan. The day after Edward's death he was crowned in Westminster Abbey. William of Normandy immediately denounced him, claiming that Harold had promised him the throne of England after Edward's death.

Eleven hundred years earlier, Julius Caesar had brought the propaganda of his pen to bear on the story of the Channel. The museum in the Norman town of Bayeux displays a first example of the propaganda of the needle: William the Conqueror's Tapestry. In it, shortly after the conquest, English needlewomen spelt out his version of the events of 1066. It stretches for nearly a hundred yards in length, beautiful in its colours and naïve forms, exquisite in its craftsmanship, haunting in its evocation of politics, life, war and death a thousand years ago. It must, indeed, be the most artistically and historically moving piece of political argument known to history.

The Tapestry tells a complex cross-Channel story. It shows Harold embarking at Bosham on a diplomatic mission to Normandy and wrecked by a Channel storm on a French beach. It shows William coming to rescue him from the man who captured him there. Next comes Harold as an honoured guest (yet implicitly also a prisoner) at William's court at Rouen. Another frame shows William and Harold campaigning together as brothers in arms in Brittany. In the essential frame for William's propaganda purposes, Harold is taking an oath of fealty to William on the bones of English martyrs and promising him the English crown. Then, back in England, Harold treacherously snatches Edward's crown for himself. William goes to war, making his preparations, his men arming, his horses embarked for the cross-Channel journey. Finally William lands in England and the Tapestry shows the Battle of Hastings, Harold cut down, God's justice done to the perjurer and his just inheritance delivered to William the Conqueror.

The Bayeux Tapestry may be movingly beautiful, but it remains propaganda. We shall never know whether Harold promised William the crown of England nor, if he did, whether as a prisoner he had any alternative. We know, in any event, that when William heard that Harold had seized the throne of England he first raged like a man made mad, then quickly obtained papal support for his claim – a papal blessing, in effect, for a holy war against England. A Channel naval campaign, a cross-Channel invasion and an invasion of England were in the making.

But Harold faced a threat from across the North Sea also. There his own brother, Tostig, supported Harald Hardrada's claim to the English throne. Each man was, in his different way, quite as serious an enemy as William of Normandy. Tostig was passionately embittered against his brother. Hardrada was the foremost warrior of his age, tall as a tree, with a fighter's reputation that stretched as far as Byzantium. It was an open question whether Tostig, Hardrada or William would be the first to carry the war to Harold.

In the event, Tostig struck first. Early in May he appeared in force off the Isle of Wight, harried the Sussex coast and landed in Sandwich. Harold believed that Tostig was acting in concert with William, whose more formidable invasion must be imminent. But Tostig, easily driven off by Harold's levies, sailed away northwards to join forces with Hardrada. His failure had shown that local English defences on the Channel coast were perfectly capable of dealing with small-scale attack. Harold, his ships and his professional soldiers would be needed only to counter full-scale invasion.

William of Normandy was preparing just that. He had mobilised his forces and called in the debts of his Breton, French and Flemish allies. At the mouth of the little river Dives, which flows through Calvados and into the Bay of the Seine at today's Cabourg, he began to assemble an army and an invasion fleet to carry it to England. The Bayeux Tapestry shows men felling trees, planing planks, building ships and dragging them into the water. Ships are loaded with wine, provisions and suits of chain armour. This is the first depiction in history of a Channel port at work.

This force assembled by William was the most formidable to be organised for a cross-Channel invasion since that of the Emperor Claudius, a thousand years earlier; and its like would not be seen again until the coming of the Armada, half a millennium later. He had 200 ships, perhaps 3,000 cavalry, an army of anything up to 7,000 men in all. Preparations complete, William waited for the only wind that could get his fleet out of the Dives, a rare south wind.

In his own way, Harold had as formidable a reputation as Hardrada, more formidable than William or Tostig. He had made it as old King Edward's indispensable fighting man. His power ran throughout southern England. The northern barons were more doubtful allies, but they could be cowed. Harold prepared himself for war on two fronts, but looked first to the south, to the Channel.

'Then King Harold came to Sandwich,' says *The Anglo-Saxon Chronicle*, 'and waited for his fleet there, because it was long before it could be gathered. And then when his fleet was gathered, he went into Wight, and lay there all the summer and the autumn; and a land-army was kept everywhere by the sea . . .'[27] But the wind that delayed William worked to Harold's disadvantage, for he could not keep his ships at sea or his men under arms indefinitely. In early September the militia were sent about their harvesting and the ships were brought to London. At about the same time William at last got out of the Dives and used a westerly wind to move his invasion force up Channel, to the mouth of the Somme at St Valéry. Only a short Channel crossing now separated him from England.

At this juncture, Harold learned that Hardrada and Tostig were at large in Yorkshire. By a forced march that still borders on the miraculous, he moved his army 190 miles to the north in five days. On 25 September he descended on the invaders at Stamford Bridge, just east of York, and overwhelmed them. Three days later, on 28 September, William sailed across 70 miles of sea and landed at Pevensey on the Sussex coast of England.

The remains of the Roman fortress at Pevensey, built all those centuries ago as part of the Saxon Shore defences, can still be seen. Within its shell,

William constructed an inner fortress of bank and ditch to give his army immediate shelter. But to the east and north lay marshy levels, shutting the invaders in. William needed to be able to go foraging. He shifted his fleet and army ten miles eastward, to Hastings, and there he built an earth and timber castle. Still he stayed close to his ships, his only line of retreat if his enemies proved too strong for him. He did not even know whom he would meet when battle came. It might be Harold, the false King of England, or Harald Hardrada, the terrifying King of Norway.

In the event, Harold settled matters in the north and marched his men back to London, still covering nearly 40 miles a day, and then on into Sussex, gathering an army around him as he came. His aim must have been to bottle William up beside the sea, deprive him of room to forage, and drive him back to his ships in a rebuff comparable to Julius Caesar's 1,100 years earlier. The consequence was that Harold arrived on the battlefield with only half his army: no more than 7,000 men in all, ranging from the lethally professional warriors of his household to half-armed peasants.

William's army was almost certainly somewhat smaller, but better trained, more cohesive, more flexible. His Norman knights brought their own retinues, his Flemish and Breton allies contingents of men-at-arms. As soon as he knew that Harold was near, he moved his army out of Hastings, marching towards today's town of Battle, nine miles away, determined to break out of Harold's trap beside the seaside. On the morning of Saturday, 14 October, his scouts sighted Harold's army drawn up on a ridge at Senlac that blocked the road to London. According to *The Anglo-Saxon Chronicle* it had gathered around 'the grey apple tree'.[28]

William's and Harold's field of battle slopes down into a little valley from the high ground on which Battle Abbey School for girls stands today. It is no more than three-quarters of a mile wide. The line on which Harold's army was drawn up was across the slope immediately below the walls of the school. William's army gathered in the valley below. Today, the slope below the Anglo-Saxon position does not look formidable. It was steep enough to slow a cavalry attack but certainly not steep enough to block one.

Harold's aim was to hold his position and let the Normans waste their strength in up-hill attacks on his waiting warriors. He deployed them ten or twelve deep behind their shield wall, all on foot, even their commanders. The regular troops were in the centre, the militia on the flanks. Their main weapon was the deadly two-handed axe. Against them, William deployed his infantry, archers and armoured cavalry, Breton allies on the left, French and Flemings on the right and his own men of Normandy in the centre.

Battle started at nine in the morning. William of Poitiers, a committed propagandist for William, claims that Harold prayed, 'May the Lord decide this day between William and me, and may he pronounce which of us has the right.'[29] As the Normans advanced, they shouted *Deus aie* ('God help us'), the Saxons answering with their battle cry 'Out, out' – the cry to which English rioters or demonstrators still instinctively resort when a football match or a poll tax inflames their blood. Archers, infantry and Norman knights attacked in turn, each of them unsuccessfully. The English line held rock solid, its defenders packed together so tightly that 'the dead could scarcely fall'. The hours dragged bloodily by, and still the attackers could make no impression on the shield wall. Then the Breton knights, their attacks as ineffectual as all the rest, broke and fled. They left the Norman flank exposed; there was a moment of panic, the rumour spread that William himself was dead, and even his Normans began to retreat.

The militia on Harold's right flank now abandoned their defensive positions and charged down the hill to complete the Normans' confusion. But William threw back his helmet to show himself and encourage his men into counter-attack. The militia were slowly cut to pieces, the main Saxon army on the ridge watching impotent to help them. Now, to replace his lost right wing Harold had to thin out his centre and left. His two brothers were dead. The shield wall began to look less formidable.

But still it held, until William feigned retreat. Again the Saxons came down into the valley from their ridge and again the Norman knights got among them and butchered them. Where the shield wall still endured, its shields still turning Norman arrows aside, William told his archers to fire high. Their falling arrows took their toll, and eventually, in that most famous and probably fictitious wounding of all military history, took out Harold's eye. His bodyguard gathered round him, fighting to the last to protect him, but the Normans broke in and cut them down. The surviving Saxons fled, the Norman cavalry in pursuit.

The battle was over. *The Anglo-Saxon Chronicle* gives it cursory treatment and ascribes the victory to God's will rather than William's efforts: 'There were killed King Harold, and Earl Leofwine his brother, and Earl Gyrth his brother, and many good men. And the French had possession of the place of slaughter, just as God granted them because of the people's sins.'[30] In fact Hastings is one of the most significant battles ever to be fought beside the Channel, to be compared with the defeat of the Armada or the great clashes of 1940 and 1944. Yet however much later sentiment may have turned the affair into the destruction of a good Anglo-Saxon king by a brutal Norman on the make, as did Charles Kingsley in his poem 'The Swan-Neck' –

> Thus fell Harold, bracelet-giver;
> Jesu rest his soul for ever;
> Angles all from thrall deliver;
> Miserere Domine –

it was in fact simply the victory of one warlord over another, both of them descended from the Vikings.

After the battle, Harold's mistress, Edith Swan-Neck, walked across the field to find the body of the dead king. His mother offered to buy it from William and give it a decent burial. The Conqueror refused. Harold's ships had failed to stop him at sea. Harold's army had failed to defeat him on land. Anglo-Saxon England had gone down to defeat before him. Henceforth the Norman machine would rule both England and Normandy. William of Poitiers records or perhaps invents a jibe: 'They said in jest that he who had guarded the coast with such insensate zeal should be buried by the seashore.'[31] In any event, William told his men to bury Harold's body on a Channel beach and put a stone on top of it. History records that later, when passions were cooler, it was reburied at Waltham Abbey, but some Sussex antiquaries still argue instead that, like Canute's daughter, Harold lies beneath the chancel floor in Bosham church beside Chichester harbour, on the Channel coast of England.

CHAPTER 3

CROSS-CHANNEL EMPIRE

W illiam's victory changed the nature of England. Much of the Anglo-Saxon nobility had died at Battle beside Harold. His sons and other notables fled to Ireland, others to Scotland or Denmark. William expropriated the property of the Anglo-Saxon ruling class, taking it for himself or presenting it to his barons and ecclesiastical administrators. Norman French became the language of English law and administration. A Norman bishop, Lanfranc, became Archbishop of Canterbury. The same families now ruled in Normandy and England, forming a little western European empire composed essentially of their land holdings. Throughout the rest of his reign William had to struggle with domestic enemies within his empire, and with threats to it from outside. He never succeeded in imposing a lasting peace throughout his dominions but he held his cross-Channel empire together and built a strong government and administration, always vigorous and usually fair and dispassionate by the standards of the time.

The requirements of this empire gave the Channel a new and different importance. The middle Channel became a thoroughfare of government, administration and trade. When William travelled to Normandy he rode from his castles at Windsor or Woodstock, through Clarendon near Winchester, and on to Southampton or Portsmouth. There he took ship across the Channel to the little port of Barfleur on the point of Normandy, before continuing to Bayeux, Rouen or Caen. A courtly entourage moved with him; and royal counsellors, administrators and messengers followed.

The Channel was an essential link of empire and its ports and shipping adapted themselves to its requirements. Ships had been using coastal waters regularly and usually safely for centuries. Angles, Saxons and Jutes had crossed the North Sea in their open boats, and from the Sutton Hoo excavations of a Saxon boat-burial in Suffolk we have precise ideas of their construction. Later the Vikings added fierce figureheads and a square sail to their own ships, still open boats like the Saxons'. Small as these ships were, they were seaworthy in all except ferocious weather. The Normans' ships evolved from these origins, and the Bayeux Tapestry shows them in use in the great cross-Channel invasion. They are clinker-built, driven by a single square sail, steered with a side rudder. They carry three horses, or provisions and wine, or a score of men, their shields lining the bulwarks. Ships such as these were used in William's cross-Channel ferry service, capable with a fair wind of making the crossing between Normandy and the Solent in a long day or a day and a night. At Barfleur they moored in a small but sheltered harbour on an exposed coast close to dangerous rocks, at Southampton beside primitive wharves on a sheltered river mouth with unusually favourable tides.

The shift to this north–south focus of attention is reflected in *The Anglo-Saxon Chronicle*, which now becomes essentially an account of the doings of the new Norman masters of England. In the north, west and east they face attacks from Scotland, from Harold's surviving sons raiding out of Ireland, and from continued Danish incursions across the North Sea. But in the south the *Chronicle* describes cross-Channel comings and goings as something commonplace among the ruling classes. Above all, it documents the king's regular travels between England and Normandy.

Six months after his victory at Battle, William went back to Normandy to receive a hero's welcome in the streets of Rouen and attend the dedication of the new church at the Abbey of Jumièges beside the Seine. Then, in 1074, 'King William led an English and French raiding-army across the sea and won the land of Maine.'[1] In 1075 he is in Normandy when he hears that a kinsman, Earl Roger, is plotting with a half-Breton, Earl Ralph, against him. The king's supporters frustrate the plan, until 'the king afterwards came to England and seized his relative, Earl Roger, and secured him'. Next, at Westminster that winter, he deals with Ralph's Bretons: 'Some were blinded and some driven from the land. Thus were traitors to William laid low.'[2] But by 1079 William is at odds with his own son, Robert, because he 'would not let him govern his earldom in Normandy which he himself . . . had given him'.[3] The story of a clash between them captures the inconsequentiality that so often offset Norman efficiency and brutality. In the battle Robert wounds his father. Then he gives him his own horse to carry him to safety. Then, filial duty done, he takes refuge from paternal revenge at the court of Flanders.

Lesser men are recorded as crossing the Channel too, sometimes in search of booty or some more enduring advantage, such as ecclesiastical preferment. The monks of Peterborough, writing their own version of *The Anglo-Saxon Chronicle*, describe two episodes of cross-Channel villainy that show how intimately the societies on the two sides of the Channel were linked together. Into accounts of the doings of kings and earls, which can be found in all versions of the *Chronicle*, they insert the story of a group of thieves who came to Peterborough at Pentecost in 1102 from Auvergne (or, on another reading of the monastic handwriting, from Alemannia – Germany). They broke into the cathedral and 'there took much of value in gold and in silver, that was: crosses and chalices and candlesticks'.[4]

The second malefactor, who arouses more extended monastic anger, is a white-collar villain, an ecclesiastical carpet-bagger, one Abbot Henry of Poitou. 'He had his abbacy at St Jean d'Angély in hand, and all the archbishops and bishops said that it was against the law, and that he could not have two abbacies in hand'; 'through his tricks' he therefore persuades someone to make him Archbishop of Besançon, but holds it for only three days and 'then he lost it, justly, because earlier he had got hold of it unjustly'. He 'gets hold of' the bishopric of Saintes, but the abbot of Cluny 'got him out of there'. Finally he turns to England and persuades the king that as 'an old and a broken-down man'[5] he could not endure the injustice and cruelty that was done to him in France.

He begs the king to give him Peterborough. 'Thus wretchedly the abbacy was given ... he came to Peterborough, and there he stayed exactly as drones do in a hive. All that the bees carry in, drones devour and carry off; and so did he.' It comes as no surprise to the chronicler that after all this villainy hauntings follow, with visions of huntsmen 'black and huge and loathesome', riding on black horses and black billy-goats, with their hounds 'all black and wide-eyed and loathesome'. This, says the chronicle of the carpet-bagger, 'was his entrance: of his exit we cannot yet say. May God provide!'[6]

That Flanders gave refuge to a rebel against William is a reminder that the Straits of Dover more often than not separated hostile powers: no cross-Channel empire linked England to the continent here. The eastern Channel in the eleventh century saw pirates and freebooters at work, privateers licensed by kings or dukes or counts, towns banding together for their own protection and to attack others. It is a very different scene from the passage of the regular imperial ferry boats on the route between Southampton and Barfleur. Imposing some kind of order on this chaos was the task of the Cinque Ports.

The Cinque Ports are not really five but seven in number, and their correct title is 'the Cinque Ports and Two Ancient Towns'. The seven lie on or close to the Kent and Sussex coast. Hastings today is a rather run-down Victorian resort, Dover a dynamo of a place powering cross-Straits ferry traffic. Sandwich is a sleepy little town, tucked away between Ramsgate and Deal, with Roman Richborough at its back gate. Romney looks across the darkly mysterious levels of Romney Marsh, while Hythe is a far brasher place, facing out to sea towards Boulogne. Rye, once a seaport, now sits on its inland hill overlooking the marshes, a beautiful old town, over-precious to the baleful eye, stuffed with history to the more appreciative. Its neighbour, Winchelsea, is different again, built to order for defensive purposes, its layout based on the model of a French fortified town, a dreamy sort of place today, in which the ideas of the medieval town planners have never quite reached fulfilment. Over the centuries the Cinque Ports and Two Ancient Towns have, in short, gone their separate ways and become very different from one another, but they have origins and founding myth in common.

They guarded a coastline greatly different from today's. The Isle of Thanet was still an island, separated from the mainland by those sheltered waters in which Aulus Plautius's ships had anchored at Richborough. The headland of Dungeness jutted into the Channel as it does today, and behind it lay marshes and some areas of level agricultural land reclaimed by the Romans. But behind it also were areas of sheltered water, navigable little rivers and shallow lagoons. In effect these carried the coastline inland, to the point where now the levels meet the hills. Rye and Winchelsea were busy ports rather than the Rip Van Winkle towns they are today.

The story of the Cinque Ports' special responsibilities for maritime defence goes back to the reign of Edward the Confessor and persists into the high Middle Ages. The men of these fishing and trading ports were charged by the king with the defence of the Kent and Sussex coast and the security of the Channel crossing. Between them they had to make fifty-seven ships available for fifty-seven days' service a year. In return the Crown gave the Portsmen trading privileges and exemptions, which they jealously guarded and wherever possible enlarged. On the back of these privileges they built a strong trading position in the Channel and further afield. In particular they controlled the export of wool and iron and the import of wine and salt.

The individual ports were banded together in a loose confederation, equally loosely subject to the Crown. At times the men of the Ports allied themselves with ports in Normandy and Spain, but essentially they were out for themselves. They were ready to fight to protect their monopolies, as much against fellow Englishmen from East Anglia and the West Country as against Frenchmen or Flemings from the other side of the Channel. They tried their hands at piracy and port-raiding themselves, 'cruelly exceeding', says Matthew Paris, a chronicler of that age, 'the limit prescribed by the King and robbing and killing English as well as French'. They went raiding in part to punish others' villainies, in part for their own advantage; and they were slow to draw clear distinctions between such activities, honest trade and the righteous defence of the realm. They dominated fifty miles of coastline from East Sussex to the Downs off the eastern face of Kent, and satellite towns as far apart as Faversham and Pevensey supported them. Together they constituted a maritime and trading force of great substance in medieval England.

William I died in 1087. He died campaigning, from a fall from his horse while besieging Mantes on the Seine. There is a flavour of waspish *Schadenfreude* behind the conventional monastic piety in *The Anglo-Saxon Chronicle*'s commentary on his end: 'Alas! how false and unstable is the prosperity of this world. He who was earlier a powerful king, and lord of many a land, he had nothing of any land but a seven-foot measure; and he who was at times clothed with gold and with jewels, he lay then covered over with earth.'[7]

Another chronicler talks of William dying stripped naked, his room stripped bare. Before he had breathed his last his sons who were there hurried off on their separate ways. The eldest, Robert, went to assert his claim to Normandy; the second, William Rufus, to take ship to England and seize the English Treasury. With moderation and good will they might have transformed the old cross-Channel empire into a loose alliance between brothers, but neither son inherited the father's political skills. They soon turned to fruitless, inconclusive campaigns against one another in Normandy and Brittany. It was only in 1100, when a third son, Henry, succeeded Rufus on the English throne (having perhaps first contrived his murder while Rufus was hunting in the New Forest) that someone approaching William I's authority set about restoring the link between England and Normandy.

First Henry had to deal with his other brother, Robert. In 1101 Robert hatched a plot with dissident barons in England and launched a little-remembered cross-Channel expedition to seize the crown. Expecting it, Henry 'sent his ships out to sea to the damage and hindrance of his brother'. But treachery was at work among his captains: 'some of them . . . turned away from the king and submitted to the earl Robert'[8] before Henry could bring the invader to battle. He drew up his army at Pevensey, where his father had first landed when he came to conquer England, but for once in his life Robert outwitted an opponent and landed at Portsmouth instead. At this point he lost his tenuous hold on the initiative, however, and made peace with his brother 'on the condition that the king relinquish all that he held within Normandy by force against the earl'. Robert went back to Normandy, and soon, peace treaty or no treaty, Henry went over to the attack, invading Normandy. By 1106 he had reunited the Duchy with England.

Henry I ruled England and Normandy for thirty-five years, gradually building an authority over his barons and his neighbours as imposing as his father's. The price of power was restless energy, untiring watchfulness and constant journeying. But he seemed destined to be disappointed in his children. He fathered many, but in 1120 he lost his only legitimate male heir, William the Atheling.

He lost him in a Channel shipping disaster, the first in recorded history. On 25 November 1120, already dangerously late in the season, Henry set off with his court from Barfleur, near the tip of the Normandy peninsula, on his way to Southampton. The king travelled in one ship, his son in another, the *White Ship*, which, a chronicler tells us, 'flew swifter than the winged arrow, sweeping the rippling surface of the deep; but the carelessness of the intoxicated crew drove her on to a rock'.[9] *The Anglo-Saxon Chronicle* gives more detail: 'the king's two sons, William and Richard [a bastard] were drowned – and Richard earl of Chester and Ottuel his brother, and very many of the king's court: stewards, and chamberlains, and cup-bearers, and various officials, and countless very distinguished people among them'. And then the *Chronicle*, usually a down-to-earth account of comings, goings and doings, brings a vivid psychological insight to the human tragedy of the disaster. 'To their friends the death of these was a double grief: one that they lost this life so suddenly, the other that few of their bodies were found anywhere afterwards.'[10] 'No ship ever brought such misery to England,' wrote William of Malmesbury, 'none was ever so notorious in the history of the world.'[11]

It is said that at first William the Atheling got away from the wreck in a boat, but when he turned back to rescue his half-sister, the boat was swamped and prince and princess drowned. That chivalrous act, by a princeling who seems otherwise to have been a mere popinjay, ensured that history would remember the *White Ship* disaster, until even a Victorian poet, Dante Gabriel Rossetti, added his own two penn'orth to the saga in 'The White Ship':

> Then o'er the splitting bulwark's brim
> The Prince's sister screamed to him.
>
> He gazed aloft, still rowing apace,
> And through the whirled surf he knew her face.
>
> He knew her face and he heard her cry,
> And he said, 'Put back! She must not die!'

Keith Feiling's treatment of the tragedy is more incisive. 'Fate dealt mercilessly with the hard heart of Henry I,' he wrote. 'His affections, like his foreign policy, were centred in his only son William; both were cut in half by the tragedy of November 1120.'[12]

Henry's hopes of keeping the crown of England and Normandy together in his immediate family's hands now depended on his only other legitimate child, and she was a woman. In 1114 his daughter Matilda had married Henry V, the Holy Roman Emperor. He died after nine years of marriage and she returned to her father's court a childless widow. Two years later her father committed her to a second marriage, this time with a French princeling of the second rank, Geoffrey, the heir of the count of Anjou. She despised Geoffrey's youth and lack of royal blood, let alone his lack of her own imperial dignity. But this was a dynastic marriage or it was nothing, and in 1133 she produced a son, a Henry like his grandfather. The boy would inherit Normandy and Anjou. Matilda was determined that he should inherit the throne of England too.

Two years later the grandfather, Henry I, died. Out of an obscure baronial showdown came the succession not of the toddler Henry but of a second cousin, Stephen. Matilda, proud, angry and ornery at the best of times, set herself to change matters. She spent the next fifteen years quarrelling with her husband and plotting Stephen's overthrow. People said of the period that 'God and his angels slept'; there was as yet little to be seen of the cohesive, cross-Channel empire that William had created and Henry I restored.

But once he was of age, Matilda and Geoffrey married Henry off to Eleanor of Aquitaine. Eleanor had a vividly chequered past and was twice her new husband's age. She had been Queen of France but was estranged from her husband, perhaps for the most obvious of reasons: 'I have married a monk, not a king,' she said. She had to her credit beauty, intelligence and verve, but above all she had property. She brought to the marriage not just Poitou but most of the lands of France between the Loire, the Atlantic, and the Pyrenees. To put all this together with Normandy and Anjou was to re-create not merely William's old Norman empire but a western European empire that dwarfed the holdings of the King of France.

It remained to unite all this with the realm of England. There Stephen still ruled, in a state of permanent civil war. In the following year the young Henry took up the struggle where his termagant of a mother had left it, and launched a personal campaign against Stephen. He crossed the Channel in winter, was blown dangerously off course and might have met the same end as William the Atheling. But he scraped to a landing in Dorset, went on to besiege Stephen's castle at Malmesbury in 1153, and came to terms with him. 'The archbishop and the wise men' mediated between the two; 'soon it became a very good peace', judged the monks at Peterborough, almost at the end of their version of *The Anglo-Saxon Chronicle*, 'such as there never was before'.[13] Its durability was never tested, for a year later Stephen was blessed with a natural death that relieved his young opponent of the task of procuring him an unnatural one.

The way was clear for Henry to pick up the crown and make himself Henry II, King of England. Now the whole western flank of the European continent from the Cheviots to the Pyrenees was united under Henry and Eleanor. Simon Schama calls this empire the fulfilment of 'Henry I's strategic vision: of the creation of a cross-Channel superstate beside which the kings of France would be reduced to puny impotence'.[14]

Henry Plantagenet, Henry II of England, ruled this empire for thirty-five years, as long as his grandfather, Henry I, had ruled England and Normandy. He would have been a 'remarkable ruler in any age . . . clever, violent, imaginative, passionately addicted to hunting and hawking yet cultivated and intellectual, and possessed of a superabundant energy which enabled him to travel faster and further than other men, sleep with many women and comprehend the detail of great policies and the inwardness of the greatest issues.'[15] History remembers him as a king who travelled indefatigably around his possessions (crossing the Channel twenty-eight times during his reign), who imposed discipline on his barons ('Henry the castle-breaker', he was called) and who (fatally for his reputation) let himself be saddled with the martyrdom of Thomas à Becket.

The story of the quarrel that led to that murder illustrates the way the affairs of England and Normandy interlocked. It shows king and archbishop constantly travelling across the Channel, at home on either side of it and, when they fell out, pronouncing anathemas against one another across it. It illustrates how the leading men of their day thought of themselves not as Englishmen or Frenchmen but as members of a class that ruled equally in England, Normandy and the rest of the Plantagenets' dominions, and who were bound to others of their kind by membership of the universal Church. The quarrel also shows how someone out of favour at Westminster or in Rouen could turn for support to the Plantagenets' enemy, France, foreshadowing not cross-Channel empire but cross-Channel war.

Thomas à Becket was the first townsman to rise to high distinction in medieval England. He was himself half Norman. He grew up in London, the son of a merchant from Rouen who had crossed the Channel to better himself and who had prospered on Cheapside. He became a servant of the Archbishop of Canterbury and then, catching the king's eye, a bureaucrat in royal service. Henry, beguiled by his diligence and worldly ability, made him his Chancellor. 'Becket was on terms of intimate friendship with the king, and served him faithfully and well for seven years as statesman, diplomat and soldier, appearing outwardly as the court ecclesiastic of extravagant worldly tastes and brilliant abilities.'[16]

Henry convinced himself that if Becket were ordained he could use the power of the Church to discipline the king's enemies. Becket allowed himself to be ordained and then consecrated Archbishop of Canterbury, but to all appearances he was a reluctant churchman. With consecration, however, something went to his head: loyalty to his priests, fatal stubbornness, vanity, perhaps even sanctity? In his own words, he changed from being 'a patron of play-actors and a follower of hounds to being a shepherd of souls'.[17] From the king's loyal servant, Becket became the defender of the prerogatives of the Church against the monarchy. Quarrels followed, pursued by both with all the bitterness of friends turned enemies. Henry was a monarch's monarch. He was not the kind of man to share power with a civil servant turned churchman, however beloved, whose career he himself had made. The quarrels became confrontations, about the powers of the Church within the State and about the king's authority over the Church. Henry, always imperious, now faced a defiant Becket, who he believed had deliberately deceived him. Becket himself was thoroughly inconsistent: defiant, accommodating and timid by turns.

He believed, probably rightly, that his life was in danger. In the end he fled across the Channel, to the Cistercian Abbey of Pontigny, where he was safe under the protection of the King of France and the Catholic Church. There he clothed himself in the outraged anger of a prince of the Church; from there he fulminated against the Church's enemies in

England, excommunicating Henry's servants, making himself ever more resolutely Henry's enemy.

France, Church, the Pope himself all became embroiled in the quarrel. Henry threatened to drive Cistercian monks out of England if Becket was allowed to remain at Pontigny. He fled to a Benedictine abbey instead. Go-betweens went back and forth across the Channel, from England to France, from Henry to Becket. Becket remained intransigent, Henry remained incensed. Finally king and archbishop met, not in England or Normandy but far away beside the Loire. A compromise was formulated, which Becket gracelessly accepted.

They parted, Henry for Normandy, Becket for England. Henry was still seething, Becket still full of foreboding. In December 1170, he took ship from Wissant and crossed to Sandwich, the harbour whose revenues Cnut had once dedicated to the support of Canterbury Cathedral. The faithful thronged to greet him there, but a group of the king's servants stood watching. The menace of these men, the sort of people he had anathematised from Pontigny, was palpable. He responded with his own kind of weapons: 'I have come to give life and limb for Justice and Truth,' he announced. From Sandwich, he went on his way to Canterbury, and from there he threw down challenges to his enemies: 'May they be damned by Jesus Christ.' Here was a man looking for martyrdom.

Henry II was holding court at his castle of Bayeux in Normandy, still thinking he had come to terms with Becket. But the archbishop's enemies brought the king accounts of his continuing defiance. Sickness intensified Henry's rage, provoking his famous outburst: 'Will no one rid me of this turbulent priest?' The four knights, Hugh de Morville, William de Tracy, Reginald Fitzurse and Richard le Breton, rushed off to do what they took to be Henry's will. They crossed to Kent and gathered at Saltwood Castle above Romney Marsh (the very Saltwood with whose grandeur the Tory MP Alan Clark would beguile the readers of his diaries so many centuries later). In the morning, they rode away up the road to Canterbury, and there at the hour of a December Vespers they murdered the archbishop in his cathedral.

'Christendom was aghast; all over western Europe Thomas was

spontaneously acclaimed as a martyr.'[18] The way the archbishop had brought his troubles on himself went for nothing. A reluctant Pope felt obliged to give Thomas à Becket what looks in retrospect like a very questionable canonisation. Henry was undone, overwhelmed by profound unpopularity, a papal interdict against his continental possessions and, when he sought forgiveness at Canterbury, by a grievous papal penance.

Henry II continued to fight the French and the Welsh; he invaded Ireland; and he went on quarrelling with his barons. As for Eleanor, she retained into old age much of her beauty and all her vitality. Her marriage with Henry and their great imperial relationship gradually drifted into detachment and then enmity. She had borne him eight children; but his mistresses had borne him more. Now king and queen watched each other from a distance. For years he held her prisoner and when she was free she held court of her own at Poitiers, he at Westminster or Bayeux. She took to signing herself 'by the wrath of God, Queen of England'. In the end she turned her passionate abilities actively against her husband, lending encouragement and then practical support to his sons' machinations against him. When he died at Chinon on the Loire in 1189 he had just lost a province to the King of France, the French were encroaching on all his possessions and the glory days of the cross-Channel empire were over.

Henry was succeeded by his eldest son Richard; and Richard, when he died in 1199, by his brother John. Between them they provide a long dying fall to the story of the Plantagenet Empire. Richard dissipated his energies and wealth in crusading and pointless Mediterranean warfare, achieving nothing except reputation as the Saracen-slayer who was nicknamed 'Lionheart'. John's reign was as pointless and less glorious. He spent it locked in faithless dealings with his faithless barons, who in the end, in the year before he died, reduced him to the indignity of sharing his power with them in the signing of the Magna Carta.

Both Richard and John saw the old cross-Channel links strained to breaking-point. They both lost ground to the fast-reviving kingdom of

France. John sought allies in an anti-French coalition, joining hands with the Counts of Flanders, Boulogne and Toulouse and with the Holy Roman Emperor himself. But on a summer's day in 1214 King Philip II of France shattered the coalition's armies at the Battle of Bouvines in Flanders. His victory set France on the road to greatness. Maine, Anjou, Touraine, Poitou, Brittany and even Normandy itself fell into the hands of the French. The whole Channel coast was united under French authority. Of all the Plantagenets' possessions in France, only the far south-western provinces of Guyenne and Gascony were left.

Now the French king saw an opportunity to carry war to his enemies. He may even have dreamed of creating a cross-Channel empire of his own. A French army got ashore in England, joined forces with rebellious barons, and took control of all south-east England. Of all the Channel strongpoints, only Dover Castle, the 'key to England', held out. 'By May 1216 Louis and his English allies had taken London and it looked very much as if the next king of England would be Lewis I.'[19]

The French and the barons marched north and in October John, still campaigning bitterly against them, went north also, lost his treasure in the Wash and his life at Newark. His eight-year-old son, Henry III, succeeded him. A regency was scratched together to hold the country against its many enemies. Only in 1217 were the French invaders defeated, and only after a French fleet had been beaten off in a battle off Sandwich was the threat to England over.

The English were to go on campaigning in France for another 300 years, but the days when their rulers overshadowed the kings of France were gone for good. The balance of power between England and France was altered. The significance of the Channel was changed also. The old empire that had run through Normandy all the way from the Scottish border to the Spanish frontier was lost, and the cross-Channel link destroyed. From now on the Channel was no longer an imperial thoroughfare. It had become instead a demarcation line between two kingdoms. For almost 600 years they were to be always at odds and more often than not at war with one another.

CHAPTER 4

FROGS AND GODDAMS

Henry III spent his life trying to contain and subdue his barons. The next king, Edward I, turned his formidable energies to building an insular empire by subduing the Welsh and Scots. For the time being the stand-off with France, and therefore cross-Channel affairs, become secondary considerations.

Edward II succeeded to the throne in 1307. He turned out to be a weak and unwise king, who was widely believed to have unorthodox sexual tastes. He nevertheless tried to bind England and France together by marrying Princess Isabella of France, and in 1308 most of Europe's crowned heads came to the splendid celebration of their marriage in Boulogne. It produced a son but no immediate political dividends, however, and it was only when Edward III came to the throne in 1327 and set about recovering the old inheritance in France that the barons got a king bellicose enough to suit them.

Yet it was the King of France who made the first move to rekindle the old English–French wars. He brought a fleet from the Mediterranean to the Channel, attacked the Isle of Wight and the English-held Channel Islands, and declared Aquitaine, for which Edward owed him fealty, confiscated to the French crown. Edward's response was to claim the French crown for himself. These were the first moves in the tangle of manoeuvre, diplomacy and occasional battles of the Hundred Years War. It was to be an episodic war, with long stops and short starts, fought out all over France, with the regular involvement of allies and proxies. For the purposes of our Channel story, seven episodes stand out. They are the sea battle at Sluys in Flanders; Edward III's Crécy campaign; his siege of Calais; the Cinque Ports' little local difficulties with their neighbours; Henry V's war that culminated at Agincourt; the judicial murder of Joan of Arc in the Place du Vieux-Marché in Rouen; and the Battle of Formigny, little known to English history but which marked a final defeat for England's hopes of retaining Normandy. Each of these events took place within 30 miles of the narrow seas. They were interrupted in 1348 by the coming of the Black Death.

First, Sluys. Trouble started with a fierce little Anglo-French maritime war, with the French burning Portsmouth and the English (with the Cinque Ports' ships well to the fore) raiding Boulogne in return. Edward sought something more decisive and planned a great landing in Flanders, to be followed by a combined operation against France. Philip of France assembled a fleet in the harbour at Sluys to block his way, saying unconvincingly that he was going crusading. The English believed he intended a cross-Channel invasion, and on 24 June 1340 they attacked his fleet, bringing the French to history's first great naval battle in the narrow seas.

Sluys today is a cheerful little holiday town just over the Dutch border from Bruges in Belgium, close to the Scheldt approaches to Antwerp. Philip's ships were massed in the estuary of the Zwin, the little river on which Sluys stands. Today the Zwin is shut in behind the sand dunes on which the summer resort of Knocke stands, forming an area of sandbanks, marshes, little rivulets and dry land.

Here 650 years ago the English and the French fought each other to the death. In a letter to his son, King Edward described his advance to battle: 'On Saturday, St John's Day, soon after the hour of noon at high tide in the name of God, and confident in our just quarrel, we entered the said port upon our said enemies, who had assembled their ships in very strong array, and who made a most noble defence all that day and the night following.'[1] The English closed with the enemy in a style which Roger Keyes was to try to emulate on this same coast when he stormed the German defences at Zeebrugge in April 1918. There was no question of manoeuvre. The French ships were moored and chained together in a solid wall. By now, ships were usually equipped with fore and stern castles, and topcastles at the mast heads, from which archers could shoot down on to the enemy's decks. At Sluys the English advanced with each shipload of archers secured between two ships filled with pikemen; this was a seaborne infantry battle, with archers and pikemen and axemen packed together into the little ships of the two fleets.

In the course of that bloody day and night the English cut the Frenchmen down or drove them across their decks and overboard; 190 ships were captured and an astonishing total of 16,000 men are supposed to have been killed. The French king's jester, with the courage of a very brave man, told his master afterwards that the English must be cowards, for they would not jump into the sea in pursuit of the French.[2] For their part the English bragged that so many Frenchmen were drowned that the very fish were learning French. In proportion to populations it was a far bloodier battle than the one the English and Spanish were to fight off this same coast 250 years later. Its outcome more or less guaranteed England's safety from invasion. The big battles to come would be fought in France, not on the English side of the Channel.

Nothing came of Edward's hopes for a grand invasion of France after his victory at Sluys, but six years later he determined to try his luck again, this time from a different direction. In the summer of 1346 he massed 15,000 men and more than 700 ships at Southampton and Portsmouth, pretending that he was on his way to Bordeaux in English Aquitaine. But the Channel gives an attacker who commands the sea the flexibility to achieve strategic surprise in his choice of destination. Once he was safely out of sight of land, Edward revealed that his real destination was Normandy, from where he intended to march on Paris. The armada landed at St Vaast-La-Hougue in the Cotentin peninsula, and Edward marched his army through Normandy to the Seine. He turned towards Paris, but it was too big to besiege, too prickly to attack. Having penetrated as far as its suburbs, Edward turned away to the north. A purposeful invasion of France was becoming what looks to posterity suspiciously like a *chevauchée* – a mere military promenade from one Channel port to another.

When Edward reached the Somme, the next obstacle to his promenade, he found the bridges destroyed or blocked. He turned aside, not inland but towards the sea. There was no sign of his fleet and the Somme on his right was widening into an estuary. Philip with a far larger army was coming up behind him and Edward was marching into a trap. But a prisoner told him of a ford across the estuary, two miles in length, at a place called Blanchetaque near Le Crotoy. He got his men away across it, an escape in its way as perilous and miraculous as the evacuation from Dunkirk was to be in 1940, and stationed his army on a little hill at Crécy-en-Ponthieu, just north of Abbeville and ten miles inland from the Channel coast. He himself surveyed the field from a windmill on the hilltop.

The role of Edward's windmill is played today by a wooden look-out tower for sightseers. Before it stretches a gentle rolling countryside, the land sloping slightly away to the south-east, terraced in places, fields interspersed with trees. This is *la France profonde*, an untroubled landscape.

There, late on an August evening, the French army stumbled into battle. A band of mercenary Genoese crossbowmen was in the van, with French cavalry in all their aristocratic splendour massed behind them. The French army was unprepared for battle, its ranks disordered even before the fighting began. The Genoese turned tail under English longbow fire. Suspecting treachery or incensed by cowardice, the French cavalry rode them down and pressed forward against the English. 'There is no man,' wrote the chronicler Jean Froissart, 'unless he had been present, that can imagine or describe truly the confusion of that day, especially the bad management and disorder of the French, whose troops were out of number.'[3] On one part of the front, the English discharged three cannons, the first ever fired on an open battlefield. On another, where Edward's young son the Black Prince commanded, the French seemed close to breaking through, and messengers were despatched to beg the king for reinforcements. 'Let the boy win his spurs,' was his reply, 'for I am determined, if it please God, that all the glory of this day be given to him, and to those into whose care I have entrusted him.'[4] The attack was turned back, the French routed.

A French account of the campaign displayed at Crécy describes the English king's military promenade as 'The raid and retreat of Edward III'. It is accurate enough as a description of Edward's strategy, but Crécy, the high point of this retreat, was a crushing tactical defeat for French arms. As for the victors, they indulged in the usual butchery of that majority of prisoners too poor to be worth a ransom, but they organised a grand funeral for the blind king of Bohemia, who had been killed at Philip's side. From the old king's coat of arms the Black Prince took the feathers that form the Prince of Wales's own arms to this day.

The English had won a famous victory. It gave them an evil reputation among their enemies and a warm sense among themselves that they had done great things against odds, and far from home.

The French had lost perhaps as many men as at Sluys. Edward might have marched on Paris and taken it, but his army was exhausted. He turned north, and marched undisturbed to the coast. At Calais he found the town resolutely held against him. Building a camp to the west of the town and urging his Flemish allies to blockade it from the east, he settled down for a long siege. Nothing, not even a Scottish invasion of northern England, distracted him from it. In hopes of raising the siege, Philip brought an army to Sangatte, where today Channel Tunnel trains break surface, but he lacked the men or the guts to attack the besiegers.

The governor of Calais reported 'Everything is eaten up – dogs, cats, horses – and we have nothing left to subsist on, unless we eat each other.'[5] Then in August 1347, exactly a year after Crécy, he surrendered the town. Edward's queen, Philippa, famously interceded for the lives of burghers whom the great Rodin sculpture equally famously shows coming out of the city gates with halters round their necks. Although pregnant, she had come across the Channel to be with the king. 'Ah, gentle sir,' Froissart reports her saying, 'since I have crossed the sea with great danger to see you, I have never asked one favour; now I most humbly ask as a gift, for the sake of the Son of the blessed Mary, and for your love to me, that you will be merciful to these six men.'

Edward seems to have been the sort of man who only very reluctantly rises to an occasion. He replied, 'Ah, lady, I wish you had been anywhere else but here.'[6] Grudgingly, however, he gave her what she asked. The men's lives were spared but they lost their livelihood, for Edward cleared the inhabitants from the town. In their place he settled English traders, giving them the monopoly, the 'staple', of several trades with the continent, particularly in English wool. For Edward, Calais was not a place to be traded away at the next peace but a conquest to be turned into an English port, town and stronghold on the French side of the Channel. It remained in English hands for two centuries, a cross-Channel twin of Dover, gathering to itself the most profitable elements of English trade with the continent. As over the years the English kings lost other French provinces and finally Normandy and Aquitaine, Calais and the countryside immediately around it became the most important and finally the last of their holdings on the mainland. They behaved as if it would be theirs for ever, and Henry VIII built a citadel there a few years before the town passed out of English control for good.

In the summer of 1348, just a year after the surrender of Calais, an unremarkable merchant ship entered the little harbour of Melcombe Regis in Weymouth Bay in Dorset. Among its cargo were the germs of the Black Death, which had been advancing across Europe from the Crimea for the past year. The plague quickly spread in England as it already had in France. It embraced the bubonic plague and two other strains and, modern opinion suggests, perhaps anthrax also. It brought dreadful and certain death, consuming anything from 30 to 50 per cent of the population. No group escaped entirely, though the death toll was higher among the poor than the rich and in the town than the countryside. The psychic damage was as great as the physical, as survivors sought an explanation for the disaster in man's sinfulness and God's anger. In the longer term the plague tipped the economic scales in the poor man's favour, against the employer and landowner, but to stricken townsmen and villagers at the time it represented unmitigated horror. Seen in retrospect, it represents the most marked caesura in European development between the tenth century and the fifteenth.

Yet to history's eye the most surprising aspect of the Black Death is how little impact it seems to have had on affairs of state. By any social or economic measure, its impact was far more important than the innumerable raids, invasions, sieges and pitched battles that make up the Hundred Years War. But only when they were confronted by the Peasants' Revolt in 1381 do we see the attention of the nations' leaders and of chroniclers like Froissart turning away from the cross-Channel struggle to domestic matters.

However, the thirteenth and fourteenth centuries saw intense social and economic change throughout Europe. Despite the wars, despite the Black Death, France and England gradually became more sophisticated, ordered societies. They came to know one another better, as much in peaceful contacts as in war. Trade, pilgrimages, diplomacy and war all stimulated cross-Channel travel. Ships grew larger in consequence. Laws were drafted to govern maritime affairs, and in the course of the fourteenth century England established Courts of Admiralty to pass judgement on disputes in the narrow seas. The Channel ports grew busier and larger. Southampton received annual merchant convoys from the Mediterranean, exporting wool and importing wine. Boulogne became a vigorous fishing and trading port, as well as an insistent rival of the Cinque Ports across the water. Dunkirk flourished as the principal Channel port of an independent Flanders. And Calais, England's window on the Low Countries, Germany and the north European members of the Hanseatic League, prospered even more mightily than all the others.

Yet politics and war remain the best-documented pursuits of these centuries of the high Middle Ages. Frivolous as much of the politics seems, futile so many of the military campaigns, this politics and these campaigns did more than anything else to shape the attitudes of the English and French to one another. In doing so, they shaped the development of all western Europe, and the significance of the Channel that simultaneously separated them and brought them together.

* * *

Beside the kings' pursuit of politics and war, the story of the Cinque Ports' troubles with the French is a sideshow, but it is worth marking. For whether England and France were at peace or war, the ports on either side of the Channel were uneasy near neighbours. The seamen of the Cinque Ports were always turbulent, constantly at odds with rivals, as often fighting fellow Englishmen from Yarmouth as foreigners from across the Channel. The story is one of regular raiding, with the Portsmen lamenting the cruelty of French raids and mounting equally vicious raids on their neighbours. Commercial rivalry and piracy merged into one another and easily led to war.

So in 1283 a French fleet approached Hythe and landed 200 men, but 'the townsmen came upon them and slew every one of them; upon which the rest of the fleet hoisted sail, and made no further attempt'. Sometimes the attackers did better. In 1359 a force of 3,000 Frenchmen landed at Winchelsea. Forty men of Winchelsea were killed, 400 other Portsmen who came to the town's support were drowned, thirteen ships laden with wine and stores were taken away to France in lucrative triumph, and 'nine illustrious women ravished'.[7] A year later the French came again and the Cinque Ports orchestrated reprisals. Then in 1377 the French burned Rye. Again the Ports hit back and the following year ships from Rye and Winchelsea went raiding French ports to recover the towns' church bells. But three years later the French, operating wholesale now, burned three of the Cinque ports, Winchelsea, Rye and Hastings, as well as Appledore.

In much of all this, the Cinque Portsmen and the French were acting as licensed surrogates for their kings, as privateers. At other times, their kings made ineffectual efforts to discipline them, but the Portsmen, for all their talk of service to the Crown, were a law unto themselves. If they could not be privateers they would turn to open piracy. In all this cross-Channel warfare, the fact of private profit weighed with both sides more heavily than any argument of *raison d'état.*

Turning back to the doings of the kings of France and England, we reach the story of Agincourt. The year 1413 brought Henry V to the throne, and with him an approach to cross-Channel warfare different from the Cinque Ports' and their opponents'. He was Edward III's great-great-grandson, twenty-six years old, vigorous and ambitious. A war of guerrillas and privateers was not for him; he wanted the glory of building a continental empire. He allied himself with the Duke of Burgundy and in August 1415 he set off from the Solent with 10,000 men to conquer France. Like Edward before him, he kept his destination a secret, and once again the Channel gave him the chance of strategic surprise. The French watched all the Channel ports, but expected that Henry would choose Boulogne. Instead he chose Normandy like Edward before him; though he landed not in the Cotentin peninsula but at the mouth of the Seine, at Harfleur.

Harfleur was a formidable place. Despite the impression that Shakespeare has left us, it fell not to direct assault but to siege, and it took Henry two months of shelling and mining and fire-raising to do the job.

Henry had intended, as Edward had before him, to march up the Seine and seize Paris, but he had lost time and it was now too late in the year for a serious campaign. A council of war voted for withdrawal to their ships. Royal honour, however, demanded a show of fight, so Henry set off, like Edward, to promenade across northern France to Calais. For him Calais was an English stronghold, as it had not been in Edward's time. He decided he could afford to travel light, leaving wheeled vehicles behind. Each man carried eight days' supplies; in that time Henry calculated on being safely within the walls of Calais.

He moved up the Channel coast, intending to cross the Somme estuary at the ford that Edward had discovered at Blanchetaque. This time, however, the French held it in force. For five days Henry marched up the left bank of the Somme, his army growing hungrier, the French army shadowing him along the other bank. Finally, between Albert and Peronne Henry slipped past the French and set off towards the safety of Calais. His line of march led across the open country that was to form the First World War's Somme battlefields. The two armies' routes were slowly converging, and again the French got in front of Henry. On 24 October, the eve of St Crispin's Day, he found them blocking the road to Calais.

The French were deployed across a stretch of open country between two woods, one surrounding the village of Tramecourt, the other Agincourt. The arena in front of them was roughly rectangular, but it tapered slightly towards the British position, from about 1,200 yards in width to just under a thousand. The battlefield can be seen today, lying like Crécy in deeply peaceful countryside. The landscape itself has apparently altered little over six centuries. As killing-fields go, it is a bucolic, even idyllic place.

Henry seems to have had 6,000 men, the French four times that number. To his men he was all confidence, but Shakespeare puts an anxious prayer on his lips:

> O God of battles! steel my soldiers' hearts
> Possess them not with fear; take from them now
> The sense of reckoning, if the opposed numbers
> Pluck their hearts from them. Not today, O Lord![8]

Yet Henry's men were hardened soldiers, if weary and hungry, while the French, from horsemen to men-at-arms, were ill-disciplined and ill-organised. In this, the story is like that of Crécy. But there the French had been eager for battle, whereas here they at first hung back. Finally Henry's men advanced into the arena and his archers opened fire. The French pressed forward, and at once their indiscipline began to count against them. Once again, the English archers took a terrible toll, then the two armies met in hand-to-hand combat as intense as on the ships at Sluys. The French, their ranks compressed by the taper of the open field into which they were advancing, were soon packed together so closely that they could not use their weapons. Their dead and wounded piled up in mounds, over which the English clambered. Within an hour they began to get the upper hand, hacking and stabbing through chinks in the body armour, taking prisoners, marching them away to the rear. The French ranks had been torn apart; but a real danger was developing that in victory the English army would dissolve into little bands of booty hunters.

The surviving French withdrew to join their own third line of men-at-arms, so far unbloodied and still hovering at the edge of battle.

Henry watched them anxiously. Now three French horsemen were seen, leading a group of armed peasants towards the English baggage train. They were coming, or the English thought they were coming, to liberate the French prisoners. Henry was taking no chances, or perhaps his lust for blood was up. He gave the order to butcher the prisoners, and posted archers to ensure that it was done. Butchered they were, while the remains of the French army withdrew.

The next day the English marched on across the battlefield, slaughtering any wounded who still stirred. The French may have lost 10,000 men in all. They were buried on the battlefield, and over the pits where the chivalry of France lies has sprung up a desolate copse. In the village of Agincourt itself a concern for the needs of today's visitor has the last word, and a 'medieval history centre' recaptures the story of 25 October 1415. It offers French and British visitors a narrative that gives a careful, dispassionate account of this most terrible and pointless of battles between the old cross-Channel rivals. John Keegan sums up its significance:

> Agincourt is one of the most instantly and vividly visualised of all epic passages in English history, and one of the most satisfactory to contemplate. It is a victory of the weak over the strong, of the common soldier over the mounted knight, of resolution over bombast, of the desperate, cornered and far from home, over the proprietorial and cocksure . . . It is also a story of slaughter-yard behaviour and of outright atrocity.[9]

We come now to the story of Joan of Arc, who in a meteoric two-year career briefly turned the story of the Hundred Years War upside-down. Mark Twain produced the best brief summary of her achievement:

> Joan of Arc stands alone, and must continue to stand alone . . . There is no one to compare her with, none to measure her by . . . There have been other young generals, but they were not girls; young generals, but they were soldiers before they were generals; she *began* as a general; she commanded the first army she

ever saw; she led it from victory to victory, and never lost a battle with it; there have been young commanders-in-chief, but none so young as she; she is the only soldier in history who has held the supreme command of a nation's armies at the age of seventeen.[10]

The facts behind that splendid piece of phrase-making are familiar ones. Joan of Arc was a peasant girl from Lorraine. She heard celestial voices telling her to drive the English from France, and in 1429 she went to the court of the king of France at Chinon to tell him what she had heard. Somehow she convinced first the king and then an investigatory committee that she came from God. They put her in command of a French army, with which she raised the siege of Orléans and drove the English from the Loire. For a time she seems to have paralysed the will of her opponents; as Alfred Burne says of her achievement in stealing the initiative from her enemies, 'all the credit for starting the pendulum in its backward swing, and for starting it in no uncertain manner, must go to that marvellous soul, the pure and peerless Maid of Orléans'.[11]

Joan led King Charles across France to be crowned at Rheims and then turned again to fighting his enemies. At the siege of Compiègne she fell into the hands of the Burgundians, who were campaigning in loose alliance with the English. Charles could have ransomed her but did not: 'Put not your trust in princes.' The Burgundians sold her to the English, who imprisoned her in Rouen, and the French church turned its attentions to 'the witch'. The churchmen told her that her visions were 'false and diabolical'. She was put on trial for heresy before the Bishop of Beauvais and condemned to death. Recanting on the scaffold, she got her sentence reduced to life imprisonment. More ecclesiastical chicanery led her to another trial and this time made no mistake. On 30 May 1431, she was burned to death in the old marketplace of Rouen, where today a twentieth-century church honours her memory.

The French Church had quite as big a part as English policy in the destruction of Joan of Arc. But the Church's persecution served temporal policy, and the English got all the blame. They must have thought it worth bearing, for the flames seemed to have disposed of the French challenge to their position in Normandy as thoroughly as they had consumed the Maid of Orléans. Instead they rekindled it. Sluys, Crécy and Agincourt, innumerable bloody skirmishes, rapes and lootings, above all the goings-on in Rouen marketplace, taught Frenchmen to hate their enemies, the English soldiers they called the 'Goddams'. What would eventually emerge as a sense of nationhood was stirring.

Meanwhile, the luxury of fighting wars in other peoples' countries from an inviolable island base had taught the English arrogance. Froissart had noticed this long ago, campaigning beside the English in Gascony: 'I, Sir John Froissart, was at Bordeaux when the Prince of Wales marched into Spain, and myself witnessed the great haughtiness of the English, who are affable to no other nation but their own.'[12] But after Henry V's death the English lacked the will to support their arrogance with men and money. They lost Maine, and soon found themselves fighting a bitter defensive war to hold on to what was left of their old French empire in Normandy. Without enough men to put an army in the field, the English could do little more than try to hold fortified Norman towns. The French laid siege to them one by one, and one by one they surrendered, till only Caen, Bayeux and Cherbourg remained.

The process came to a head in 1450. In that year London at last despatched a small expeditionary force to the support of Normandy's remaining garrisons. It landed at Cherbourg, and set off under Sir Thomas Kyriell, an experienced fighter, to march to the relief of Bayeux. On 15 April, it reached the little village of Formigny. It lies just inland from Omaha beach, where the Americans were to land in June 1944, and not much more than a mile from the great American military cemetery at St Laurent-sur-Mer.

Kyriell with perhaps 4,000 men faced a French force of about the same size. The French advanced and the armies engaged in the same sort of battle that archers and men-at-arms had fought at Agincourt. The English seized a few French guns and were having the better of the fight when another French army appeared on the English flank. The French to their front rallied; the English, attacked from south as well as west, were overwhelmed. Kyriell was captured and his little army broken.

As a lost battle, Formigny passes for very little in English legend or historiography, but in it the French got their revenge for Sluys, Crécy and Agincourt. Strategically it was more important than any of them, for after it England lost Normandy and everything it held north of the Loire except Calais. The next year it lost even Aquitaine.

The Hundred Years War was over. For a time there was to be no more campaigning in the fair land of France, but no amity either. France had grown as self-consciously French as England had long been English. The old order that had made the Channel an interior sea of a western European empire had been swept away. Instead, two self-consciously different and frequently hostile nations, the arch-exemplars of nation-hood in western Europe, now saw it as a frontier between them.

CHAPTER 5

THE FAITH DIVIDES

I n the summer of 1485, Henry of Richmond, a self-made Welsh adventurer with tenuous connections with the English monarchy, set out from Honfleur to seize the throne of England. From that exquisite little jewel of a port in Normandy he sailed to Milford Haven in south Wales. Then he marched north gathering his supporters, turned east to victory at Bosworth, and went on from there to London. His coronation as Henry VII at Westminster marked the beginning of the Tudor dynasty.

Henry reigned for a quarter of a century. Although he had to confront such strange characters as Lambert Simnel and Perkin Warbeck, pretenders to his throne with shadowy backers inside England and on the continent, and though he fought little wars, some of them on the Channel and usually at other men's expense, he was by instinct a man of peace. He wanted a stable, orderly monarchy, and for that he needed money. Peace generated money, war consumed it. So he looked to the towns of the Channel coast not as sally-ports against continental enemies but as shipping, trading and industrial centres, places that could generate tax revenues.

The Channel ports, of France as much as England, had been in all these businesses for centuries. Inshore fishing was a universal activity. The only way to move heavy goods within a country was by water, between coastal or river ports. Cross-Channel trade was equally well established. Many Channel ports had longer-range business also. Most of them traded with the Hanseatic League and hence into the Baltic. Others had old-established links with the Mediterranean and with what had once been English ports of the Gironde. And privateering, raiding and downright piracy rode on the back of all these more clearly legitimate activities.

These Channel ports mostly stood to benefit from the revolutionary growth in trade that shaped the affairs of early modern Europe, but they did so in differing degrees; and some saw their position decline. Europe's greatest economic centres were the city states of northern Italy and the cities of the Low Countries and Germany. Trade between the two passed mainly through the Channel and benefited some Channel ports. So Southampton, for example, long traded with Genoa and Venice, whose representatives settled in the city; but in 1534 the Venetians' annual trading fleet came for the last time. Southampton had suffered too from the loss of trade with the Gironde when England lost Aquitaine. The fighting navy's Channel base was shifted to Portsmouth. And the growth of London attracted shipping away from the Channel ports and up the Thames. The consequence of all this was that in the early sixteenth century Southampton, a major Channel port since the time of the kingdom of Wessex, was gradually eclipsed.

English cross-Channel trade with the continent, on the other hand, flourished. Calais, still in English hands, continued to benefit from its monopoly on wool exports. The export of wool was beginning to be replaced by the export of finished cloth, but the Merchants of the Staple still enjoyed the monopoly and made Calais one of the richest of English towns. Most business with northern Europe passed through Calais, and it was also England's bridge to the culture and sophistication of Flanders. On the other side of the Channel the old Cinque Ports did well with the export of iron goods from the foundries of the Kent and Sussex Weald. But their old role as the defenders of south-east England and of English shipping in the Channel declined as English kings equipped themselves with battle fleets of their own.

In the middle of Henry VII's reign, in 1492, Columbus 'sailed the ocean blue'. The French and English kings encouraged their subjects to follow where the Portuguese and Spanish had gone into the oceans of the world. Plymouth and St Malo both particularly benefited from the opening of new worlds, though Bristol did better than either. In the course of the sixteenth century almost all the Channel ports took in their different ways to that mixture of voyages of global discovery, honest trade, privateering and downright piracy which the Plymouth buccaneer Francis Drake was to bring to such perfection.

By contrast with the more flamboyant Henrys who went before and after him, Henry VII was a dull king but a good one: 'He tamed the barons, calmed the Church, fought off all pretenders, established an efficient legal and financial system, conducted an energetic policy in France and Spain, provided for his children, and died in his bed.'[1] He bequeathed to his heir, Henry VIII, a solid base from which to make what impact he chose upon the world.

The new king looked like a throwback to earlier times. He was six feet tall and powerfully built, a giant among his contemporaries. He had the glamour, restlessness, ambition and bellicosity of much earlier kings, most memorably Henry V. He had also the facility of mind and breadth of interest which, had he put himself to it seriously, would have made him a scholar. His brutality and self-indulgence were slower in coming to the surface. In time they made of him an evil and in the end a grotesque figure, destructive of anything and anyone he touched. But he started out a popular monarch and despite everything he never lost the admiration of his people.

In Henry's lifetime, England changed in two fundamental ways. The Renaissance, the hesitant transition from the medieval centuries to modern times, had had its imperceptible beginnings in Britain under his father. Under the son, it gathered momentum, but it was a change that owed little to the king himself. The second, however, was more his doing than any other man's. His lust, his matrimonial politics and his thirst for monastic property drove him to the breach with Rome that gave England a church of its own and divided it by faith from most of its continental neighbours.

So Henry changed the face of England, yet he would never have become king but for the death of his elder brother, Arthur. Henry was then betrothed to Arthur's widow, Catherine of Aragon, and they were married in time for her to be beside him at his coronation. The bridegroom was eighteen years of age, handsome, strong, lusty and impatient of his father's parsimonious ways. So to win cheap popularity he sacrificed his father's taxmen to the axeman, and turned his ambition to war, that traditional royal road to glory.

His wife's family gave him the excuse for his first war. Catherine's father, the King of Aragon, wanted to take Navarre from the King of France. Henry went to cross-Channel war in loyal support of his father-in-law. In 1512, still only twenty-one, he set out to invade Normandy. By now ships of war, 'King's ships', were becoming distinct from merchantmen, and Henry had inherited from his father half a dozen powerful three-masters capable of outfacing anything the French sent against them. They displaced close on 1,000 tons, carried up to 200 guns capable of immobilising an enemy by destroying his rigging, if not of sinking him, and they went to war packed with soldiers ready, if they could get alongside the enemy, to fight a land battle at sea.

Henry may have imagined that he would reconquer the Normandy possessions that his predecessors had lost, but his army achieved little. In the following year he tried again, this time in northern France, taking an army of 25,000 men to Calais and from there to the siege of Thérouanne. This time things went better, and Henry's army defeated a French army that came to break the siege. At the same time another English army overwhelmed France's allies, the Scots, at Flodden. So when the time came for peace Henry could make it on his own terms. He gathered Thérouanne and more of northern France into his hands. At little cost he had transformed the little English colony around Calais into an extensive English holding. He must have told himself that in time he would restore the old English empire in France.

The glory of sixteenth-century war now gives way for a time to the splendours of sixteenth-century diplomacy. Three young men were determined to star on the European stage. The Emperor Charles V dreamed of uniting all Europe; Francis I of France stood in his way; and Henry was determined to muscle his way into the game. With his father's treasure as a war chest and with his base protected by the sea, he had something of value to offer to either Charles or Francis, for any two of the three who banded together could outweigh the third. The whole of the year 1520 was given up to the search for the partner who could deliver most. It was played out on both sides of the Straits of Dover.

The minuet started with an unprecedented imperial visit to England. In May, Charles V came to woo Henry. The emperor landed to royal and civic acclaim at Dover and processed up Watling Street on his way to meet the king at Canterbury. There they talked and partied, both of them arrayed in splendour. The fanfares and the extravagance failed to produce a treaty, however, and Henry turned his attention to wooing Francis.

This time it was Henry who crossed the Channel, but the meeting nevertheless took place on English territory within the Pale. He sailed with the queen from Dover to Calais, 'at the charges of the Cinque Ports', accompanied by Cardinal Wolsey and a vast retinue of nobles and ecclesiastics. 'Be it noted,' say the Dover town records, 'that never in the memory of man was seen so vast a multitude; so bravely arrayed and adorned – the servants as well as the nobles.'[2] The plan had been to accommodate the two kings in the castles of Guines and Ardres, just outside Calais in the English colony. Both, it turned out, were too dilapidated for the purpose. Wolsey went to work, therefore, to create a temporary, prefabricated setting worthy of the occasion – the Field of the Cloth of Gold. It was intended 'to demonstrate to the new Holy Roman Emperor, Charles V... that if need be the two old cross-Channel foes could stand together against Habsburg intimidation'.[3]

Given the history of centuries of warfare between England and France, that was a difficult argument to sustain, but diplomacy would do what it could. Meanwhile, there was glory to be enjoyed, for both kings knew that conscious splendour was part of the performance, to impress both the emperor Charles and one another. So Wolsey brought 5,000 English aristocrats to the party, Francis as many of his own. Fantastic castles and pavilions of wood and cloth and plaster housed the participants. Fountains, music, eating and drinking, displays of courtly love and knightly valour were all on offer. Sir Thomas More was there in attendance on the king. So was Anne Boleyn as a lady-in-waiting to the queen, and it may have been here that she first caught Henry's eye.

Even at the time, the great event was all for nothing. A wrestling match between Henry and Francis was arranged as a part of the festivities. Henry lost, and kings hate to lose. His chagrin may have added to his diplomats' difficulties. In any event they failed to conjure an Anglo-French agreement out of the perfumed air of the Field of the Cloth of Gold. The French knights rode away on their chargers, their ladies on their palfreys. The English aristocrats took to their ships and sailed away.

As for Henry, he decided to try his hand again with the emperor. He went off to Gravelines, a town on the Flanders coast between Calais and Dunkirk, and proved himself third time lucky. His negotiations with Charles were successful and produced a secret treaty against the French. It led to an attempt to make a concerted invasion of France from south, east and north. But England's part in it amounted to very little and at the end of it, in 1525, Henry was happy enough to make his peace with France.

Now the focus shifts to amatory, matrimonial and ecclesiastical politics. Henry was tiring of Catherine, disappointed that she seemed unable to bear him a son, and increasingly besotted with Anne Boleyn. He addressed himself to the problems involved in disposing of a wife, marrying a mistress, begetting a male heir, and coping with the consequences of all this for relations with the papacy and with neighbouring kings. The story is too familiar to need retelling. It brought Henry into conflict with the Pope, the Spanish royal house, German theologians and Italian canon lawyers, as well as most of Europe. At the end of it, he had divided his people religiously, committed the judicial murder of Thomas More and John Fisher, expropriated the monasteries, separated England from the universal Church and made himself head of a new national Church instead. For the first time since Augustine, England was an off-shore island at odds with the rest of Christendom.

Having done all this, Henry felt himself vulnerable. While in England he had been shaking the tree of faith for his own essentially worldly purposes, on the continent true religious reformers had been at work. They had aroused strong passions, which soon took political as well as doctrinal form. In doing so, they split national societies. The continent was in ferment, and religious, political and military considerations played on one another. Henry already had political enemies. Now he had religious ones as well.

He turned again to diplomacy, and again he went to a meeting with the King of France near Calais. In October 1532, a contemporary account tells us, 'the King's Grace took his ship called the *Swallow*: and so came to Calais by ten o'clock'. (In fair weather the crossing from Dover took about five hours in the ships of that age.) He rode out to meet the French king 'within the English Pale three miles', each of them accompanied by an escort 600 strong. 'Then was the lovingest meeting that ever was seen; for the one embraced the other five or six times on horseback; and so did the lords on either party to other; and so did ride hand in hand with great love the space of a mile.'[4]

But even this lovingest meeting guaranteed nothing. Henry still feared cross-Channel attack. To meet it, he embarked on the most ambitious programme of building Channel-coast fortifications since the coming of the Normans.

Many of Henry's defensive works are visible to this day. On the east coast of Kent he built castles at Deal and Walmer, long since converted into desirable marine residences for Wardens of the Cinque Ports such as the first Duke of Wellington and Winston Churchill. He gave Calais a new citadel and added to Dover's formidable medieval defences. He fortified Portsmouth, the Solent and the Isle of Wight and built a castle on England's rock of Gibraltar, Portland, overlooking Weymouth Bay.

Away in the west he fortified the approaches to Dartmouth and Falmouth and strengthened the Channel Islands' defences.

Each of his fortresses was built to the best standards of the day, each equipped with bastions of its own. Perhaps the most intriguing is Hurst Castle. It stands far out in the western Solent, commanding the passage between the mainland and the Isle of Wight, approached by a gruelling mile-long walk along a spit of shingle or a ten-minute ferry ride. It is encased now in a much greater fortification, erected in the 1850s when a war scare consumed Victorian society. But within its Victorian carapace Henry's castle is still there at Hurst, as it was when he built it to deter French ships from creeping past the Needles and approaching Portsmouth and Southampton through the western Solent.

His castles built, and feeling himself secure at last at home, Henry once again committed himself to alliance with the Emperor. He led 40,000 men across the Channel and, although the campaign that followed achieved no outright victory, it brought Henry possession of Boulogne to add to Calais in his little colony in northern France. But no sixteenth-century alliance was constant. The Emperor made his peace with the French, who now were free to carry the war to the English. They planned a naval assault across the Channel and an attack on the Solent ports.

Henry had reinforced his navy as well as his land defences. Since early in his reign his navy had contained two of the most formidable ships of their age. One was the *Henry Grâce à Dieu*, usually known as the *Great Harry*, at 1,500 tons twice as big as many of her contemporaries, a four-master, bristling with guns. The other was the *Mary Rose*. She fought in Henry's early battles against the French at Brest and Cherbourg, went north to help stem a Scottish invasion in 1513, and escorted Henry when he crossed the Channel to the Field of the Cross of Gold in 1520. The Admiral, Sir Edward Howard, reported to the king, 'The *Mary Rose*, Sir, she is the noblest ship of sail and a great ship at this hour that I trow to be in Christendom, 'adding 'A ship of 100 tons will not be sooner about than she.'[5] To the *Great Harry* and the *Mary Rose* Henry added three more ships bought from Baltic shipowners. By the time French invasion threatened in the summer of 1545, eighty ships were moored in Portsmouth harbour waiting to counter it.

If the English fleet had got smartly away to sea, the result might have been the first great mid-Channel naval battle. But the French were able to evade the few English ships that got out of Portsmouth, and themselves penetrated into the Solent. They seized the Isle of Wight and set about burning villages there. It was nothing more than a campaign of pin-pricks but Henry's pride was hurt, his prestige damaged. All his expenditure on fortifications seemed to have gone for nothing. He hastened down to Portsmouth, and when he arrived 'he fretted and his teeth stood on an edge to see the bravery of his enemies who come so near his nose and he not able to encounter with them'.[6]

Alarm beacons were lit, the local militia called to arms, ships summoned from the Thames: 'The king as soon as his whole fleet was come together willed them to set things in order and to go to sea.' The Vice-Admiral was placed in command of the *Mary Rose* and the fleet sailed out into the Solent to confront the French. The French began to withdraw, when disaster happened. Suddenly the *Mary Rose* capsized. The ambassador of the Holy Roman Emperor reported to his master, 'One of the survivors, a Fleming, told me that the disaster was caused by their not having closed the lowest row of gun ports on one side. Having fired the guns on that side, the ship was turning in order to fire from the other side, when the wind caught her sails so strongly as to heel her over . . .'[7]

The *Mary Rose* took 470 of her crew to the bottom with her. She took also Henry's pride. As a young man thirty years earlier he had presided at her launching, blowing a silver whistle a yard long in celebration. Now, in his fifties, he stood on the shore at Southsea and watched the *Mary Rose* go down. Her hull and her guns, parts of her standing rigging and her people's bits-and-pieces, have been recovered from the deep and are displayed today in Portsmouth Dockyard.

In the end, England and France once again came to terms, this time at Ardres, the little town in the outskirts of Calais beside the Field of the Cloth of Gold. The following year, Henry died, having involved his country in painful and costly convulsions for the best part of his thirty-six years upon the throne. He left three children who succeeded him in turn: Edward, the boy king who died young; Catholic Mary, whose enemies christened her 'Bloody Mary'; and Elizabeth, 'Good Queen Bess' to her ordinary subjects and 'Gloriana' to the more high-flown, who for better or for worse imposed a religious settlement of her own. With their differing ecclesiastical policies, Henry's children added to the religious turmoil that he had let loose upon England.

The details of those religious policies would take us far from our Channel theme. The essentials, however, are familiar. In the course of Edward's short reign England lurched towards all-out Protestantism; Mary, in her equally brief reign, brought back the orthodoxy of Catholicism; and Elizabeth, secure on her throne for almost half a century, gradually worked her way to the settlement of half-measures and compromises which has survived, as far as any religious policy survives in modern England, to this day.

Their doings had different impacts on the story of the Channel. The effect of Edward's was to bring Protestant fanatics from Germany and the Low Countries hastening across the water to England, determined to make it a godly country according to their own beliefs. In reversing that and making England Catholic again, Mary made a bigger but short-lived mark. She started the process of restoring her country's relations with the Catholic powers, France among them. But her alliance with Spain set her at odds with France, and in the last year of her life she lost to the French England's last foothold on the continent – the town, port and fortress of Calais – remarking, according to the chronicler Holinshed, 'When I am dead and opened, you shall find "Calais" lying in my heart.'[8] That loss removed a thorn from France's paw. In the long term, therefore, it altered the long-term relationship between England and France for the better. But in the short term it shifted the balance of power in the Channel between England and France and it left the English angry and resentful.

* * *

The French had resented the English occupation of Calais and the Pale for two centuries, constantly reminded of the even longer centuries in which more than half of France had fallen under the power of the English kings. In seizing more French lands and incorporating them in the colony, Henry VIII had aggravated the offence that Calais represented. When Mary came to the throne, and with her Spanish marriage joined in the Spanish war against France, the French wanted Calais even more urgently than they had wanted it for two centuries. English weakness offered them the chance to get it. George Ferrers, the Tudor politician and poet, has left an account of what happened.

The loss of Calais, he wrote, 'was such a buffet to England as had not happened in more than an hundred years before; and a dishonour wherewith this realm shall be blotted until GOD shall give power to redubbe it with some like requital to the French'.[9] The garrisons of Calais and its outlying forts were under strength, no more than 500 men in all, 'which negligence was not unknown to the enemy'. The commanders of Calais warned London, and London did nothing to reinforce them. The French commander, the Duke of Guise, 'proceeded in this enterprise with marvellous policy'. He approached Calais as if his only object was to resupply the French garrisons in Boulogne and Ardres, then seized one of Calais's outlying fortifications at Sangatte. Dividing his artillery, he battered two more forts into surrender, and then brought his guns into play against Calais Castle itself. The castle was old and the English thought it indefensible against artillery. They therefore 'devised to make a train with certain barrels of powder to this purpose, that when the Frenchmen should enter, as they well knew, that there they would, to have fired the said train, and blown up the Keep; and for that purpose left never a man to defend it'. But the French 'espied the train, and so avoided the same. So that device came to no purpose.' The French captured the castle and advanced into the town.

The English counter-attacked and drove the French back, but the French-held castle dominated the town. The Lord Deputy, Lord Wentworth, sought terms, and 'The next morning, the Frenchmen entered the town, summoned the citizens to gather in two churches, held them there for a day and a night without food or drink, and meanwhile rifled their houses.' The next day, 'all the Englishmen, except the Lord Deputy and the others reserved for prisoners, were suffered to pass out of the town in safety', escorted, to rub salt into the wounds of English pride, by a troop of light horsemen from France's ally, Scotland. Wentworth and 'others of the chief of the town, to the number of fifty... such as it pleased the Duke of Guise to appoint, were sent prisoners into France'.

One of those Channel storms that so often blow its history off course had frustrated efforts to send reinforcements to the garrison of Calais. 'But such terrible tempests then arose,' Ferrers tells us, 'and continued the space of four or five days together, that the like had not been seen before in the remembrance of man; wherefore some said "That same was done by necromancy, and that the Devil was raised up and become French".' Ferrers's own judgement is more all-embracing: 'Thus by the negligence of the Council at home, conspiracy of traitors elsewhere, force and false practice of enemies, helped by the rage of the most terrible tempests of contrary winds and weather; this famous Fort of Calais was brought again to the hands and possession of the French.' He did not add Queen Mary to his list of culprits, but her name can be read between his lines.

Mary's half-sister, Elizabeth, has left a very different imprint on the history of England. Her story, and her impact on the story of the Channel, is best looked at in the next chapter, when the Armada threatens and the political and religious divides between England and the Catholic powers come into sharpest focus. But it is worth summing up here what half a century of religious turmoil had done by 1558 to England's relationship with the countries of the continent, and hence to the significance of the Channel.

At the heart of the convulsions that Henry provoked and bequeathed to his children were the break with Rome and the creation, under him, of a church in England that acknowledged no authority outside the realm. Henry died still thinking himself a Catholic king of a Catholic country, but he had broken the essential link that had bound England to Rome ever since the coming of St Augustine. His heir made further changes, giving Protestantism deeper inroads into English life and involving the country, emotionally as much as practically, in the religious disputes of half Europe. When Queen Mary tried to take her country back to Catholicism she also brought back into it the Spanish influences that had faded with the destruction of her mother's marriage by Henry VIII. In doing so, bringing Philip of Spain as her suitor and then her bridegroom to her court at Westminster, for example, she invited Spanish concern for England, a sense almost of proprietorship, which came home to roost when her successor Elizabeth embarked on courses at odds with those of Spain.

But the biggest change brought about by the convulsions of the reigns of Henry VIII, Edward VI and Mary was the creation of a sense among the English that their country truly was different from its continental neighbours. The sense had always been there, but usually inchoate and latent. Now the religious excitements of the age added to the concern for national identity. Shakespeare was not yet a gleam in his father's eye when Mary died; but England was already pregnant with the ideas about itself, about the world, and about the distinctions to be drawn between the two, which the brilliance of his mind and pen were to make immortal.

The historian Norman Davies argues that the Reformation 'drove a wedge down the Channel' for which there was no historical precedent.[10] 'All the great shifts of previous times, whether the establishment of the Celts, the rule of the Romans, the arrival of the Anglo-Saxons, or the conquests of Normans and Angevins, had usually fostered a rapprochement between the experiences of the islanders and that of the Continentals. But the Reformation set them apart.'

The significance of this changed relationship between England and the continent emerged slowly in the course of the reigns of Henry VIII, his son and his two daughters. At first it seemed less important than the changes that were taking place within the kingdom: the expulsion of the 'good, shaven men' from their monasteries, the seizure of church lands by the king's new, hard-faced friends, the appearance of married clergy in the parish churches, the enclosure of hitherto common land. But over time, the skilled publicity of Church and State started to build a new awareness of Englishness as something different from and better than the identities on offer on the continent.

In the French wars, Englishmen and Frenchmen had begun to reinforce their own sense of identity by contrasting their own ways with their enemies'. They still did so under the Tudors, with a contempt that had become commonplace. As they searched for new ways to build a sense of identity between themselves and their peoples, Renaissance sovereigns based themselves on these time-honoured prejudices. Now they could point to religious as well as political and social differences. The rift between England and her neighbours provided ample material. Englishmen ate roast beef, foreigners ate fish on Fridays, and, to go by the Protestant handbills, cardinals in Rome ate babies. In the French wars, Englishmen had learned to despise French ways and Frenchmen to hate English ones. Now even the foreigners' forms of worship were different, suspect.

Of course, Englishmen were divided. Many hankered after the old ways and rejoiced when Queen Mary restored them. Others wanted root-and-branch reform, going far beyond Henry's changes and Elizabeth's settlement; they got what they wanted, if only very briefly, under Edward. Many, perhaps most, were satisfied in the end by the Elizabethan settlement. But whatever they wanted and whatever they gained by the breach with Rome, Englishmen paid a price for it too. In Norman Davies's words, the religious change that consumed the country in the sixteenth century 'cut England off from the cultural and intellectual community to which she had belonged for nearly a thousand years; and it forced her to develop along isolated, eccentric lines'. It forced on the English a perversity that is with them to this day. 'The English have had little chance but to take pride in their isolation and eccentricity... Their habit of harping on the story of their survival without any foreign invasion since 1066 is an essential part of the exercise. It conceals the fact that England's cultural isolation dates not from 1066 but from 1534.'[11]

This sharper awareness of distinction between island and continent increased the significance of the Channel. Its physical role had always been obvious; now it acquired also a psychological significance as a line of demarcation between two quite different worlds. And in the end it was an event in the Channel itself that brought that sense of difference to a white-heat of conviction. That event was the coming of the great Spanish Armada.

CHAPTER 6

SPANIARDS IN THE CHANNEL

The great Spanish Armada of 1588 turned Europe's attention to the Channel, but its origins are to be found all over Europe and in the New World. So this chapter ranges wide, taking us further from the Channel than any other. In San Juan de Uloa in Mexico, for example, English pirates finally convinced the King of Spain of the need for action against the pestilent islanders. The ruins at Fotheringay in the English Midlands are a reminder of the execution of Mary Queen of Scots which finally provoked the enterprise. The bleak monastery at the Escorial outside Madrid houses the modest rooms in which Philip II planned the Armada. In Lisbon, the fleet set out down the Tagus to the sea; it would sail up the English Channel coast from the Lizard, past Plymouth and Torbay to the Isle of Wight. On Plymouth Hoe, Francis Drake played his famous game of bowls. In Calais, the English fireships were sent about their diabolical business. The Armada's ships were wrecked on the Blasket Islands off the west coast of Ireland, and its starving survivors finally reached home at Santander in northern Spain.

The 'Enterprise of England', Catholic Europe's plan to destroy

Elizabeth's power and bring her kingdom back to Catholicism, was thirty years of religious argument and political chicanery in the making. When at last the Armada sailed, in May 1588, its course took it out into the Atlantic from Lisbon, to Corunna, across the Bay of Biscay to the entrance of the Channel, and then up-Channel to the Straits of Dover and the Calais roads. Nowhere off the coast of Portugal and Spain, in the Bay of Biscay nor in the Channel itself, is there one single decisive engagement that spelt the Armada's fate. Not even at Calais was the outcome of the English fireship attack clear-cut. After Calais, when the English commanders pursued the Spanish and closed in on them off Gravelines, they knew the damage they had done but remained uncertain that they had prevailed. When the Spanish fleet withdrew to the north they still feared its return. Only when so many of its ships went to their destruction on the Irish coast was its failure certain, and only when the survivors crept home broken and starving was the extent of the defeat apparent to the world.

The Armada's story, therefore, starts not in the Channel in 1588 but in London thirty years earlier, on 17 November 1558, the day Queen Mary of England died of the stomach tumour that she had too long mistaken for a child. Catholic hopes of restoring the old religion died with her. So did Spanish hopes of binding England into a coalition of Catholic princes who between them would rule Europe with the Pope and against his Protestant enemies.

Mary's half-sister Elizabeth brought very different convictions and temperament to the throne. Like her sister, she had lived in fear of the assassin or the executioner. But whereas Mary's experiences had channelled her single-mindedness into commitment to the Catholic faith, Elizabeth's life as a princess in peril had made her cautious, ambiguous in utterance, hesitant in decision. At the age of eighteen she was pressed on her belief of the nature of the Eucharist. In reply she produced those four lines of masterly equivocation:

> 'Twas God the word that spake it,
> He took the bread and brake it;

And what the word did make it;
That I believe, and take it.

She took this talent for equivocation with her to the throne and in the end to the grave, and applied it as much to politics as to faith. It balanced her enemies against one another. While to the radical Protestants in England she was little better than a Papist, to the Catholics she was the scourge of true religion. To Spain and the Papacy she was the enemy who put herself at the head of Satan's legions; to the Protestant Dutch, as they struggled to hold Spain's armies at bay, she was an inconstant, unreliable friend. France, her nearest neighbour, was divided; but neither the king nor his rivals of the House of Guise nor the Protestant minority could put their faith in her. To her counsellors she was evasive and indecisive, relying finally more on her own instincts than their advice. To increasingly large numbers of people, she made herself the least of all evils. Out of equivocation, evasion, ambiguity and pro-crastination, she built the Elizabethan settlement.

It was a policy that kept other European heads of state at a loss to divine the queen's real intentions. The Pope, Philip, the French, the Dutch all sought clarity and certainty; none achieved it. Some of the Pope's advisers saw in her religious settlement an attachment to the ways of the old faith in the face of Protestant fanaticism; to others it was the betrayal of her duty of submission to the Vicar of Christ. Philip II urged an alliance against the French, in a war that might have won back the Calais that Mary had lost. Against the French, England cherished ancient enmities, but Elizabeth would commit herself to neither war nor peace. The Protestant Dutch, at war with the Spanish armies in the Netherlands, looked to her for salvation. She wanted no war if she could avoid it, however, and when the Dutch offered her their throne she rejected it. English aid to the Dutch remained parsimonious, fitful, more often than not in the form of deniable volunteers. And England's naval heroes, whose pursuit of the Spanish treasure galleons Philip saw as piracy, were in turn licensed, criticised, caressed, abused and sometimes disowned by the queen they claimed to serve.

Slowly, however, the irreconcilables became manifest. Émigré English Catholics brought to the papacy evidence of the queen's malignancy. The Pope twisted and turned, but in 1570 came the bull of her excommunication, *Regnans in Excelsis*. She needed her share of Spain's South American treasure, and the pretence that English seamen served themselves alone wore increasingly threadbare: Philip turned decisively against her. Faced with defeat, the Protestant enemies of Spain and France became more and more dependent on the queen's support. She still hung back, but little by little she 'was drawn in at one time or another, and usually with reluctance, along the whole Channel littoral from Brittany and Normandy to Flanders, Zealand and Holland. It was war on land as well as at sea.'[1] She found herself supporting Protestant rebels from the Low Countries to La Rochelle.

The excommunication of Elizabeth encouraged Catholic resistance to her. At Douai, St Omer and other centres just across the Channel, seminaries trained priests for the English mission, and in particular the first English recruits to the new Jesuit order. The atmosphere was highly charged: 'Martyrdom was in the air of Douai. It was spoken of, and in secret prayed for, as the supreme privilege of which only divine grace could make them worthy.'[2] Priests trained in such an atmosphere slipped across the Channel and through quiet little ports secretly entered England. One of them was the Jesuit Edmund Campion, who wrote 'The expense is reckoned, the enterprise begun; it is of God, it cannot be withstood. So the faith was planted: so it must be restored.'[3] When missionaries like Campion were caught, put to the torture and executed, English Catholicism had its martyrs to set in the balance against Bloody Mary's protestant victims.

The bull of excommunication also encouraged the men who plotted the queen's overthrow. The Pope's secretary told would-be assassins that Elizabeth was 'that guilty woman of England . . . whoever sends her out of the world . . . not only does not sin but gains merit . . .'.[4] Such men wanted to replace her with the Catholic Mary Queen of Scots, who had been Elizabeth's prisoner ever since she fled to England from Scottish civil war in 1568. Even under house arrest and worse, she kept up her contacts with those 'daring subtle men who slipped in and out of the Channel ports in disguise',[5] bringing now word of the Pope's wishes, now of support for those who would execute them.

Mary's doings were clandestine, but they were not secret from Elizabeth's agents. Now, with the Spanish menace growing, Elizabeth had to scotch them, yet repeatedly she drew back from her cousin's destruction. In the end, Mary was brought to trial and found guilty of 'disobedience ... incitement to insurrection ... high treason'. Still Elizabeth vacillated, but in the end, in February 1587, Mary died on the scaffold at Fotheringay, asserting to the Anglican pastor who pressed his advice upon her the Catholic faith that made her so dangerous: 'I shall die as I have lived, in the true and Catholic faith. All you can say to me on that score is but vain, and all your prayers, I think, can avail me but little.'[6]

The deed done, Elizabeth turned against her servants, declaring that she had not wanted Mary's head. But the fact was that the heir-apparent to the throne of England, a Queen of Scotland, a Princess of France, and a somewhat besmirched icon of Catholicism, had died a traitor's death in Elizabeth's England. The battle lines between England and Catholic Europe could not have been more clearly drawn.

The focus shifts from Mary's death at Fotheringay to Philip II's strange, duty-driven life in the Escorial, thirty miles outside Madrid, 'this bare mountainside whence I rule the affairs of half the world'.[7] Like Elizabeth, Philip was assailed by contradictory pressures. Unlike her, he immersed himself in detail. He lived the ascetic life of the monks, and when he took his siesta he did so in his chair, holding in his hand a pebble whose fall would wake him as soon as sleep overcame him. Like Elizabeth, he knew how to encourage, warn and dissimulate, while reserving decision to himself. But whereas she ruled by fits and starts, using favourites who bore her anger and basked in her praise, his reign was one of steadfast isolation, writing in his own tortured hand long minutes of comment and instruction to his secretaries at their desks in the next room, maintaining a monastic calm in face alike of triumph and disaster.

Now, as the word of Mary's execution went round Europe, Philip at last committed himself to the destruction of Elizabeth. He would launch the Enterprise of England, so long discussed. He knew nothing of the sea; and he ordered that the Spanish fleet should move against England like one of his implacable armies. It would advance up the Channel, brushing aside English ships that blocked its way. Meanwhile, the Duke of Parma in the Spanish Low Countries, today's Belgium, would put his soldiers to work digging canals and building barges. When the Armada arrived, he would shift his forces from their positions on the Scheldt facing the Dutch to Dunkirk on the coast facing England. Arrived off the North Foreland, which the Spanish called 'the cape of Margate', the Armada would take Parma's flotilla under its protection. Within twenty-four hours the Spanish troops would be ashore on the coast of Kent or Essex, with the road to London open before them.

But first, Spain had to get those formidable fighting men ashore in England. In command of the fleet that would put them there Philip had placed the Marquis of Santa Cruz, hero of the victory over the Turkish fleet at Lepanto. Santa Cruz brought the same heroism to the desperate work of getting the fleet ready for sea. But he saw the unpreparedness of ships and men for a seaborne enterprise far greater than any nation had ever attempted before. Philip, instinctively a cautious procrastinator (he had once written 'in so great an enterprise as that of England, it is fitting to move with feet of lead'), now urged haste: 'Success depends mostly on speed. Be quick!'[8] Santa Cruz remained cautious. Finally, in February 1588, he died in harness.

In his place Philip put the Duke of Medina Sidonia, grandee of Spain. Unlike Santa Cruz, the duke knew nothing of the sea. Repeatedly he pleaded his own inadequacy for the job. In a world of aristocratic fire-eaters, he had the moral courage to risk the charge of cowardice, begging the king to find a more experienced commander. But the king was unwavering, the duke bound by his sense of duty to the Crown. He took himself off to Lisbon to assume command of the fleet assembling there.

He found, as Santa Cruz had done, that ships and men were unprepared for war. He flung himself into the work. He knew his limitations but he was honest, diligent and an able administrator. His rank gave him authority over quarrelsome subordinates. He listened to expert advice. Gradually the elements of the enterprise fell into place. The Portuguese contingent of the fleet was composed of good ships. A new and powerful Tuscan galleon was pressed into service. Slowly the Spanish ships were manned, victualled and equipped. In the end the fleet still fell short of its gigantic task but was as fit for its purpose as effort could make it.

The Spaniards were not left at peace while they made their preparations. English raids on the Iberian coast, like English attacks on the treasure fleets from the Indies, had tormented Philip into committing himself to this Enterprise of England. They continued while Medina Sidonia pressed ahead with the Armada's preparation. Francis Drake attacked Cadiz and Sagres, destroying Spanish ships and stores. Off the Azores he intercepted a Portuguese carrack loaded with the wealth of the Indies. But his talk of bottling up the Spanish fleet in the estuary of the Tagus promised more than he could deliver. Far from his base, on a hostile coast, he could mount only the flimsiest of blockades. When at last the great Armada put to sea it was unmolested.

On 28 May 1588, Medina Sidonia led his fleet to sea. He had ten first-line Portuguese galleons, fourteen Spanish, the Tuscan ship and four Spanish galleasses – half galleon, half galley. Behind them came forty ships of the second line, large armed merchantmen. Medina Sidonia had also thirty-four lighter, faster vessels to screen his fleet, seek out the enemy and carry messages between his commanders; twenty-three freighters; and four galleys, oar-driven Mediterranean fighting ships, easily swamped by high Atlantic seas.

Documentary evidence of Medina Sidonia's fleet gives details of tonnage, numbers of guns, size of crews, and place and date of building. At one end of the scale his flagship, *San Martin*, displaced 1,000 tons, mounted forty-eight guns, carried 160 sailors and 300 soldiers. At the other were the pinnaces, under a hundred tons, with a crew of fourteen or fifteen men and a single gun. In the middle were the lumbering merchantmen, which proved more a hindrance than a help. There are similar details of the English ships the Spaniards were to meet. *Ark Royal*, the flagship, was an 800-tonner, with thirty guns, a crew of 270 and 120 soldiers, and, again at the other end of the scale, the English too had their 100- and 50-tonners. In all the English sent out 197 ships to meet the Spanish, 15,925 men against perhaps 26,000.[9]

Naval history knows a great deal about the strengths and weaknesses of the ships that composed the English and Spanish fleets. The best among them were the best in the world. The Spanish warships regularly crossed the Atlantic to convoy their treasure galleons home from the Main, and the English as regularly sailed to the West Indies to lie in wait for them. For ten years before the Armada, John Hawkins had had control of the building and maintenance of the queen's ships. He forced through many changes in their design, building them lower, longer, leaner, crowding them with guns and abolishing the old high bow and stern castles. There are records of the problems of command, seamanship and tactics both sides faced; for example, in some ways the Spaniards' greatest weakness was that they took so many scarcely seaworthy vessels with them – they might have done better with fewer ships, all first-raters. It is also clear that the English myth that their ships were so very much smaller and frailer than the Spaniards' was just that, a myth.

No ship that fought on either side has been preserved, but two historic ships give a good impression of what the English and Spanish ships looked like, and how they functioned. The *Mary Rose* would have been among the queen's ships in the fleet that fought the Armada had she not gone down forty years earlier. In a museum in Stockholm lies the flagship of the Swedish fleet, the 1,200-ton *Vasa*, which capsized on her maiden voyage forty years after the Armada. A generation younger than the Armada ships, she demonstrates the terrifying face of sixteenth- and seventeenth-century sea power. Also, in the Thames just above London Bridge, lies something towards the other end of the scale, a 300-ton, 20-gun, 100-foot long replica of Francis Drake's *Golden Hinde* – it seems a marvel that anything so small could have circumnavigated the globe.

Medina Sidonia still had to get his ships to the junction with Parma, and it took him twenty days of adverse winds, lost ships and dwindling food supplies to get them as far as Corunna in the north-western corner of Spain. There a sudden storm, vicious as no June storm in living memory, struck the fleet, scattering or destroying many ships and ravaging the rest. Already the crews were hungry; there was disease about and the beginnings of fear. By now Medina Sidonia was quite convinced that his ships were incapable of the mission they had been set. He wrote to Philip, urging him to make peace or at least postpone the enterprise by a year. He got an unbending response. The king ordered him to sea with what ships he could muster. Finally, a month after the storm, Medina Sidonia set sail once more, north-east across the Bay of Biscay with the mouth of the Channel for his landfall.

For all their earlier successes on the Iberian coast, the English too faced difficulties. Drake talked vaingloriously of taking fifty ships back to the coast of Spain and destroying the Armada there. Elizabeth decided that if such a stroke were to be attempted she would commit to it all available ships, merchantmen as well as queen's ships. She put Howard of Effingham, Lord High Admiral of England, in command, with Drake as his Vice-Admiral. Like Medina Sidonia, Howard was delayed by storms, but on 23 May he reached Plymouth and joined forces with Drake. For three weeks the same weather that scattered Medina Sidonia's ships held him fast in Plymouth. When finally he could get to sea the queen's uncertainties kept him back. At last more ships and supplies reached Howard, and with ninety ships of all kinds he and Drake set off to look for Medina Sidonia off the coast of Spain.

In less than a week, on 22 July, he was back in Plymouth, driven there by adverse winds. On the same day, Medina Sidonia left Corunna. As he came northwards across the Bay of Biscay, Howard was frantically engaged in getting his ships fit for sea again. Then, on 29 July, it was reported that a part of the Spanish fleet had been sighted off the Scillies. It was clear that the decisive battles would be fought not off the Spanish coast but in the Channel. Francis Drake may or may not have said, 'There is plenty of time to win this game, and to thrash the Spaniards too,' but on the evening of 29 July Howard led his fleet to sea. At sea, Medina Sidonia held a council of war. On land, the first beacons warning that the Spaniards were coming were lit.

Hindsight tells us that the great Spanish Armada was doomed to failure, unfit to challenge the superior seamanship and gunnery of the English commanders. Howard had no such assurance. He had spent months getting the fleet together, persuading the queen to foot the bill, locked in argument about tactics and command, concerned about manning and supplies. Like Medina Sidonia, he was asked to deliver something beyond the material and administrative resources of his age. What he had achieved so far was a triumph of making do. Now he faced battle with Medina Sidonia with worries to match his enemy's.

Medina knew how far he was from home, his lines of communication and retreat at his opponent's mercy. Howard faced many of Medina Sidonia's problems of victualling, manning and maintaining his ships. Like him he faced the unprecedented challenge of handling large numbers of ships in combat. He knew how fatal a single mistake could be. The Armada might escape him up-Channel, join forces with Parma unobserved and land his remorseless infantry on the shores of Kent. Alternatively, Medina Sidonia might slip into Falmouth or Plymouth or Weymouth, or seize the Isle of Wight and sail up the Solent. He could put raiding parties ashore, or something more formidable. And in England there were fears that Spanish invaders would meet Catholic insurgents flocking to join them. England thought it was in great danger in the summer of 1588, and its fears weighed heavily on Howard's shoulders.

On 30 July, the Armada's slow advance up the Channel began. Warning beacons had been lit the length of the coast as soon as the fleet was first sighted, but here were the ships themselves. Medina Sidonia placed them in a great crescent, with his weakest ships in the thickest part of the crescent, behind the van, and his most manoeuvrable in the horns. It was a formation derived from experience of war on land, and in hindsight it looks like a ludicrous way to position fighting ships under sail. But Sidonia knew his ships' weaknesses: they were scarcely capable of tactical manoeuvre, or of fighting a gun battle at anything beyond point blank range. The crescent kept his ships together, relatively safe from being picked off by the English. If it held, it would carry him to his rendezvous with Parma.

Medina Sidonia kept close to the English coast, and in the oldest privately occupied house in Devon there is a contemporary record of his passing. There, incised into the stone embrasure of a window opening on to a combe leading down to the distant sea, are profiles of three sixteenth-century ships. To the expert eye, each of them is identifiable as one of the principal ships of the Armada. The fleet sailed eastwards from the Lizard to Dodman Point, past Plymouth, inshore of Eddystone, round Start Point and across Tor Bay. Like Howard, Medina Sidonia knew the importance of the weather gauge, the wind blowing steadily up-Channel from the west, but most of his ships lacked the ability to capture it. For them safety lay not in manoeuvre but in close-packed unity. The English fleet was capable of seizing the weather gauge, but if it did so it lost the ability to attack the Spanish vanguard and to stand between Medina Sidonia and Parma when the moment of their junction came. There were sea-fights to the west of the Eddystone, off Start Point, and off Portland Bill. Each was indecisive, ships damaged rather than sunk, and after each the Armada's advance continued.

The English were surprised and impressed by Spanish discipline, which kept the ungainly fleet together; conscious of their own failure to bring Medina Sidonia to a real battle; and concerned that once he had won through to join Parma the strategic balance would be tipped against them. There was another clash, this time off the Isle of Wight. Still Medina Sidonia sailed on, into the very throat of the Straits of Dover, his advance unchecked by everything the English guns had been able to throw at him. The game so far was his.

As the Armada advanced, Howard hung back, reluctant to commit himself till he knew where Parma's forces were. The same question troubled Medina Sidonia, for he was approaching the rendezvous without word from Parma. Finally he decided to take shelter on the French coast and wait for news from the Netherlands. He anchored on the French coast two leagues from Calais citadel. Howard, reinforced by Seymour's squadron coming south from blockading Dunkirk, anchored near him.

Spanish and English knew that they were anchored on a dangerous lee shore, unwelcome visitors to a French governor who would commit himself to neither. They did not know, as we do, the other elements in the strategic picture. They did not know, for example, that the Dutch had taken up the blockade that Seymour had abandoned and were capable in their light and agile pinnaces of destroying in the shallows any barges Parma sent to sea. Medina Sidonia did not know that Parma had no light boats of his own able to fight the Dutch. Neither side knew that in Dunkirk, only 30 miles away, Parma had few barges ready for sea, and that against the Dutch those few would be the coffins of any infantry embarked in them. Spanish hopes and English fears were engaged by an invasion force that could never survive if it put to sea.

On the other hand, Howard and Medina Sidonia could see the dangers of their position. The next gale in that stormy summer would drive both fleets ashore. They could not stay where they were. The passage up the Channel had shown that no decision was likely to be achieved by cannon fire. The English knew that they must use fireships. So did the Spanish; and they knew from Parma's experiences in the Netherlands the horrors that they could inflict upon an enemy. 'The hellburners of Antwerp' were 'the most terrible weapons ever used by men in war, fireships which were actually enormous bombs capable of killing more men in one blast than might fall in a great battle, and of strewing a circle more than a mile across with a litter of flaming wreckage.'[10] The Spaniards faced the sixteenth-century equivalent of nuclear weapons.

In the event, the English proved themselves less effective hellburners than the Dutch had been at Antwerp. They quickly identified eight vessels to be sacrificed in a fireship attack. These were filled with combustibles, their guns double shotted. The Spanish prepared their defences — essentially, light pinnaces with orders to hook on to the fireships and beach them before they got in among the galleons. On the night of 6 August, with a spring tide and a strong wind at their backs, the English launched their fireships into the Spanish anchorage. Seeing that his pinnaces had succeeded in beaching only two of the eight fireships, Medina Sidonia ordered his fleet to put to sea.

Four of his best ships succeeded in following him offshore to windward. The rest, panicking, fled before the wind along the coast to the north-eastward. At dawn the English saw that the fireships had not succeeded in burning the Armada to the water line; but they had driven some Spanish ships ashore and scattered many others. Medina Sidonia's invincible crescent was no more. Instead he faced them with only a short line of ships. Howard weighed anchor and set off in pursuit. The Spanish admiral prepared to give battle, while he sent pinnaces to recall his fleeing captains to their duty. The English, Drake in the lead, closed in to attack the Spanish at close gunshot range.

Naval historians ever since have explored the rights and wrongs of the fighting that followed. Some believe that Drake did right when he suddenly turned away from Medina Sidonia's strong ships and attacked others that were struggling to rejoin him. Others say that he was after glory in beating ships whose crews were already demoralised, and reserve their praise for Martin Frobisher, who pressed the attack against the Spaniards' greatest strength and criticised Drake's tactics afterwards.

Gradually the Spanish ships rejoined their commander and re-formed the close-order half-moon formation that the English had found so formidable. In time, however, the close-range battering fire of the English guns – piercing hulls, sweeping decks, butchering crews – wiped out the Spaniards' capacity to fight their ships. Even the English, full of blood-lust and pride, admired their gallantry; but it looked as if the Armada's last hour had come. Then, yet again, the weather played a hand. A squall blinded the combatants, and when it cleared the English saw that the Spanish had hauled away to the northwards, to re-form and – still gallant – offer battle once again. The English, mauled themselves and short of victuals, powder and shot, declined it.

From now on, the Armada's voyage goes far from the Channel and can be quickly described. The battered ships moved away towards the Zeeland coast, the English still harrying them: 'Their force is wonderful great and strong,' Howard reported, 'and yet we pluck their feathers little and little.'[11] It was a perilous, shoaling coast, and soon the Spanish ships were in danger of running aground. Rather than accept that, Medina Sidonia prepared to stand and fight yet again; but in the nick of time the God of the Catholics sent a change in the wind and what was left of the Armada was able to stand out into deeper water. Northwards sailed the Spanish ships, with the English, down to their last few cannonballs, shepherding them as they went, until, off the Scottish coast, the English could turn away, their job done, their country's salvation secured.

The Spaniards sailed on, ships battered, wounds festering, water foul, food mouldering. The only feasible way home was around Scotland and Ireland. Every ship was put on short rations, the same for every grandee, officer, soldier or sailor. They rounded the Shetlands and bore away to the west. Then the weather turned against them, south-west gales that drove them on to the Irish coast. Here the Spanish began at last to lose the ships that English gunfire and fireships had failed to destroy. The crews drowned, were done to death by the Irish, or were hunted down and butchered by the handful of Englishmen who served the queen in Ireland. The ships that escaped destruction struggled on towards home and safety. After nineteen more days of torment, Medina Sidonia brought his flagship and the rest of his fleet home to Santander.

So what was left of the Armada came home in failure. Philip had brought Messianic faith to its success, defying the evidence and the consistent pessimism of his admirals. Now he appeared to accept defeat with monastic stoicism, but behind that carapace he underwent a 'profound spiritual crisis'.[12] Medina Sidonia had done all that a man faced with such difficulties could have done; now he withdrew into quiet retirement. Parma, who had never believed that the Enterprise of England could be carried to success, remained in the Spanish Netherlands, to continue campaigning against the Dutch.

In retrospect we can see how right those Spanish pessimists had been from the beginning. The Enterprise of England far exceeded the technology, resources and organisational skills of the day. That Medina Sidonia got the Armada to the Channel at all was close to miraculous. That his unwieldy fleet held together against attacks by more experienced English captains and their superior ships is a tribute to Spanish courage, discipline and determination. That the English could wound yet so often fail to destroy illustrates the difficulty of fighting a fleet action with sixteenth-century ships and guns. We know now that Parma could never hope to get his soldiers in their barges to a rendezvous at sea with Medina Sidonia's great ships before the Dutch pinnaces got among them and destroyed them. That in the end Sidonia could bring so many of his men and ships home to Spain was another miracle or, as he would have seen it, the work of a merciful Catholic God. It was no miracle, only a favourable balance of forces, which accounted for England's safety from Spanish invasion in the summer of 1588.

But to the English at the time, it all seemed miraculous, God-given. They were left to rejoice in their victory and their salvation, the work of their incomparable sea captains. On 10 August, only four days after the fireships had been sent against the Spanish ships off Calais, Thomas Deloney entered 'Three Ballads on the Armada fight' at Stationers' Hall in London. They bear all the marks of their hasty composition, but they capture the spirit of vainglorious rejoicing at the Spanish failure:

> O Noble England,
> fall down upon thy knee!
> And praise thy GOD, with thankful heart
> which still maintaineth thee!
> The foreign forces
> that seek thy utter spoil,
> Shall then, through His especial grace,
> be brought to shameful foil.
> With mighty power,
> they come unto our coast;
> To overrun our country quite,
> they make their brags and boast.
> In strength of men
> they set their only stay;
> But we, upon the LORD our GOD
> will put our trust alway![13]

Men who penned sentiments such as these were reacting spontaneously and instantly to the news of the great naval victory. But they were also irresistibly drawn to the religious myth which in the last chapter we saw developing around the English Reformation. Noble or commoner, literate or unlettered, the English began to lay the foundations of a great national myth about themselves, now political and military as much as religious.

It had many elements. One was a myth of invincibility at sea and of the protection given by its waters. It partnered a myth of national and religious unity that Elizabeth and her churchmen did everything they could to reinforce. Like most myths, it had a starting-point in fact, to which wishful thinking, hindsight, second thoughts, legend and pure fiction brought their elaborations.

The queen herself contributed mightily. On 18 August, as the Armada had sailed away up the coast of Scotland and the first English ships came back to report, she set off down the Thames in her royal barge to visit the armed camp at Tilbury. It had been created to bar the approach to London along the Thames, and was garrisoned by the rag-tag army of nobles, retainers, trained bands and armed peasantry which was all England could put into the field against invasion. Her gentlemen-at-arms accompanied her and her Captain-General, Leicester, was waiting to welcome her.

As the Armada had advanced up the Channel, England had been filled with rumour of the Catholic uprising that would greet the arrival of Parma's terrible infantry. Now the Spaniards were in retreat, but there was still fear of a Catholic assassin. But as she set out to inspect her army, Elizabeth rejected the escort that Leicester pressed upon her. Instead she went out on horseback among the men, escorted by nothing more formidable than four of her nobles and two boys. Afterwards she clothed the gesture in words that helped create the national myth of modern England. 'I do not desire,' she said, 'to live to distrust my faithful and loving people . . . I am come amongst you . . . to live or die amongst you . . . I know I have the body of a weak and feeble woman, but I have the heart and stomach of a king, and a king of England too.' Should Parma or any other prince of Europe invade England, 'I myself will take up arms, I myself will be your general.'[14]

With that speech was born the legend of Good Queen Bess, beloved of her people. It enhanced still further her reputation abroad, which the victory over the Armada established. 'She is a great woman,' Pope Sixtus V said of her, 'and were she only Catholic she would be without her match ... Just look how well she governs; she is only a woman, only mistress of half an island, and yet she makes herself feared by Spain, by France, by the Emperor, by all.'[15]

The idea of England united against the world and of the trusting fellowship of Englishmen has shaped the minds of the English people through much of their modern history. The sea and the waters of the Channel in particular play a great part in the story. Shakespeare used John of Gaunt's dying words in *Richard II* to give poetic wings to the role of the sea in the national story:

> This precious stone, set in the silver sea,
> Which serves it in the office of a wall,
> Or as a moat defensive to a house,
> Against the envy of less happier lands,
> This blessed plot, this earth, this realm, this England.[16]

Francis Bacon, the seventeenth-century essayist, gave the idea more practical form. 'This much is certain,' he wrote, 'that he that commands the sea is at great liberty, and may take as much or as little of the war as he will; whereas those that be strongest by land are many times, nevertheless, in great straits.'[17] We shall find eighteenth-century English admirals returning to the theme: 'I do not say the French cannot come. I only say they cannot come by water.' Napoleon, his Army of the Coasts of the Ocean defeated by the unseen presence of English warships, expressed his frustration in the face of English sea power. 'With 30,000 men in transports at the Downs,' he said, 'the English can paralyse 300,000 of my army, and that will reduce us to the rank of a second-class power.' In time it became a story not of England alone but of Britain against the rest, of a Britain conjured out of that very idea that the islanders were different from and superior to the continentals arrayed against them.

Only a miracle could have brought the Spanish success in their Enterprise of England, yet the English treated its defeat as a miracle of their own, its failure as God-sent; and out of it they made a story which gave them a new view of themselves and of their country. The Channel was central to the story, a precious piece of water that English seamen had made as English as any of England's counties. To the English, it seemed that God had created it to separate them from other, always unreliable, and often dangerous human beings.

CHAPTER 7

THE ROAD
TO DUTCH
INVASION

The defeat of the Armada did not mark the end of Philip II's designs on England. In 1597 he sent another naval expedition into the Channel and, though it failed, it put ashore a strong raiding party in Cornwall. It terrorised half the county, captured Mousehole, celebrated mass in an Anglican church (which the Catholic Spaniards called a mosque), and devastated the old centre of Penzance. But in 1598 Philip died and over the years that followed Spain's quarrel with England gradually died also. England devoted most of the seventeenth century to domestic disagreements, and when it turned against foreigners it was mostly against those formidable commercial rivals, the Dutch. Finally, a Dutch invader in the form of William of Orange arrived, landing with an army at Brixham on Torbay to sweep away his father-in-law, James II, the last Catholic King of England, and make himself king on terms agreed with England's Whig oligarchy.

Between the Armada and Dutch William's invasion stretch exactly 100 years of history. As far as the Channel is concerned, it is a period bereft of any clear sense of direction, although four themes can be picked out that really matter. The first is the growth of exploration, trade and settlement in the New World, bringing a new vocation to the Channel ports and new rivalries to Channel waters. The second is the English Civil War and the Commonwealth. Commercial rivalry with the Dutch, leading to the Dutch wars and a serious challenge to Britannia's dominance, comes third. Lastly, there are the events that provoked William of Orange's descent on the coast of Devon, and its importance for the future of England and the Channel.

There are subordinate themes too. There is the greatest scene in the greatest play in English literature, played out on Shakespeare Cliff at Dover. There are such things as Channel pirates and privateers; the Battle of the Dunes, with English regiments engaged in a battle of the continental titans on the beach just east of Dunkirk; Samuel Pepys's voyage to Holland to bring Charles II home to his kingdom in 1660; and a determined lady's exploration of the English Channel ports in the 1690s.

First, *King Lear*. In 1603, James, son of Mary Queen of Scots, succeeded Elizabeth on the throne of England. In the next few years William Shakespeare produced four of the greatest of his tragedies: *Othello*, *Macbeth*, *Coriolanus* and, above all, *Lear*. In it he used two classic Elizabethan metaphors for madness and chaos, the vastness of the sea and the horrors of vertigo, as signposts pointing the way down the road to national and personal redemption.

In Act IV, Scene 6 of *Lear*, the triple tragedy – of the old king's betrayal by his daughters, of Gloucester's blinding, and of the state of Albion 'come to great confusion' – is played out, in the words of the stage direction, in 'The country near Dover'. Edgar persuades his blinded father that he stands on the very edge of the cliff:

> How fearful
> And dizzy 'tis to cast one's eyes so low! . . .
> The fishermen that walk upon the beach
> Appear like mice . . .
> . . . you are now within a foot
> Of the extreme verge.

Gloucester falls forward, as he imagines to his death; and out of the shock of the anti-climax his son constructs a way to rescue him from his despair.

Enter King Lear, garlanded in flowers and mentally quite unhinged, with a speech full of powerful and radical criticism of the faults inherent in the very society over which he once ruled as an arrogant and absolute monarch. He is reunited with Cordelia, the only one of his daughters who has not turned against him. Later she is murdered, Lear emotionally destroyed. But the way is cleared for a happier future for the play's survivors, and for society. Lear, like Gloucester, has found emotional redemption on Dover Cliff, and so has Albion's political kingdom. Heady, and perhaps dangerous, stuff to offer to the courtiers of England's new king.

After the theatrical and metaphysical comes the material – the growth of western Europe's overseas contacts and trade. The Portuguese and Spanish discovery of the wider world had begun in the fifteenth century but, in the sixteenth and seventeenth, France, the Netherlands and England all joined in. In 1524, the Italian explorer Verrazano sailed from Dieppe to explore the mouth of the Hudson River, establish a settlement on the site of New York and leave a more lasting mark on the new world than Christopher Columbus ever did. Between 1577 and 1580, Francis Drake, a Plymouth seaman, took the little *Golden Hinde* right round the globe. In 1608 Samuel Champlain sailed from Honfleur in Normandy to found French Canada. Jacques Cartier from St Malo in Brittany was one of the first Europeans to explore Canada, and to this day the old city of Quebec on the St Lawrence has a feel about it of the city from which he set out. By 1614 English and French colonists were squabbling over rival settlements in Maine and Nova Scotia. Finally, and in English eyes most memorable of all these adventurers, in 1620 the Pilgrim Fathers sailed away from Plymouth Hoe in the Mayflower on their way to found New England.

At the same time, European fishermen were exploiting new grounds across the Atlantic. They went out in their open boats every season to the rich and virgin cod fisheries on the Grand Banks off Newfoundland.

They dried their catch on North American beaches and brought it home to sell in European markets, doing well enough to make the difficulty, discomfort and danger of the voyage worth the candle.

Other explorers and traders were going still further afield. By the beginning of the sixteenth century the Portuguese had explored the west coast of Africa. By its end the Spanish had built a rich and sophisticated South American empire, whose gold first enriched and then enervated Spain itself. The Dutch went to the East Indies and established trading bases there, and by 1623 Dutch officials and traders at Amboina were at bloody odds with English merchants trying to break into their monopoly of nutmeg. In the course of a century and a half, Europe's presence in the wider world had become a fact, perhaps the most important fact of modern history.

All these voyages of exploration, settlement, trade and conquest brought change to the Channel ports. The ships that crossed the oceans were built in Channel estuaries or on Channel beaches. Men from the English, French and Dutch ports manned them. The returning argosies were landed in French or English ports or carried through the Straits of Dover to the Antwerp and Amsterdam markets or the cities of the Baltic. Places such as Plymouth, St Malo, Falmouth, Honfleur and Brest prospered. The harbour at Le Havre was developed when its neighbour, Harfleur, fell victim to silting sands. The explosion of Europe into the world meant that the very nature of the Channel's business was altered. To its age-old cross-Channel concerns it had now added business down-Channel into the oceans as well.

With the new prosperity came troubles. Disputes over land and trade at the other side of the world became disputes between governments at home. A defeat in the East or West Indies became something to be avenged in the narrow seas. Governments reasserted ancient claims in order to revenge themselves for insults or damage suffered by their seamen a hemisphere away. The English Navigation Acts had long demanded, for example, that imports and exports should be shipped in English vessels. Now they were deployed to protect English fisheries by barring the import of foreign fish into England – fish stolen from under the noses of honest English fishermen on the Grand Banks. Similarly,

England asserted the rights of its Court of Admiralty to rule the affairs of the narrow seas. 'The dominion of the sea,' said Thomas Coventry in the House of Commons, 'as it is an ancient and undoubted right of the crown of England, so is it the best security of the land. The wooden walls are the best security of this kingdom.'[1] When it demanded salutes from every foreign ship that passed through the Straits of Dover the English crown was asserting that the very seas were English, and throwing down a challenge to seamen of every other nation.

Yet the Netherlands was rapidly emerging as the leading European seafaring nation, its merchants more thrusting than its English rivals, its seamen as skilled. For the Dutch the Straits of Dover were the way to the ocean. But even in peacetime English law and English seamen harassed them, and the islanders, sitting between the narrow seas and the ocean, had the geographical advantage. In time of war the Dutch would have to drive the English back into harbour if their own ships were not to be bottled up in port and their trade destroyed. In the course of the seventeenth century these essentially commercial disputes were to lead to repeated naval wars between England and Holland. Samuel Pepys's diaries reveal the human, political and commercial grief they caused. But the even bigger fact for England, Holland and the other naval powers of the day was the new wealth they were fighting for, which the discovery of new worlds was bringing them. Both the wealth and the wars fed the Channel with new importance. It is an importance that over the centuries since it has never lost.

Throughout the sixteenth century, piracy in the Channel in its most simple and brutal form declined. But piracy licensed by governments – privateering – flourished. It was an instrument of governmental policy, effective but whenever necessary disavowable; and at the same time a source of profit to monarch, investor and privateering captain.

Pirates had operated in the Channel since the beginnings of recorded history. The Romans built the Classis Britanniae and the forts of the Saxon Shore to contain them. Pirates, or people very like pirates, brought Anglo-Saxon and Viking raiders to Britain. The seamen of the Cinque Ports fought pirates and themselves indulged in piracy. Dunkirk was for centuries a notorious haunt of pirates. In the sixteenth century religion and piracy became intertwined, with the Dutch corsairs who called themselves the Sea Beggars defending Protestantism against the Spanish at one entrance to the Channel, and the corsairs of La Rochelle raiding the shipping of the Catholic King of France at the other.

In the early seventeenth century a new and terrible form of piracy came to the Channel. Naval wars in the Mediterranean were fought in galleys and the demand for galley-slaves to pull their oars was inexhaustible. The Barbary pirates from the ports of North Africa moved out into the Atlantic in search of them. Soon they took to operating in the Channel approaches and deep into the Channel itself. They took seamen out of ships in the Channel, inshore fishermen off their little boats, and farm labourers out of French and English fields. Justified fear of 'the Turk' ran up and down the Channel, and for a time governments and navies proved ineffective in dealing with them.

Meanwhile governments patronised pirates of their own or made them respectable as privateers with letters of marque to their names. So Henry VIII's favourite privateer, Robert Reneger, made himself an ornament of the royal court and a respected citizen of Southampton at a time when that city's more conventional commercial activities were in decline. Elizabeth's benevolence towards English piracy on the Spanish Main is a famous fact of history, but she also turned a blind eye to privateers harassing Spanish shipping in the Channel on its way from Spain to the Spanish Netherlands, taking a cut of Spanish treasure when it was brought into her ports. In the course of the sixteenth century, royal navies grew more powerful and effective. They were increasingly capable of dealing with unlicensed piracy. But in times of trouble, as when the Armada came, men who had made their fortunes as privateers were welcome auxiliaries. They gained respectability as well as wealth.

Jean Bart, for example, a member of a proud family of Dunkirk privateers, turned himself into a French naval hero. At first he served Holland, and he was in Ruyter's fleet that stormed England's Medway defences in 1667. But he switched his allegiance to France, and in the French–Dutch wars of the 1670s he took eighty-one Dutch prizes.

Twenty years later, when France faced famine, he captured a 100-ship convoy loaded with wheat from the Baltic. But his most extraordinary exploit involved not privateers or men-of-war but an open boat. Captured by the English, he broke out of his prison in Plymouth, stole a boat, and rowed across to France. It was a hundred-mile haul across the western Channel, and it took him fifty-two hours. Louis XIV ennobled him and in the twentieth century the French Republic gave his name to a battleship.

While England struggled for maritime commercial prosperity it was increasingly preoccupied with different issues at home. The claims of its Stuart king rubbed against the ambitions of its parliamentary and merchant classes. Its sailors and merchants may have gone out into the wide world, but most of seventeenth-century England's attention was still turned in upon itself. Preoccupation with political and religious issues was on the increase, leading the country towards constitutional deadlock and civil war.

So from the accession of Charles I to the last years of Cromwell's Protectorate, England largely turned its back upon the Channel. When at last civil war broke out, Charles made his headquarters in Oxford, while his opponents made theirs in London. His strength lay in the north and the west, theirs in the south-east and East Anglia. So the war was fought essentially in the English Midlands, just as when it was resumed the fighting was mainly in Scotland, Ireland and the English North.

The Channel counties were therefore largely spared the fighting, though their ports had a certain utility for both sides, not least for the import of arms, and the Channel's role is an episodic matter of bits and pieces. The king's ships by and large declared for the parliamentary cause, throwing the royalists on the defensive at sea: the ships that remained to them spent their time evading blockade and attacking lone ships of the other side, and their cavalry hero, Prince Rupert, turned privateer and attacked parliamentary ships and seaside fortresses. A parliamentary garrison held Plymouth, and parliamentary armies made repeated attempts to penetrate the royalist counties of Dorset,

Devonshire and Cornwall. They devoted inordinate efforts, for example, to the siege of Weymouth. Kent and Sussex by contrast were solidly parliamentarian, and Hampshire mostly so. When things went badly for the king, Falmouth saw Queen Henrietta Maria escaping to her native France, where she pawned her jewels to buy arms for his cause. For a time the teenage Prince of Wales took refugee in the Scilly Isles. The Channel Islands saw out the war divided: Jersey royalist, Guernsey mostly parliamentarian. And throughout the war, as before it, the king held his political prisoners under lock and key in Jersey and the Scillies.

At the end of the war, however, the focus of great events suddenly settled on the Isle of Wight. In 1646 Charles surrendered to the invading Scottish army. They sold him to Parliament, which held him prisoner at Hampton Court, while Parliament and army tried to agree on his fate. Finally, fearing assassination, he escaped from what was no more than house arrest and fled to the Isle of Wight. There, in the great castle of Carisbrooke, he hoped to reassert his tarnished royal authority. The governor, however, treated him with the courtesy due to a king, but as a prisoner. Plans to rescue him failed, even though royalist ships were cruising off the coast of the Isle of Wight to take him to France and freedom.

Unbending about his own position, Charles tried to play Scots, New Model Army and Parliament off against one another. He only exasperated his captors. They took him to the little Isle of Wight town of Newport, and in the unlikely setting of the Grammar School there formal council meetings were held to find a settlement that would satisfy the army, the parliamentary commissioners and the king himself. Eventually the king was removed, now entirely a prisoner, to the strict isolation of Henry VIII's Hurst Castle in the western Solent. From there he was brought back at last to Whitehall, a farce of a trial in Westminster Hall, and execution.

Charles's execution did not mark the end of the civil wars of England, but the defeat of his son, Charles II, at the Battle of Worcester in 1651 did. After that disaster Charles famously escaped pursuit by hiding in an oak tree. Then he made his way in disguise to the Channel coast. At the little port of Shoreham in Sussex a 30-foot coasting collier, *Surprise*, was waiting for him. She took him over the water to the French port of Fécamp and into exile. (At the Restoration he bought the little ship from her owner, a ship's master from Brighton, renamed her *Royal Escape*, and moored her at the Tower of London, perhaps to remind himself that come what may he should never go on his travels again.)

Charles's departure was followed by nine years of republican rule, seven of them dominated by the personality of Oliver Cromwell. The Commonwealth took up the old commercial quarrels with the Dutch, pursuing them in a maritime war. But in 1656, two years before his death, Cromwell found himself involved in a war not with the Netherlands but between France and Spain. It culminated in June 1658 in a battle on the seashore a few miles east of Dunkirk. For the Spaniards, it was the Last Hurrah of their long presence in the Low Countries, for the French a milestone on their road to pre-eminence in Europe. For the British troops engaged on both sides, this was the last battle of their civil war.

This Battle of the Dunes took place in France's most northerly point, up against the Belgian frontier, at a place called Bray Dunes. It is a bleak and shabby resort, blessed only by splendid beaches. From these beaches a broken British army was to be so memorably rescued in 1940. To the west lie the shoals on which the Armada's ships ran aground as they scattered before the English fireships. Behind Bray, a little way inland, flows one of Flanders's innumerable canals. Parma had hoped to shift his barges along it to Dunkirk on their way to the invasion of England. The same canal held the Germans back from the Dunkirk beaches in 1940. So Bray has seen the making of much British history.

Between beach and canal lies a stretch of heath, giving way in places to sand dunes held in place by scrawny vegetation. Here, on 13 June 1658, the French and Spanish armies met. At issue was what was left of the Spanish presence in the Low Countries. The Dutch had at last fought their way free of Spanish occupation; now a newly assertive France wanted to drive the Spanish out altogether. At the head of the French army was the great soldier, Marshal Turenne; in the background among the civilians the young Louis XIV and the great French statesman, Mazarin.

To secure Cromwell's help, Mazarin had promised him Dunkirk, which would serve, in the words of Cromwell's diplomatic adviser John Thurloe, as 'a bridle to the Dutch and a door into the continent'.[2] So six scarlet-clad English regiments fought beside the French in what was to be the New Model Army's last battle. Cromwell's ambassador in Paris, Sir William Lockhart, took the day off from diplomacy and turned soldier to command them. The opposing army was led by a Spanish prince of the blood, advised by the great Condé himself. The Spanish infantry were supported by five regiments – English, Irish and Scottish – loyal to the next King of England, Charles II. Charles's brother, the Duke of York, commanded them.

It was a brutal battle, viciously fought by infantry in close combat. Eventually, victory went to Turenne and his English allies, sweeping their enemies to destruction 'at push of pike' across the sand dunes. Cromwell got his promised reward, took possession of Dunkirk, and had 'the keys of the continent at his girdle'. To some it seemed a worthy replacement for Calais, lost a century earlier, which could be developed as a new English foothold on the continent. But within three months Cromwell was dead, and within two years the system he had built was swept away. In the early summer of 1660, Charles II was restored to the English throne. He was impoverished, and in retrospect wiser than Cromwell's diplomatic adviser. He sold Dunkirk to the French, giving up his country's doorway to the continent and its bridle on the Dutch. He rid it also of what in time would have become as solid an obstacle as Calais once had been to reasonable relations with the French, an enduring *casus belli* at the very entrance to the Channel.

When Oliver Cromwell died, his son Richard succeeded him, but to most intents and purposes the Protectorate died with the father. Before long, discreet emissaries from England and Scotland were waiting upon Charles II to discuss his return to the throne. Finally an English fleet sailed to bring the king and the royal family home. It was a splendid event in the history of the North Sea and the Channel. Fortunately

Samuel Pepys was there, to enjoy every minute and record it in his diary.

On 23 March 1660, Pepys took ship with his master, Edward Mountagu. He knew they were on a confidential mission, and little by little it became clear that its purpose was to bring the king home from his travels. Pepys's diaries take us with the fleet from Gravesend down the Thames ('I begin to be dizzy and squeamish'), into the Estuary ('I saw many wracks and masts, which are now the greatest guides for ships') and out into the sea lanes ('... overtook two good merchant-men ... going to the East Indies'). Soon Pepys tires of straight travel-reporting ('the lieutenant and I lay out of his window with his glass, looking at the women that were on board them, being pretty handsome').[3] He sees the Goodwin Sands; Deal Castle; the accelerating replacement of republican emblems with royalist ones; and the passing tragedy of 'the Coxon of the Cheriton boate; who dropping overboard, could not be saved, but was drowned'.

While the fleet waits in the Straits of Dover, the tide of opinion is setting in favour of the restoration of the monarchy. It dawns on Pepys that actions and correspondence he had thought insignificant have all played a part in the change, which Mountagu is orchestrating. His master sends Pepys off in a ship's boat to take a royalist proclamation round the fleet. He records 'the great joy that I brought to all men', but when the ships fire their *feu de joie* they nearly make an end of him as 'bullets go hissing over our heads as we were in the boat'.[4]

The fleet sails for the Dutch coast. The great men go off to kiss the king's hand, and the Duke of York's, and the Queen of Bohemia's. Pepys goes to Delft, and closely examines the Dutch ladies' charms. The royal party come on board and rename the *Nazeby* the *Charles*, something one cannot help feeling Mountagu might have been wise to attend to earlier. On 25 May the fleet disembarks the king and his court at Dover. There George Monck, general of the New Model Army, self-made admiral of the Protectorate's navy, wise statesman and wiser turncoat, welcomes them. Two days later Mountagu is rewarded for all his efforts with his appointment 'Companion-Elect of our Noble Order of the Garter'. 'We will rise together,' he promises Pepys; and the course of the diarist's career as a great naval administrator is set to follow in his wake.[5]

* * *

The story of England's naval wars with the Netherlands, fought in the North Sea, the Thames Estuary and the Channel, has its roots in the years of Cromwell's Protectorate. For him, Holland was as much a commercial rival and naval threat as it had been to Charles I. The City merchants wanted a foreign policy that served their money-making, and action that put the Dutch in their place. Now, as a result of the Civil War, England had an army comparable with those of continental nations. It had an effective fleet. And both army and navy needed to be kept usefully and if possible gainfully employed.

The result was the first of three wars with the Netherlands, which were fought off and on from 1652 to 1674, first by Cromwell and then by Charles II, and which generated more battles in the Channel and the narrow seas than have ever been fought there since. Naval science had come a long way since the Armada. Now fleets could cruise and fight far from their home bases. Admirals and captains could manoeuvre their ships and fleets to seize the weather gauge and put their enemies downwind. Their gunners could do serious damage at longer distances. Naval warfare no longer followed the rules of war on land and admirals were ceasing to be 'generals at sea'. These were changes that gave an extra advantage to the seagoing nations, and to England and Holland above all. They were well-matched enemies.

In 1652, England wanted war. To bring it about, the government determined to make the most of the ancient English claim that foreigners should salute the English flag at Dover. They tried and failed to choke the Dutch by attacks on their fisheries and trade, in the course of which a British fleet commander, Robert Blake, was beaten off by the Dutch admiral Ruyter in a battle off the Lizard. Matters rapidly escalated, with an English success in an action between the two battle fleets off the Kentish Knock and an English defeat off Dungeness. The English withdrew into the Thames, the Dutch made free of the Channel. It was only in 1653 when the English recalled a squadron they had sent to the Mediterranean (in itself a sign of the new flexibility of naval warfare) that they could match the Dutch in numbers, defeat them in battle off the Dutch coast and end the war on reasonably dignified terms.

The Protectorate now turned for a time against Spain. But Spain was a declining power, the Netherlands an assertive one. Within five years of Charles's restoration, England was again at war with the Dutch. The cause was the same as in Cromwell's war: commercial rivalry at sea. To it the king added his dislike of republicanism; but it was commercial interest at Court and in the City, not politics, which in 1664 sent a fleet commanded by the Duke of York and Prince Rupert of the Rhine to patrol the Channel and snap up Dutch merchant convoys. This licensed piracy drove the Dutch to a formal declaration of war, and soon Pepys's old patron Mountagu, now Lord Sandwich and admiral of the narrow seas, was out on blockade duty off the Dutch coast.

By now Pepys was Clerk of the Acts to the Navy Board, 'the right hand of the navy' and the man in overall charge of its support and supply. His diaries describe the war through the eyes of the man behind the scenes. He takes a seaman just home from the fleet to tell the king how the battle of 1 June 1666 has gone: 'we found the Dutch fleet at anchor . . . between Dunkirke and Ostend, and made them let slip their anchors – they about 90, and we less than 60. We fought them and put them to the run, till they met with about 16 sail of fresh ships and so bore up again. The fight continued till night, and then again the next morning . . . they chasing us for the most part of Saturday and yesterday; we fleeing from them.' No one of note has been killed, and Sir W. Clerke, 'who hath lost his leg . . . bore it bravely'. The king rewards the sailor, 'And so parted, mightily pleased with the account he did give him of the fight and the success it ended with.' But Pepys is shrewder than his monarch: 'It seems the Duke [of York] did give way again and again.'[6]

Soon, however, the English ships handle the Dutch roughly off Orfordness on the Sussex coast, and might have taken the war to Holland. But in September 1666 comes the Great Fire, and by the summer of the following year, as London sets about rebuilding, Ruyter and his fleet are in the Thames, moving steadily upstream. Pepys goes out to inspect the defences and finds the amateurs in ineffectual charge: 'Down to Gravesend, where I find the Duke of Albemarle just come, with a great many idle lords and gentlemen, with their pistols and fooleries; and the bulworke not able to have stood half an hour had they [the Dutch] come up.'[7]

Pepys does his duty, and casts around to find vessels that can be used as fireships against the Dutch, but he also takes the precaution of moving his money to the country in case the Dutch take London. Ruyter gets into the Medway, burns Rochester and Chatham, and seizes the pride of the English fleet, the *Royal Charles*. Pepys fumes in his diary that she should have been moved further upstream and that the officer who failed to move her 'deserves . . . to be hanged for not doing it'.[8] The summer of 1667 marked the nadir of England's fortunes, and there was a danger that Pepys and the men around him, like the man who had lost the *Royal Charles*, might be sacrificed to popular anger. France threatened to join the war in support of the Dutch and the time had come to end it on any terms. England made peace as best it could, yielding to the Dutch on commercial traffic in the narrow seas.

The third Dutch war, five years later, was a different matter, in which political chicanery as well as commercial interests got involved. Louis XIV had wearied of his Dutch alliance and wanted to destroy Holland's power to sustain alliances against him. In the secret Treaty of Dover of 1670, he bribed Charles II to help him, promising him in return control of the mouths of the Rhine and Scheldt, which English policy through-out modern history has sought to keep out of hostile hands.

By now Pepys, convinced that he is going blind, has closed his diary for the last time, 'that course which is almost as much as to see myself go into my grave',[9] and seventeenth-century English history becomes duller·in consequence. To start the war with Holland, Charles picked a typical narrow seas fight, reiterating the ancient demand that ships of any nation using the Straits of Dover should salute any English man of war. The Royal Navy's very Articles of War asserted that 'It is upon the navy under the good Providence of God that the safety, honour and welfare of this realm do chiefly depend.' But even with French support the English could not prevail. The Dutch were Davids against Goliaths. They had the better of a fight with the combined English and French fleets off Southwold and again at Camperdown, and on land they flooded the French army out of their country. In the Treaty of Westminster in

February 1674 that ended the fighting, England was lucky to get Dutch acceptance of that symbol of her sovereignty at sea, the right to stop and search others' merchantmen. The Dutch commercial wars were over.

All these wars leave little sense of the towns and ports and houses that punctuate the Channel coast of England. Pepys gives a fine description of Charles II's landing at Dover and reception by its mayor and citizenry; but he was a Londoner through and through and never explored the south coast. The journals of Celia Fiennes, an indefatigable gentlewoman of progressive but religious tastes, come to fill the gap. They describe two long journeys of exploration in seventeenth-century England which took her as far north as Newcastle and as far west as Penzance. In the course of them she visited Deal and Sandwich, Dover, Rye and Winchelsea, Portsmouth, the Isle of Wight, Lymington, Lyme Regis, Purbeck, Exeter, Plymouth, Penzance and Truro, and Land's End. She has an eye for everything, from the possibilities of invasion to the prospects for industry. Her comments are shrewd and naïve by turns. They provide a sharp-eyed view of the English coast of the Channel at the very end of the seventeenth century.

South of Deal, Celia Fiennes looks out on the coast on which Julius Caesar had landed. 'The Downs seemes to be so open a place and the shoar so easye for landing I should think it no difficulty to land a good army of men in a little tyme, there is only 3 little forts [at Deal, Sandwich and Walmer] . . . which hold a few Guns but I should think they would be of little effect and give the enemy no great trouble.' At Dover she sees the room in which, she is told, Queen Elizabeth heard of the death of Queen Mary: 'the balcony just by in which she saw the Messenger coming which she supposed was of Death to take off her head, but proved the Messenger that brought the news of the Crowne and Kingdoms falling to her by the death of her sister.' She goes on to Winchelsea and finds it a decayed little place with 'major and aldermen which 13 makes most of the inhabitants'. Rye will be as bad 'in a little tyme if the sea leaves it, which is in a very fair way to do . . .'[10]

'Portsmouth is a very good town well built with Stone and Brick its not a large town.' The defences seem strong on the landward side but not to seaward: 'the great schipps lye at anchor here', and Celia Fiennes goes aboard the *Royal Charles* and the *Royal James*. 'The Castle looks very fine but think it's but of little Strength or Service.' In the Isle of Wight she visits Yarmouth, Cowes and Carisbrooke, and finds that 'the fertility of the whole island produces corn of all sorts in great plenty, and all sorts of cattle and butter cheese as also great stores of fish and fowle'.

At Lymington she turns her attention away from buildings and ships because 'the greatest trade is by their Salterns' – the salt pans whose workings she describes at length. At Lyme Regis, by contrast, it is the Cobb which captures her attention, and in the Isle of Purbeck the crabs and lobsters. Exeter impresses by its cloth business: 'the whole town and country is employ'd for at least 20 mile round in spinning, weaveing, dressing, and scouring, fulling and drying of the serges, it turns the most money in a weeke of anything in England'.[11]

The streets of Plymouth are 'inhabitted with seamen and those which have affaires on the sea, for here up to the town there is a depth of water for shipps of the first rate to ride'. From Plymouth westwards the way is hard, but at Truro and Redruth she explores the copper mines. The miners ship the tin to Bristol rather than Plymouth 'because since the warre they could not double the poynt at the Lands End being so neer France, the pirates or privateers met them'. And lastly to Penzance, passing by a church 'which was almost sunck into the sands'. Penzance itself 'looks soe snugg and warme and truely it needs shelter haveing the sea on the other side and no fewell: turf and furse and ferne; they have little or noe wood and noe coale . . .'[12] – and the thought takes her off on a racing, tumbling stream of consciousness to Derbyshire, which has both.

English history, which was for so long Whig history, recognises no successful foreign invasion since 1066. Yet when William of Orange landed in Torbay in 1688 he came in Dutch ships with a Dutch army against the country's legitimate king, his father-in-law, James II. So this was in very deed a foreign invasion, accomplished exactly 100 years after the failure of the Armada. It stands on its head the myth of

Albion, inviolate since 1066. It is a major, much ignored, feature of the English Channel's story.

Its origins go back to 1685, when James II succeeded his brother on the throne of England. As Duke of York, James had given Restoration England much service. His brother made him Lord High Admiral. As Pepys's master, he comes across in the diaries as a strong and effective chief, loyal and generous to those who served him. He instituted naval procedures that have lasted down the centuries; and he repeatedly took the fleet to sea and brought back victories. If the Royal Navy has commanded the Channel and the narrow seas from his day to ours, with the fatal exception of the day of William's crossing, it is in large part due to the sense of duty that he bred in it.

But James was to prove himself a better admiral than king. Whereas Charles reserved his inclination towards Catholicism for a deathbed conversion, James made no secret of his faith and, succeeding to the throne, at once declared himself a Catholic. He was crowned in the Anglican rite, but his faith seemed to align him with a totalitarian Catholic Church, just as his brisk naval authoritarianism identified him with continental tyrants.

Next came two events, each with a West Country flavour, which brought popular support to the new king's Whig opponents. On 11 June 1685, James Fitzroy, Duke of Monmouth, landed at Lyme Regis and proclaimed himself 'head and captain-general of Protestant forces of the kingdom'. Monmouth was Charles II's eldest natural son, who had made a troubled career in his father's service, been banished from court, and established a relationship in exile with William of Orange. Now he sought to put himself at the head of opposition to his uncle, the new king.

From Lyme Regis Monmouth marched with his little army to Taunton, where his followers proclaimed him King of England. At Sedgemoor he was captured and taken to London. There he threw himself in vain on his uncle's mercy; and nine days later he was executed as a traitor in the Tower. In defeat his absurd adventure would have been forgotten but for the brutal trials of his supporters which followed. At his 'Bloody Assizes' the king's judge, George Jeffreys, showed little justice and no mercy. Monmouth's men were judicially butchered on the beach at Lyme. These, James's enemies argued, were not the ways of honest Protestant England but a throwback to the days of 'Bloody Mary', an example of the continental tyranny that James wanted to establish in England.

Next James suspended the penal laws against Catholics and nonconformists. He saw the move as an act of toleration, but it met with vociferous resistance, and Anglicans complained that they were being required to connive at their own destruction. Seven bishops stood out against the king and were arrested and put on trial. One of them was Jonathan Trelawny, bishop of Exeter. His cause provoked the last threat in English history that the West Country was prepared to use armed force against central authority. In the words of R. S. Hawker's 'The Song of the Western Men':

> Trelawny, he's in keep and hold,
> Trelawny, he may die;
> But here's twenty thousand Cornish bold
> Will know the reason why!

Finally, James added a very human little offence to all his other affronts to Protestant England. In 1688, his queen presented him with a son. The child was christened James Edward and was to become the Old Pretender. His immediate significance was that he embodied the prospect of a Catholic Stuart son succeeding a Catholic father on the throne of England. Whereas James's opponents might have hoped that his religious and authoritarian innovations would die with him (and he was already fifty-five), now they suddenly acquired the prospect of permanence.

The Whigs had long been in contact with William and Mary. Now they urged them to take possession of James's forfeit throne. Mary was reluctant to turn against her father. William was cautious, but if he were to save the Netherlands from the growing threat of Louis XIV's ambitions he would need English support. They committed themselves to seizing control of England.

Sympathisers in England promised them support, but they could only rally around an invading army. A naval expedition, successful where the Spanish had failed, was necessary to get it there. For the Dutch this was a high-risk gamble against French as well as English sea power. But for once the wind in the narrow seas blew from the east. It brought the pretenders smartly out of harbour while it pinned James's ships down in the Thames. Once again the narrow seas, often thought of as an obstacle to movement, in fact provide an invader with strategic flexibility. William could have gone to Yorkshire, to East Anglia or into the Thames. His advisers persuaded him instead to sail down-Channel and land in the same West Country where Monmouth had come looking for support.

So the Dutch fleet advanced to the Straits of Dover. On 3 November 1688, it entered the straits, 'its flanking ships coming close to the shores of England and France, with braying of trumpets and beating of drums'.[13] The English tailed along, far behind; and a French fleet that had been sent to intercept the Dutch was easily evaded. Then faulty navigation took a hand against Dutch William, and his fleet sailed past its designated landing point. But a Protestant change of wind brought it back from the west, and on 5 November 1688 William landed at Brixham in Devon, across the bay from Torquay. Hilaire Belloc, the Catholic poet and polemicist who was also an impassioned small-boat sailor in the Channel, imagined the scene: 'I should like to have seen that big Dutch fleet, with its few English renegades on board come sweeping into Torbay. I should like to have seen the crowded boats passing to and fro, landing the Dutchmen and other foreign troops, and the great lords who were conspiring against their king, and the saturnine William himself.' For profoundly as Belloc despised this invasion to end 'the age-long, but dying, tradition of monarchy in Britain, and put the rich in the saddle for good', not even he could deny that 'From the moment when the huge armament bowled through the Straits of Dover under a south-east wind ... to that afternoon, two days later, when the high gilded poops of the Dutchmen stood out in line across Torbay, the whole evil thing was full of grandeur and of colour.'[14]

The Whig historian Lord Macaulay took another view of the Dutch adventure. To him, it was not 'the whole evil thing' but the Glorious Revolution. In his excitement he thinks not just about the revolution but about the progress that it was to bring to England. So Torbay, he says, was a primitive place when William landed there, its quiet shores 'undisturbed by the bustle either of commerce or of pleasure'. How different it had become, with its 'crowded marts' and 'luxurious pavilions', by his own time, a century and a half later.[15]

William had 11,000 troops with him. Only 4,000 of them were English or Scots. James marched to Salisbury, but as one magnate after another went over to the invaders, support for his cause ebbed away. He still hoped for support from France, and he sent the baby Prince of Wales to Portsmouth on the way to Paris and safety. But even the nobleman to whom he entrusted his son turned renegade and brought the baby back to London. Finally, the royal family fled. Their boat was intercepted by a fisherman in the Thames Estuary and brought back. They spent tense days in Whitehall under Dutch guard, a matter of yards from the Banqueting House through whose windows James's father had stepped to his execution, and finally were glad to be despatched into exile in France. They left the country in the hands of the king's daughter, her Dutch husband, the Whig oligarchy of England and a foreign army of occupation.

Of course, William and Mary would not have taken the risk of invading England if they had not known that powerful English interests would welcome their coming and join them in James II's overthrow. Once power was theirs, so was the writing of history. As the Elizabethan wit, Sir John Harington, pronounced:

> Treason doth never prosper; what's the reason?
> For if it prosper, none dare call it treason.

The Dutch invasion of November 1688 became the Glorious Revolution; and so it has remained in English history ever since. But that interpretation does less than justice to the facts. It perpetuates the myth that no one has successfully invaded England since 1066. And it denies the story of the Channel an elegant symmetry. In 1588 a foreign Armada had sailed up the Channel from the Lizard to the Straits on its way to conquer England. It failed, and the fact of its failure has been a glory of English history and historiography ever since. One hundred years later, a foreign fleet sailed down the Channel from the Straits to the Devon coast on its way, too, to conquer England. This one succeeded, a Dutch triumph over an English king. But in the hands of English historiography, this triumph, like the Armada's defeat, also became a glory of English history, for this invader was a good Protestant king, not a Catholic tyrant like Philip II. So his victory has been transformed by the sleight of hand of Whig historians into a home-grown triumph of honest Englishmen.

CHAPTER 8

THE WHALE
AND THE
ELEPHANT

W e are approaching the half-way point in this story of the
Channel. It is time to take a break from the political
narrative and look in more general terms at what the
Channel was becoming in the course of the eighteenth century.

To start, there is the condition of the two countries that between
them shape the Channel and dictate much of its character. In the
sixteenth and seventeenth centuries England and France developed a
new sense of self-awareness as nations. In the course of the eighteenth
they took that process further, becoming centralised, nation-based
territorial monarchies, the two most important such entities in western
Europe.

In France the ambitions and achievements of King Louis XIV were
central to the process. By the time he died in 1715 the French state
extended roughly to the borders it enjoys today. The Sun King and his
successors concentrated power at Versailles. The splendours of their
court and aristocracy aroused an awareness of Frenchness among more
humble men and women. Despite the class differences that in the end
destroyed the *ancien régime*, France was united, and had become

unambiguously a nation – *la grande nation* – in some ways *the* western European nation, imposing itself on the attention of its neighbours as a cultural and commercial giant as well as a political and military force.

Something similar was happening in 'Britain' (which at this point mostly replaces 'England' in this narrative). Wales had long been subordinated to England's sense of identity. In 1707 came the union between England and Scotland. Englishmen, and some Scotsmen, took to calling Scotland 'North Britain', and ambitious North Britons took the high road to England, 'the noblest prospect', Dr Johnson famously asserted, 'which a Scotchman ever sees'. In the eighteenth century, the British ruling classes started to propagate a sense of a common British identity among subjects of the Crown. Over the course of a century the concept of Great Britain gradually came to absorb all three countries, overlaying old national and local loyalties and rendering them increasingly subordinate to the central authority of King and Parliament in London.

The best way to teach the French and the British to identify themselves as belonging to national entities was to indoctrinate them in their differences from other people, and in particular from each other. Indoctrination fell on fertile ground, for the English and French had long been accustomed to make cross-Channel comparisons, usually to the other's detriment. In Britain, Protestantism as expressed in the moderate ceremonies of the Anglican Church had been promoted as the Englishman's birthright, setting him apart from those who followed Rome. France reversed the image, and Europe's 'most Christian king' was seen as a stalwart of Catholicism. Now both countries added secular characteristics to the list of things which made people distinctively French or British. Inevitably, things military and naval were added to these lists of characteristics, and each country took pride in its victories over the other; so in the course of the eighteenth century '*gloire*' in France and 'success' in Britain became specifically French and British concerns.

The story of the artist William Hogarth's visit to Calais illustrates the cross-Channel disparagement that fed this sense of national distinctiveness. In 1748 he went to France and in Calais got into a fracas with the authorities. 'Ignorant of the customs of France,' his biographer John Ireland explains, 'and considering the gate of Calais merely as a piece of ancient architecture, he began to make a sketch. This was soon observed; he was seized as a spy, who intended to draw a plan of the fortifications, and escorted by a file of musqueteers to M. la Commandant. His sketch-book was examined leaf by leaf, and found to contain drawings that had not the most distant relation to tactics.'[1] Nevertheless, the governor politely tells him, 'that had not a treaty between the nations actually been signed, he should have been under the disagreeable necessity of hanging him upon the ramparts'. As it is, Hogarth is marched between two guards back to his ship: 'nor did they quit their prisoner, until he was a league from shore; when, seizing him by the shoulders, and spinning him round upon the deck, they said he was now at liberty to pursue his voyage without further molestation'.

Inevitably, Hogarth had his own back. 'The first time anyone goes from hence to france by way of Calais,' he wrote, 'he cannot avoid being struck with the Extreem different face things appear with at so little a distance from Dover. A farcical pomp of war, parade of religion and Bustle with very little business, in short, poverty, slavery and Insolence (with an affectation of politeness) give you even here the first specimen of the whole country.'[2] Then he turned to his brush and produced his painting *O the Roast Beef of Old England: The Gate of Calais* (reproduced in picture section). It is a great painting as well as an effective piece of cross-Channel propaganda. In it Hogarth shows the circumstances of his arrest as an incidental to his depiction of everything that he and all honest Englishmen think wrong in France: poverty, sloth, dirt, arrogance and Popery. As an engraving the work became an immensely popular diatribe against the French. 'My own figure, in the corner with the soldier's hand upon my shoulder,' Hogarth added, with a show of the self-conscious moderation of the English gentleman, 'is said to be tolerably like.'

This heightened awareness of difference from others increased the importance of the frontiers that defined these nation states. As in so many things, Britain was different: the sea had always provided a clearer delineation than uncertain borders ever could. But the growth in power of a centralised France brought Paris's authority to the Channel coast. Calais, which had once been English, and Dunkirk, which had once been Spanish, now thought of themselves as French. Brittany continued to think of itself as different, a difference that was to come to a bloody dénouement in the French Revolution, but even here France created the naval base of Brest at the very point of the peninsula, with the specific purpose of projecting its sea power into the oceans. The writ of the eighteenth-century French state might run tenuously in Brittany, but along the whole length of the Channel, France and Britain looked each other in the eye.

They took each other seriously, more seriously than they took any other European nation. They looked critically at one another as partners, rivals, competitors and enemies. It went without saying that they watched each other's diplomatic and military moves like hawks. Trade between them mattered, and so did their commercial rivalries. The complexity of the relationship extended beyond politics and business, however. It embraced cultural, scientific and intellectual issues too. The English admired French style and intellectual fireworks, while French observers such as Voltaire and Montesquieu believed that they could learn from the civility of Britain's domestic politics. Each country saw the other as its foremost rival. When Victor Hugo wrote of the two countries, 'There has never been an antipathy between them, only the desire to surpass. France is the adversary of England as the better is the enemy of the good,' he cut to the heart of the two countries' sentiments about one another as much in the eighteenth century as in his own.

Yet the strengths and weaknesses of the two neighbours were very different. The Louis were true, absolute kings, whereas the Georges had come to power by parliamentary invitation. In France the aristocracy was politically motivated and socially exclusive; in Britain it valued wealth creation as much as birth, inviting economics, even commerce, into its charmed circle. France's army threatened to dominate the continent; Britain was an island, and poured its wealth into the navy which, by mid-century, quartered the globe. The whale regarded the elephant and the tiger glared at the shark.

*　*　*

The Channel ports developed in various ways. When it acquired Dunkirk from the English in Charles II's time, France lavished subsidies on this newest possession. Calais suffered by contrast. It had by then been back in France's grasp for a century, and was allowed to drift to the very edge of Paris's attention, bereft of the business that England had sent it. Now it was Boulogne, not Calais, which handled most traffic across the eastern Channel. Le Havre grew in importance as it replaced the silted harbours of Honfleur and Harfleur, and Dieppe and St Malo continued the trade with French Canada.

On the English side, Dover Castle remained 'the key to England' and the town retained its old importance, but other places had flourishing cross-Channel business, and yet others grew to meet particular needs. So Portsmouth gained importance as France came to replace Holland as the main naval enemy and the navy shifted its weight from the Thames Estuary to the Channel. Similarly, at the end of the century Ramsgate quickly came into prominence as a base for British troops in Flanders. Plymouth, like Portsmouth, became a place where naval officers settled their families while they went away to sea and Falmouth, further down-Channel even than Plymouth, grew in importance as a reporting station for ships homeward bound from distant waters.

But Southampton, which in time would eclipse the others, remained a laggard throughout the eighteenth century. Daniel Defoe went there and wrote of it, "'Tis in a manner dying with age; the decay of the trade is the real decay of the town; and all the business of the moment that is transacted there, is the trade between us and the Islands of Jersey and Guernsey, with a little of the wine trade, and much smuggling.'[3] On the French coast opposite, the natural harbour at Cherbourg remained unexploited, largely because its land communications with the rest of France were so bad. First Louis XVI and then Napoleon made abortive efforts to build a naval port there, but it would have to wait till the mid-nineteenth century before its completion caused an invasion scare in Britain.

It was the growth of the maritime traffic of a port outside the Channel, however, which did most to change its eighteenth-century profile. London was steadily displacing Antwerp and Amsterdam as

Europe's greatest port. Of Southampton, Defoe wrote, 'London has eaten it up.' London's trade with the world beyond Europe was rapidly increasing, and it went through the Straits of Dover. There outward bound ships encountered the everlasting Channel reality of the prevailing westerly winds. So ships anchored in the Downs between Deal and the Goodwin Sands while they waited – sometimes for weeks on end – for a favourable wind that would carry them into the high seas. The towering masts of the East India Company liners sometimes made a forest out of the Downs' seascape. The East Indiamen made a comparable impact at the other end of the Channel when they touched at Falmouth, bringing hot news and rich nabobs from the east. London ships, inbound or outbound, did more than any other single influence to alter the commercial face of the Channel in the course of the eighteenth century.

However pre-eminent the port of London became in trade with the wider world, it could not displace the Channel ports' trade with France. Cross-Channel business grew, along with the increasing curiosity of England and France about one another. The regular cross-Channel packets carried people, ideas and goods. The people were anything from aristocrats setting out on the Grand Tour, through scientists eager to confer with their foreign *confrères*, to dressmakers off to eye up the latest Paris fashions. The ideas were literary, artistic, scientific and political – the common currency of a commonwealth of scholars embracing everyone from Hume, Gibbon, Johnson and Adam Smith to Voltaire and Rousseau. The goods were English woollens and French silks, bawdy books and French brandy, Newcastle coal and Étaples lobsters, and the latest scientific instrument shipped across the Channel to astonish the *cognoscenti* of France or England.

Constant development had brought the ships that served this down-Channel and cross-Channel traffic to high levels of practical sophistication. Nothing could override their dependence on the wind, their vulnerability to storms, their susceptibility to tide and currents. The sea was a hard trade served mostly by very simple men; but they worked their ships with a professional assurance based on centuries of seagoing experience. In the course of the eighteenth century most of the conundrums that had beset navigation were solved, and inshore, in the Channel particularly, other aids began to come to the mariner's assistance.

The most notable were the first offshore lighthouses. The approach to some of the Channel ports had been marked by guiding lights for centuries. Dover's goes back to Roman times, and Caligula, when he came to the Channel with his vain hopes of invading Britain, built one at Boulogne. But offshore hazards had trapped and destroyed ships by the thousand over the centuries. The Eddystone rocks off Plymouth were particularly notorious, and in 1696 Henry Winstanley, an engineer and engraver, produced plans to build a lighthouse on them. He and his men erected a 120-foot wooden tower, anchored to the exceptionally hard rock of Eddystone by twelve iron stanchions. On her travels in the West Country, Celia Fiennes observed the work in progress and was moved by it to religious speculation:

> a light house which is building on a meer rock in the middle of the sea; this . . . will be of great advantage for the guide of the shipps that pass that way; from this you have a good refflection on the great care and provision the wise God makes for all persons and things in his Creation, that there should be in some places . . . rocks even in the midst of the deep which can be made use of for a constant guide and mark for the passengers on their voyages; but the Earth is full of the goodness of the Lord and soe is this Great Sea . . .[4]

Within a year, however, a French privateer snatched Winstanley and his men off the Eddystone rocks. Louis XIV set him free and sent him home saying that he was a benefactor of humanity at large, and he went back to the Eddystone. There the great storm of 1703, one of the greatest, perhaps the greatest, storm that has ever hit the Channel, caught him; and wind and waves swept him and his creation to their destruction. It was five years before another Eddystone tower, again of wood, was erected and half a century later it too was destroyed, this time by fire, the victim of its own great light. The loss was made good in 1759 by Eddystone's first masonry tower, a brilliant piece of engineering and scientific design that lasted for more than a century until the seas undermined the rock on which it stood. Successive Eddystone lights did more than guide ships into Plymouth; they set a standard for emulation elsewhere in the Channel, until by 1835 even the rocks off Barfleur on which the White Ship had come to grief were safely marked. In this as in so many other ways, the process of taming the Channel had begun.

So in the eighteenth century the English Channel came to its fulfilment as one of Europe's great arteries, carrying its life-blood from the continent to Britain and back again, and out into Europe's every overseas extremity. Most of the vast sum of activities in and around the Channel served peaceful purposes, for though the century saw peace and war in regular alternation, war imposed itself comparatively little on the routines of peace. These peaceful purposes in themselves helped make Europe's history, as well as furnishing the resources essential for the acts of war that catch the historical eye. The European nations, and Britain and France above all, were simultaneously united and distinct. As Voltaire put it in the first sentence of his *History of the War of 1741*, 'I have always considered the Christian powers of Europe as one great republic, whose parts all correspond with each other, even when they endeavour at their mutual destruction.'[5] In this chapter, Britain and France constitute 'one great republic'. In the next 'they endeavour at their mutual destruction'.

Even in peacetime, the Royal Navy was the single most visible feature of the Channel world and on the other side of the water the French navy tried, if it never quite succeeded, to present as imposing a face to observers. By the middle of the eighteenth century the British fleet was operating in a good half of the globe, and the voyages of Admiral Anson and Captain Cook brought the other half into its ambit. The Channel was the base from which all this power was projected around the world.

The navy, and the system of land-based services that supported it, was the biggest industrial enterprise of the century, employing every kind of trade in its ships and dockyards. Portsmouth and Plymouth owed their existence to the navy. In Plymouth, the largest warships moored in the Sound close in below the town, at Portsmouth, far in the offing; but both towns were completely given over to its affairs, and the naval dockyard monopolised Portsmouth's waterfront, as it still does today. 'These docks and yards,' wrote Daniel Defoe, 'are now like a town by themselves and are a kind of marine corporation, or a government of their own kind within themselves, there being particular large rows of buildings . . . within the new works, for all the principal officers of the place . . .'[6]

Behind the fierce naval face of Portsmouth and Plymouth were all the ancillary services that helped to keep the navy in being. In the 1760s both places acquired their naval hospitals, at Haslar and Stonehouse. By the standards of the day, these were vast establishments, which belatedly brought care to the navy's sick and wounded at a standard that was far ahead of its time. Seagoing admirals needed houses for their families on the hills outside the towns, port admirals their communications with London, whether it be by fast pinnace up-Channel, messenger overland or, eventually, the semaphore that flashed messages between the roof of the Admiralty in London and Portsmouth. Innumerable boatmen were needed to ferry men and supplies between shore and ship. When they came ashore, naval officers needed their inns and their coaches to take them to London and, if they were lucky, word of promotion at the Admiralty. Sailors needed their beer houses and brothels, and too often these were the haunts of 'crimps' who delivered them into the hands of the press gang.

If it were to keep its ships manned, the navy needed its press gangs. They pursued a brutal but necessary trade. The Royal Navy was a hard employer and, the chance of prize money apart, it never offered financial rewards to compare with the merchant fleet. In wartime in particular it could never fill out all its crews with volunteers. Captains sent men ashore to cajole recruits into the service and turned a blind eye to their methods of persuasion. Gradually the machinery to press men into service became more elaborate and formal.

The men of the Impress Service roamed through coastal towns and sometimes inland, fighting street battles with men who resisted. Afloat, they went out in cutters to board incoming merchantmen, snatch trained men from their crews, and enrol them to serve in a king's ship just fitting out for distant service. A man, once pressed, would flee if he were allowed ashore. So all that a sailor home from a three-year voyage with his pay burning a hole in his pocket saw of his home country was the distant roofs of Portsmouth, espied from the deck of a man-of-war at anchor off Spithead. The Royal Navy, confessed an eighteenth-century admiral, was 'manned by violence and maintained by cruelty'.

In war the navy had an insatiable need for ships, and so, in peace and war, had the merchant fleet. Channel shipyards produced many of them. The king's line-of-battle ships were built in Portsmouth Dockyard, but little shipyards in almost any creek or estuary on either side of the Channel were capable of building colliers, merchantmen, frigates and fishing boats, and often something bigger. One of these little places can be seen at Buckler's Hard on the edge of the New Forest in Hampshire. Two rows of eighteenth-century houses and workshops face each other across an open green that slopes down to the water's edge – all have now been prettified. But at the bottom of the slope, unprettified, are the waters of the Beaulieu river, and into them, when the tide was high, eighteenth-century shipbuilders somehow succeeded in launching major ships of war for the Royal Navy. They worked the same sort of trick with smaller vessels in even more unpromising places, like the Hastings waterfront or the diminutive river at Rye.

The great warships and the Indiamen attracted most attention in the eighteenth-century Channel, but in among them, unnoticed, were the fishermen. Some went out into the blue waters, sometimes across the Atlantic to the Newfoundland cod fisheries. Others worked in the Channel, trawling, long-line fishing, following the herring shoals in their annual migration down the North Sea coast and into the Channel; and on shore an indispensable female support system worked with them, gutting the fish, salting it, getting it to market. Among the fishing ports, Brighton (in the form of Brighthelmstone) was prominent, but inshore fishing boats worked off every beach and out of every estuary the whole length of the Channel.

There were others who worked along the shore. With the new fashion on the English side of the Channel for sea-bathing came a demand for bathing machines, for women to help the ladies change, and for plungers of both sexes to help you overcome your fears and trust yourself to the briny. Other trades went back further. Seaweed scavengers, like every other kind of beachcomber, had been at work on the Channel coast since Shakespeare's day, and in *Lear* Edgar espies 'one that gathers samphire, dreadful trade!' But the Channel had a still more dreadful trade, wrecking, pursued by men and women who were not above showing a misleading light on a dirty night to lure a ship on to the rocks. A medieval law gave them the right to pillage any ship that went ashore, provided no member of the crew survived. It was a law that invited murder.

The biggest of all the eighteenth-century Channel's nefarious trades, however, was smuggling. Smugglers could turn a profit whenever commercial circumstances or the search for government revenue created too great a disparity between the cost of goods on the two sides of the Channel. People on both sides of the water, perhaps most people in the towns and counties of the Channel coast, saw them as legitimate businessmen, even benefactors, no questions asked. Others were intimidated by the smugglers' power to harm those who frustrated them, so menace came to join temptation. The business attracted men in large numbers, fishermen, longshoremen, beachcombers wanting faster profits than legitimate activity could earn. The seamen among them knew their inshore waters better than the Revenue captains and their partners on land knew every lane, every lonely farmhouse in which they could hide their cargoes, and every customer for the goods they brought ashore. Kipling may have been writing in more than a century of retrospect, but in 'A Smuggler's Song' he captured the atmosphere of many a dark night along the eighteenth-century Channel coast:

If you wake at midnight, and hear a horse's feet,
Don't go drawing back the blind, or looking in the street.

Them that asks no questions isn't told a lie.
Watch the wall, my darling, while the Gentlemen go by!

Five and twenty ponies
Trotting through the dark –
Brandy for the Parson
'Baccy for the Clerk;
Laces for a lady, letters for a spy,
And watch the wall, my darling, while the Gentlemen go by!

There is scarcely a port, beach or creek on either side of the Channel that has not been used by smugglers, but for long they were particularly active in the West Country, on the eastern coast of Kent, and in Romney Marsh. So Daphne du Maurier's Jamaica Inn in her novel of the same name was a famous smugglers' haunt. The writer Sir Arthur Quiller-Couch was a Cornishman through and through; one of his forebears was reputed to have organised hundreds of landings of contraband in the county and never lost a man. Romney Marsh offered deserted beaches and quiet lanes, and a local solidarity that went back to the time of the Cinque Ports. And the smugglers operating from Deal and Sandwich knew their way through passages in the Goodwin Sands where their pursuers could not follow them.

By the 1780s smugglers were estimated to be bringing in £3 million of contraband a year, against legal imports worth only four times as much. The 'Gentlemen' organised themselves on a military scale, with a thousand men to protect some landings from the attentions of the Revenue men, and 700 to escort the goods inland. 'Will Washington take America,' asked a member of the House of Lords in the course of the American Revolution, 'or the smugglers England first?'[7]

There was always a ready market in Britain for French spirits, lace and tobacco, but there were equally good markets in France, for goods as commonplace as English wool. When Daniel Defoe saw dragoons out patrolling near Dover in the 1720s, 'riding always about as if they were huntsmen beating up their game', they told him that their quarry were 'owlers', illegal exporters of Kentish wool. But if they were outnumbered by the smugglers they were 'oblig'd, as it were, to stand still, and see the wool carry'd off before their faces, not daring to meddle; and the boats taking it in from the very horses' backs, go immediately off, and are on the coast of France before any notice can be given of them'.[8] In the same way, France during the Napoleonic Wars was prepared to pay over their face value for golden guineas. The captains and crews of East Indiamen, newly returned from the East and temporarily at anchor in the Downs, supplemented their wages by the sale to smugglers of untaxed oriental luxuries like silks, tea and spices.

The Crown fought back, but it was decades before it got the upper hand. On land there were Defoe's dragoons or the Customs' 'Riding Officers' who patrolled the coasts and, if they were lucky, found smugglers at work. At sea, Revenue cutters intercepted suspicious vessels and if necessary attacked them. But in most winds the smugglers' luggers could outsail the cutters, and it was a rare Revenue captain who knew the inshore waters as well as the inshore fishermen turned smuggler. In 1809 a new service, the Water Guard, was formed. It was manned by retired navy men, and patrolled close inshore to intercept luggers that evaded the Revenue cutters. And in 1822 all three services were brought together under a new service, His Majesty's Coastguard.

But the smugglers were experienced, skilled and ruthless. Despite their violence, and perhaps because of it, they operated in a protective environment. Throughout the coastal counties ordinary people turned a blind eye to their business. The 'Gentlemen', after all, more often than not were their neighbours, and they had a fearful way with informers. As for the comfortably off – Kipling's squire, parson, clerk – they were happy to buy foreign luxuries, no questions asked. A smuggler dangling in chains from a gibbet was a powerful deterrent; but magistrates were reluctant to send him there as long as he had violent friends who knew where to find them.

So smuggling persisted as a lucrative trade well into the nineteenth century. In 1820, for example, a gang of smugglers fought a pitched battle with Revenue men near Herne Bay and went on to spring prisoners from Faversham gaol. And there could be no denying the sheer glamour of famous smugglers, like George Snelling. In 1829 he was presented to ten-year-old Princess Victoria as 'the great smuggler of Broadstairs', and he died at last full of years and honour at the age of ninety-six. Deal coastguards were seizing French brandy and tobacco brought ashore on moonless nights as late as the 1880s. Smugglers and their look-outs, Customs men and their informers, coastguards and Revenue cutter crews, soldiers and sailors employed to hunt down the smugglers' gangs, all of these played an essential part in the story of the eighteenth-century Channel. It was well into the nineteenth before the servants of the Crown got the upper hand.

CHAPTER 9

THE TIGER AND THE SHARK

From the arrival of William and Mary on the English throne, Britain and France lived for a century in uneasy rivalry, which often degenerated into war. Of the hundred-odd years that separated the Glorious Revolution of 1688 from the French Revolution of 1789, the English and French spent forty of them at war with one another. Whale and elephant were transmogrified into shark and tiger, each lord of its own domain. When one tried to fight its way into the other's kingdom, more often than not it came off worse. So in the wars that France and Britain fought across western Europe and all over the wider world, one never succeeded in overwhelming the other. With a few exceptional setbacks the British remained supreme at sea, the French on land. Throughout the century, the Channel remained the demarcation between the two. Occasionally war came to its coasts and waters. More often it remained the still centre of the worldwide struggle between the tiger and the shark.

William III had joined his wife in seizing the throne of England to ensure British support in keeping the French out of the Netherlands. For over a century the Dutch had been fighting the Spanish, eventually to a standstill. But Louis XIV sought to fill the vacuum left by the Spanish departure, and became as much of a threat to Dutch liberties as the Spanish had been. It was inevitable that, once ensconced in their new kingdom, William and Mary should pick up the old English rivalry with France and bend it to the defence of their old kingdom in the Netherlands.

On the other side of the Channel, Louis was as determined as William. If he could put James back on the English throne he would help him destroy the Dutch. So while Louis fought once famous and now forgotten battles against the Dutch at Fleurus, Steenkerke and Neerwinden, he put money and supplies behind James's campaigns in Ireland and Scotland against William. They led to the Battle of Killiekrankie and the massacre of Glencoe, the siege of Derry and the Battle of the Boyne. But these campaigns in Ireland and Scotland came nowhere near unseating William from the throne, and Louis and James knew that the most direct road from Paris to Whitehall lay across the Channel. If they could get a French army ashore on the coast of Kent they could seize London and the throne. All that stood in their way was the British fleet. So the story of tiger and shark starts with two naval battles in the Channel.

As Duke of York, James II had built a powerful and well-led Royal Navy which now was William and Mary's. To their Dutch fleet they could add fifty-nine English ships of the line, 173 vessels in all, and the hitting power of almost 7,000 naval guns. The combined fleets were more powerful than anything that could be sent against them, and provided they could hold the Channel they could block any descent on the coasts of Britain and Holland.

To challenge them, Louis decided to bring the Mediterranean squadron from Toulon into the Atlantic and unite it with the western squadron at Brest. He put the Comte de Tourville in command. Tourville had made an early reputation fighting with the Knights of Malta against the Muslim pirates of Algiers. Now, in June 1690, he put to sea with seventy-five ships of the line to sweep the Protestants out of the English Channel.

An English admiral commanded the allied fleet that opposed him. Like Tourville, Arthur Herbert, Earl of Torrington, had made his early reputation in the Mediterranean, losing an eye in battle against the Algiers pirates. Unlike some English naval officers, he had a staunchly Protestant reputation, and James had dismissed him from the service when he refused to support the relaxation of the law against Catholics and dissenters. Indeed, he was among the first to declare for William and Mary, and it was he who had commanded the Dutch fleet that brought them to Torbay.

Tourville felt his way up the English coast of the Channel. He found the Dutch and English fleets anchored off Beachy Head on the Sussex coast with fifty-eight ships of the line. 'The odds are great,' Torrington reported; but with wind and current behind him he took his fleets out to fight. The Dutch commander, who at first had urged Torrington to wait for reinforcements, now broke away from the English squadron and plunged headlong into battle with the French. He severely mauled the first ships he encountered, but another of Tourville's three squadrons came up and caught the Dutch ships in a murderous cross-fire. When one of them was finally taken the French found 230 men dead or wounded in her: 'There was not a foot of space above the water line that had not been hit,' an officer reported, 'and the deck was strewn with dead and dying.'[1] The Dutch were knocked out of the battle.

Throughout all this mayhem, the English ships lingered out of range. By the time they joined battle, Tourville was ready to give them the treatment he had given the Dutch. The English ships could not take the battering, and Torrington turned away from the French van to attack the weaker ships in the rear. Even here he encountered fierce resistance.

The game so far was Tourville's, and as the wind shifted to the west he prepared to pursue the retreating Dutch and destroy what was left of their fleet. But the wind dropped, and the tide turned against him. Torrington anchored, while the French drifted away. Tourville could report: 'The enemy has fled . . . We have captured one ship, dismasted eleven, sunk two . . .' And when Torrington sent fireships against him, Tourville succeeded in sinking them as well.

For the next two days, Torrington remained at anchor while Tourville pursued what was left of the Dutch fleet into Dover. The Dutch lost seventeen ships, the French none. Finally Torrington withdrew the British fleet into the Thames. The French, very amateurs at sea, had taken the war to the shores of England, destroyed the fleet of one sea-going nation and badly mauled the other. For a time, invasion and a march on London seemed likely. Most of William's army was in Ireland, and the Lords Lieutenant were reduced to calling out the militias. In the end it was wind, weather and French inertia that saved Britain, not the prowess of its fleet or amateur soldiers and their pikes. Louis and James failed to exploit the victory that Tourville had won for them.

All the same, the consequences for William and Mary were serious. After the battle was over, the Dutch brushed aside the fact of their own commander's indiscipline and blamed Torrington for what had happened. For decades afterwards they nursed suspicions of British commanders. William and Mary's old doubts of the loyalties of their naval leaders were revived. They still sat uneasy on their English throne, and now they suspected even Torrington. Had he deliberately abandoned the Dutch ships to their fate? Such were their fears that before the next British fleet went out to battle Mary demanded of its officers an oath of loyalty to her personally, the English Queen of England. It was only the news of his victory over James at the Battle of the Boyne on the day after the Channel battle that saved William from disastrous political consequences of the defeat. The Battle of Beachy Head was not an auspicious start for the shark in its struggle with the tiger.

Two years later, James and Louis agreed to try again to mount a cross-Channel invasion of England. They concentrated French troops and James's little Irish army at St Vaast-la-Hougue in Normandy. Once again the Toulon squadron was summoned and again Tourville was put in command. His orders were to seize command of the Channel and escort an invasion fleet to the English coast. This was to be a major combined operation; it was the strategy of the Armada once again.

Tourville had his reservations. For him this was a purely naval war. It would be time enough for an invasion fleet when he had cleared the

British and Dutch from the Channel. 'Let our enemies wear themselves out at sea,' he argued, 'and then we will sail out and attack them off Ushant.' But like Philip II before him, Louis was impatient of delay. Tourville's orders read: 'His Majesty definitely desires him to leave Brest on the said day, April 25th, even should he have information that the enemy is at sea with a force superior to that in readiness to sail with him.'[2] In the event, Tourville put to sea on 12 May 1692. He took thirty-nine ships with him, leaving many more behind for want of crews. The Toulon squadron was delayed by adverse weather, and so were most of the squadron from Rochefort. Only forty-four ships sailed with him in search of the British and Dutch.

This time the allied fleet was already on the enemy coast. It was again commanded by an Englishman, Edward Russell, Earl of Orford, who had with him thirty-six Dutch ships and sixty-three of his own. So it was to be ninety-nine ships to forty-four; almost 7,000 guns to 3,200; 53,000 men against 21,000. With these numbers Tourville had no chance, but he was driven into battle by insistent orders from the minister of war.

The fleets met off the north-east tip of the Normandy peninsula, off Barfleur. Tourville could have avoided battle by dropping anchor but his orders, and his own honour, drove him into a suicidal advance towards the allied fleet. Suddenly the wind dropped, and one French ship at least was reduced to being towed into battle by a pinnace. The long pounding started and the French, though so vastly outnumbered, had the best of it. The fighting lasted for fifteen hours in which the French lost 1,700 men, the allies 2,000, most of them British.

Overnight the British towed away their most badly damaged ships, and both sides tried to patch up the damage for the fighting that would surely be resumed at dawn. The allies still heavily outnumbered the French, and during the night Tourville pulled his ships back to the westward. When the morning mist cleared, daylight revealed something of the damage that had been done. But the bulk of the two fleets moved steadily westwards, still firing at one another. By the late afternoon they were off Cherbourg, anchored to avoid being carried away by the ebbing tide.

West of Cherbourg the Cap de la Hague juts out into the Channel, the furthermost tip of Normandy. Beyond it lies the British island of Alderney. Between the two the Alderney Race offers a dangerous passage to the southward, feared by yachtsmen to this day. It offered an escape from Russell's squadrons, and during this second night of the battle the ships of Tourville's vanguard broke away from the battle, turned south and made for shelter in the harbour of St Malo on the coast of Brittany.

At this point a human and individual drama intervenes as counterpoint to all the battering and bloodshed that has gone before. Robert Browning captures the flavour of it in his poem 'Hervé Riel':

> ... the thirty-first of May, helter-skelter thro' the blue,
> Like a crowd of frightened porpoises a shoal of sharks pursue,
> Came crowding ship on ship to St Malo on the Rance,
> With the English fleet in view.

But the bar outside St Malo harbour is notoriously dangerous and the French captains balk at attempting it. Then one man, a merchant seaman who has been pressed into the royal service, shows them the way:

> A Captain? A Lieutenant? A Mate – first, second, third?
> No such man of mark, and meet
> With his betters to compete!
> But a simple Breton sailor pressed by Tourville for the fleet,
> A poor coasting-pilot he, Hervé Riel ...

And Browning's hero leads the vanguard of the French fleet across the bar to safety under St Malo's guns.

The tide and currents of the Alderney Race had proved too much for fifteen of Tourville's ships. An old French Michelin Green Guide says that they were 'bounced back like corks' towards the north and towards the enemy. Rather than fight a superior enemy, they fled eastwards past Barfleur and took refuge in the roadstead at St Vaast-la-Hougue on the east side of the Normandy peninsula, behind the little island of Tahitou. At Cherbourg the English and Dutch were already burning enemy ships which had run aground there. At St Vaast they got in among the French ships and burned them at their leisure. James and the men of his army looked on, unable to do anything as their last hope of a cross-Channel passage and an invasion of England went up in flames and smoke.

French morale was shattered by the defeat. So was that of James's army. As for the British, they sailed away from St Vaast rejoicing. They had avenged their own defeat within sight of the English coast and chased the French back to their shoreline. Ever afterwards they were determined to keep them there.

Successes like St Vaast-la-Hougue reinforced a popular affection for the navy and its crews that went back to the defeat of the Armada. 'The royal navy of England,' wrote William Blackstone in his eighteenth-century *Commentary on the Laws of England*, 'has ever been its greatest defence and ornament; it is its ancient and natural strength; the floating bulwark of the island.' That conviction found more popular expression. Conditions for the men afloat might be appalling, provision for their dependants at home shamefully inadequate. But as long as the navy could bring back victories like St Vaast-la-Hougue, Jack Tar and his officers would remain national heroes. The history of the eighteenth-century navy is marred by incompetence and occasional cowardice afloat; by incompetence and persistent corruption in the dockyards; by bickering between admirals and political jobbery to advance an officer's career. Through all this, the nation's faith in the navy persisted, and its affection for sailors and admiration for their commanders flourished.

So, at Beachy Head and St Vaast-la-Hougue, began the story of the struggle between the tiger and the shark. It was to continue throughout the eighteenth century, in Germany, the Low Countries and the Mediterranean; in India, North America, the West Indies and on any ocean where hostile ships met. In France one Louis succeeded another, in England Georges, with such men as Walpole, Chatham and Pitt providing the political leadership. In the course of these campaigns the French won victories and accumulated military glory all over Europe.

For their part the British won naval battles, took India and Canada from the French, and lost America.

Antique, even quaint, as those wars of peruqued professional armies and silk-stockinged naval officers may appear, they were fought for reasons of interest and strategy that seemed solid to the men of the time and whose validity a strategic eye would acknowledge today. So in the War of the Spanish Succession the British fought to keep the French out of the old Spanish provinces in the Low Countries, and away from the estuary of the Scheldt from which an invasion of Britain might come. They fought them again in the 1740s for predominance in India, the West Indies and North America. Ten years later, in the Seven Years War, the struggle was resumed, with the British fighting French armies and fleets worldwide. From a British point of view, this was a good war, and at the end of it the Treaty of Paris confirmed them in their vastly expanded empire in India and North America. By 1779, however, they faced the powerful combination of France, Spain and the United States. Trapped at Yorktown by a French and Spanish fleet, a British army was forced to surrender to the American insurgents; and at the peace conference which put an end to the war they lost half of that North American empire, keeping only the Canadian half they had taken from France in 1763.

These wars took fleets and armies far afield, but the Channel remained at the heart of the matter. Both sides knew that if the French could seize control of the narrow seas for a week they could throw an army across the Straits of Dover, march on London and reinstate the Stuarts. The British knew that, whatever happened elsewhere on the globe, they must maintain their control of the Channel. So time after time the French came to the Channel coast and thought about invasion. Meanwhile, the British constantly reinforced the Channel fleet.

When the line-of-battle ships went to sea they did so in the full panoply of war. Yet more often than not it was their sheer potential for battle that did the business as they rode peacefully at anchor off Portsmouth or Plymouth, their great guns shut away behind their gunports. Meanwhile the cruisers and frigates maintained a close blockade of Brest, on the watch for signs that the French fleet was preparing to come out and fight. When it did, and the fleets clashed, they met in the Mediterranean or the West Indies, off America or in the Western Approaches, competing to get to windward of the enemy, before launching themselves into close combat. Quite often, therefore, the eighteenth-century Channel seems to lie at the quiet eye of a worldwide storm, the source of naval power that rarely saw its warlike face.

From time to time, however, the Channel and its nearer approaches echoed to the broadsides of ships of the line. In 1747, Admiral George Anson, newly back from circumnavigating the globe, took a squadron cruising off the island of Ouessant (always Ushant to the English) at the very tip of the Breton peninsula. There he intercepted a French convoy bound for America and wiped out its escort. A few months later, in the same area, Admiral Edward Hawke tried the same trick with less complete success and came home in dudgeon and something dangerously near disgrace. Anson went on to become First Lord of the Admiralty, the guiding conscience of the eighteenth-century navy and the leader who imposed on it 'the ingrained assumption that a man's first duty was to the good of the Service'.[3] But it was Hawke, ten years later, who went on to win the completest naval victory over the French.

For much of the eighteenth century, Britain lived in fear of French invasion. In 1745 Charles Edward Stuart, the Young Pretender, reached Derby on the road from Scotland to London. That his rag-tag army was able to advance so far from a landing in the remote west of Scotland was a standing reminder of London's vulnerability to a foreign army that succeeded in getting ashore in Kent or Sussex.

Nine years after the Young Pretender's final defeat at Culloden came a new war with France; and soon Britain was consumed by one of those fears of a cross-Channel invasion that punctuate its history. Once again Hogarth lent the genius of his etching needle to the task of arousing the English against the French. He produced two etchings, *France* and *England*, which were intended as propaganda posters. The first gave his customers a graphic warning of what a successful French invasion would mean for English liberties. The second shows the robust virtues of old England.

In *France*, Hogarth draws the same savage portrait of the French as in *The Gate of Calais*. The men of 'a starved, unwilling and fanatical French army' prepare to invade England as 'a sadistic, well-fed monk tests the edge of his executioner's axe'. He has the tools of torture in his hand, and flourishes a *'Plan pour un monastere dans Black Friar a Londre'*. The second print, *England,* on the other hand, is all jollity and well-being. A tavern sign advertises beef, 'Roast and Boil'd every Day'.* A soldier guards his own giant beefsteak with his sword. A song sheet proclaims that Britannia rules the waves. This is the well-being for which any Englishman should fight. And sure enough, a small boy stands on tip toe to be measured by the recruiting sergeant, so that he will be tall enough to join the army.

Meanwhile, the army and navy prepared pre-emptive strikes against potential invasion ports. They were typical of those combined operations so beloved of an island nation's military planners, which others criticised as an expensive game of 'breaking windows with guineas'. One expedition struck at Cherbourg, where the French had for some time been building a naval base. Their purpose was to give themselves a base on the mid-Channel coast which the British saw as a dagger pointed straight at Portsmouth and the Isle of Wight. The attackers succeeded in reducing the buildings of the docks to rubble.

But another expedition, this one directed at St Malo, turned into a Channel-coast disaster. The raiders succeeded in getting safely ashore, but French troops in superior numbers were approaching. The shark was out of his element. The raiders withdrew to St Cast near Dinard on the other side of the river Rance, where the fleet was waiting to take them off. There, beside one of those glorious north Breton fiords, the French fell on the British troops as they were embarking, shelled them and charged the rearguard with the bayonet. They killed or took prisoner 750 men. It was like the defeat at Dieppe in 1942 of a rather similar cross-Channel expedition.

The defeat became the talk of London town. The rearguard had been found by the Grenadier Guards. A little later the diarist James Boswell, in love with the idea of strolling in Whitehall in a Guards officer's uniform, got himself invited to 'a Guards party'. There he met a

Grenadier colonel, whose conversation cooled his ardour. 'He was on the expedition to St Cast, but escaped unhurt,' Boswell recorded. 'The Colonel talked of battles and dreadful wounds, which made us shudder. Really, these things are not to be talked of, for in cold blood they shock one prodigiously.'[5] There is a sense of eighteenth-century reality breaking in on eighteenth-century fantasy in Boswell's garret as he wrote his diary that night.

So offensive action at Cherbourg and St Malo had failed to dispose of the invasion threat. In the spring of 1759 Admiral Hawke was sent to blockade the French fleet in Brest. For months the ships of the Channel fleet beat back and forth off this iron-bound coast, until in November an Atlantic storm blew them off station. The French admiral took the chance to get his fleet to sea and seemed to vanish into the wide expanses of the Atlantic. Late in the year it might be, but there was at least a theoretical danger of a French descent somewhere on the coast of Britain. Hawke scotched it. He must have remembered the criticism that had followed his failure to find the French off Ushant ten years earlier. Now he hunted the French ships down, finding them in Quiberon Bay, on the south-west coast of Brittany. There, in bad light and dirty weather, he took his ships into almost unknown inshore waters, closed on the French and overwhelmed them with superior gunnery. The French lost six ships and the rest scattered. It was St Vaast-la-Hougue all over again.

The immediate threat of invasion was lifted. Almost more important, defeats such as these sapped the French naval officers' confidence in their own professional competence, just as St Cast had demoralised the Grenadiers. After Quiberon they bitterly compared the lethal efficiency of the British ships and the disorganised shambles aboard their own. Between them, Quiberon and St Cast reminded tiger and shark that they were safer in their own element than in the enemy's.

Within twenty years Britain and France were at war again, as the French and Spanish came to the support of the rebellious American colonies. It became a world war, which took the Royal Navy almost as far afield as the French Revolutionary and Napoleonic Wars were to do. As in earlier wars, power was projected from the Channel into the oceans. But a British fleet was patrolling the Breton coast once again, this time under the command of Admiral Augustus Keppel.

Keppel had been at sea for more than forty years. Like Torrington, he had fought the Algiers pirates. He had accompanied the great Anson on his circumnavigation of the earth. He was in short the complete professional. Now he was in command of the Channel fleet and preoccupied – history concludes obsessed – by the fear that a French invasion force was preparing to put to sea, evade him and land on the coast of Britain. 'I am not brave enough to go to my bed,' he wrote, 'with the confidence of the country's being in security.'[6] His anxiety made him over-cautious. He sighted the French fleet off Ushant, but when he moved to the attack he failed to find the jugular. Haphazard fighting dragged on and though several French ships were mauled none of them was sunk. So another French squadron got away across the Atlantic to bring succour to the American rebels and tighten the vice around the British army in North America.

Keppel had been a member of the court that twenty years earlier had sentenced Admiral Byng to death. Byng, it judged, had failed in his inescapable duty to seek battle with the enemy. He was shot on a ship's quarter deck in Portsmouth harbour, and Voltaire was not far off the mark when he wrote of the affair: 'In [England] it is thought well to kill an admiral from time to time to encourage the others.' Now one of Keppel's admirals accused him of incompetence or worse. He was brought before a court-martial and was at risk of suffering the fate of Byng. He was found not guilty, the charge against him condemned as 'malicious and ill-founded'. But the back-biting between Keppel and his accuser continued, each demanding the court-martial of the other. Political allegiances muddied what Anson had taught should be the clear water of loyalty to the navy's service alone. The whole episode shows the eighteenth-century navy at its worst, just as Quiberon reveals it at its finest.

* * *

The war for America continued. Against France and Spain the Royal Navy was overstretched. Now there appeared a new challenger to British control of the narrow seas. The threat it represented was minuscule beside that of the French and Spanish fleets, minuscule too beside the dangers that the British army in America faced. But it brought the infant United States Navy across the Atlantic for the first time, into British home waters, and into action against the Royal Navy.

The challenger was John Paul Jones, born in Scotland, one-time cabin boy and after that mate on an American slaver. In his little ship *Ranger* he sailed the length of the Irish Sea, taking prizes as he went, and put into Brest to a hero's welcome. American privateers came to follow his example and exploit the shortage of frigates to protect British merchant shipping. Jones had shown himself the complete master of guerrilla warfare at sea. A year later he was given command of the *Bonhomme Richard* and led a squadron of five ships right round the British Isles, taking prizes along the way. In the North Sea he attacked a convoy from the Baltic and found himself up against two British warship escorts. They called upon him to surrender. 'I have not yet begun to fight,' was his reply. After a three-hour battle and with the *Bonhomme Richard* sinking under him, he took the surrender of one of the British ships, *Serapis*, shifted his men and flag into her, captured her consort also, and sailed proudly away with his prizes. The French heaped him with honours and the Americans made him a commodore. The minnow had wounded the shark.

Two years later, the British commander in North America, Cornwallis, found himself trapped between Washington's army and the French and Spanish fleets. The projection of British power from the Channel into the oceans had failed. On 19 October 1781, Cornwallis capitulated while the band played 'The World Turned Upside Down'. Yet the shark remained a formidable foe, still capable of engaging the second and third largest navies in the world.

In 1783 the whole world made peace in the Treaty of Versailles. Britain recovered its colonies in the West Indies. Spain kept Minorca and recovered Florida. The French got back their possessions in the East Indies, the Caribbean and West Africa. Even King Heraclius II was drawn into the peace-making when he was brought to recognise Russian suzerainty over Georgia. The government of King George recognised the infant United States and the Americans set out on their road to greatness. In the Channel, the status quo was restored: shark powerful at sea, French tiger pawing the beaches in its desire to get at its enemies.

Britain and France might in the end have gone back to the old friendly rivalry of elephant and whale. But within a decade the world was again turned upside-down by the overthrow of a government yet more oppressive than King George's. The French monarchy fell, and by 1792 Europe was at war, as the continental monarchies set out to destroy the infant revolution. In 1793, Britain too joined in the war against the French, a war that was to last more or less unbroken for over twenty years.

CHAPTER 10

OLD BONEY
AT
BOULOGNE

T he French Revolution ushers in a different kind of world. Once
again France and Britain play contrasting roles, but now France
gives itself over to a long, passionate drama, in which a great
cast of actors – monarch, dissident aristocrats, bourgeois revolutionaries, bloodstained Jacobins, embattled defenders of the Republic, the
Directorate, First Consul Bonaparte and in the end Emperor Napoleon
– succeed one another at the centre of the stage. Britain is among the
powers that react against this assertive revolutionary passion, which so
rapidly developed into an attempt to remake Europe in France's image.
It becomes paymaster to all the others, trying to use its naval power to
strangle the infant French Republic and hold together a coalition of
European armies against France.

This drama is played out all over the world, from the Kremlin in
Moscow to the sugar islands of the West Indies. But it repeatedly
comes to the Channel, as when Napoleon comes to Boulogne to plan
the invasion of England, when Nelson sails away from Portsmouth to
destroy the French and Spanish fleets at Trafalgar, when the ship
bringing the first news of Wellington's victory at Waterloo is

becalmed in the Downs and the messenger has himself rowed ashore at Broadstairs, and when, at the very end of the story, Napoleon is brought, a prisoner in a British ship, to Plymouth on his way to St Helena.

More frequently the Channel plays a supporting role. French aristocrats in unconvincing disguise slip through northern French ports in flight from the guillotine. There are riots against conscription and hunger in Dieppe and Le Havre. The republican armies bring a new kind of war to the Low Countries. Their political masters close the seminaries and monasteries of northern France and Flanders that have sent recusant priests across the Channel into England ever since the reign of Queen Elizabeth. British ships prowl off the French coast and land desperate little *émigré* armies on the coast of Brittany, while privateers slip out from Boulogne to prey on any unescorted British merchantmen.

Revulsion against the revolution started slowly. William Wordsworth captured a widespread reaction to 'The French Revolution, as it Appeared to Enthusiasts' when he wrote, ten years after the event, 'Bliss was it in that dawn to be alive/But to be young was very heaven!' More practical people wanted their interests to be protected even in the ecstasy of revolution, and within months the citizens of Le Havre were complaining to Paris that the shipbuilders were replacing trained shipwrights with casual labour; that unlicensed competition was making things impossible for the coffee, lemonade and vinegar sellers of the town, and that the hat-buying public 'was cheated by persons who without any knowledge insinuate themselves into the trade'.[1] Aristocrats flee in fear, and then lesser members of the royal family; and by October 1790 the Paris press is reporting rumours of a conspiracy to rescue the king from captivity and take him to Rouen. There are suspicions too that British money is behind a mutiny among the men of the Brest squadron and garrison.

Then, in January 1793, comes the execution of Louis XVI, which scandalises all Europe. In the Vendée, on the Atlantic coast just south of the Loire, a 'Grand Royal and Catholic Army' is formed to fight the

Caesar on the Kent coast: the first landing against resistance in the Channel's recorded history

William's ships as he sails across the Channel to conquer England

The Needles: hazard to shipping at the western tip of the Isle of Wight

Thomas à Becket lands at Sandwich under the hostile eyes of the King's henchmen

Henry VIII leaves Dover on his way to meet the French King at the Field of the Cloth of Gold

The English fireships attack the Armada in Calais Roads

William of Orange at Torbay
plans the overthrow of
King James II

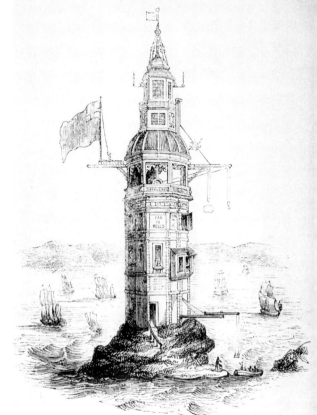

'A constant guide and mark for
the passengers on their voyages':
Winstanley's Eddystone
Lighthouse

The gate of Calais: Hogarth's first impression of England's cross-Channel neighbour

The French attack Jersey: Major Peirson dies in the defence of St Helier

The British army waits on the Dunkirk beaches for rescue by the little ships and the Royal Nav

Spitfires on patrol over the Channel coast during the Battle of Britain

Troops go ashore on D-Day under machine-gun fire

'We must take our harbour with us': Mulberry Harbour on the coast of Normandy

Channel disaster: the *Herald of Free Enterprise* off Zeebrugge

Eurostar breaks surface from the Channel Tunnel

revolution. The continental monarchies set out to destroy Revolutionary France. Its leaders turn to conscription, and soon the fishermen's wives of Dieppe are complaining that, with their husbands gone to war, they and their children are starving. The revolutionaries find counter-revolutionary conspiracy everywhere, and the town council of Le Havre is suspected of deliberately causing famine in the district by exporting wheat to southern England. More moderate men gather forces in Caen to send against the revolutionaries in command in Paris, but they are routed. The Jacobins are riding a wave of revolutionary and nationalist fervour. They send untrained, ill-equipped republican armies against the coalition of monarchs arrayed against them, and their *élan* wins them victories. In the winter of 1793 the revolutionary armies advance into the Low Countries, and:

> the ragged men carried the Three Colours and sang the terrible song of Marseilles from Fleurus to the Rhine, and captured the fortresses of Flanders and the fortresses of Holland and Brabant, and crossed the Lys, and the Scheldt, and the Dendre, and the Senne, and the Dyle, and the Meuse, and the Leek, and entered Antwerp and Rotterdam and Amsterdam and the Hague, and thundered on their horses across the ice to capture with naked swords the battle-fleet of Holland.[2]

Soon, however, the French were on the defensive. By now the Royal Navy's blockade of the French ports was biting deep. Paris was starving and the republic waited desperately for the arrival of a food convoy from America. The French admiral at Brest put to sea to escort the convoy home. The Channel fleet was anchored in Torbay. When his frigates reported that the French had put to sea, its commander, Lord Howe, set out to find and destroy them. Four hundred miles out in the Atlantic he found the French between the fog banks and brought them to battle. It was the first day of June, 1794, 'the Glorious First of June'. Howe's ships comprehensively outfought the French, seizing six warships and sinking another. It was a famous victory that, had it been complete, might have throttled the revolution. But while Howe battered the French warships, the food convoy escaped, to slip into Brest with its cargo to save France for the revolution.

In Brittany and the Vendée the revolutionaries faced effective domestic enemies. The conservative, deeply Catholic peasants of the west of France were repelled by the self-conscious atheism and iconoclasm of the revolutionary leaders. To them the execution of the king had been sacrilege. They waged bitter guerrilla war against the troops sent to put them down, who fought back with equal savagery. Royalist *émigrés* saw an opportunity, and in 1795 British ships put 8,000 royalist soldiers ashore on the Quiberon peninsula. They hoped that the peasant armies of Brittany would come to welcome them and march on Paris with them. But they wasted time in Quiberon while republican forces closed in. They let themselves be trapped on the narrow peninsula, unable even to deploy in fighting formation. There, where Hawke had won his famous victory in 1761, the republicans got in among them and massacred them.

Yet the slaughter at Quiberon failed to crush the Breton insurrection. Everywhere in Brittany and the Vendée the guerrilla war continued. The peasants were fighting for their Catholicism and freedom to be themselves, with the same bitterness that the Spanish turned a few years later against the French army of occupation. The revolution did terrible things to break the Bretons, on a scale far greater than English brutalities against the Irish about the same time. Those years reinforced ancient Breton resentment against the metropolis, a resentment of Celt against Frank, which lingers in Brittany to this day.

All England had rejoiced at the Royal Navy's First of June victory, and society from top to bottom was in love with Jack Tar. But in April 1797 the navy suddenly turned from fighting the king's enemies to terrifying his subjects. The men of the ships of the Channel fleet moored at Spithead, far offshore from Portsmouth harbour, mutinied. They were respectful, as polite as men who spent their lives in the hugger-mugger of the lower deck could ever be, and they reiterated their willingness to fight like Britons if the French fleet put to sea. But they had grievances and they wanted them redressed. In effect, thousands of sailors went on strike until long-standing complaints about pay, leave and food were attended to. 'The Channel fleet,' wrote Lord Spencer, the First Lord of the Admiralty of the day, 'is now lost to the country as much as if it was at the bottom of the sea.'[3] He exaggerated, for there was nothing revolutionary about the affair, but with the guillotine not long sated on the other side of the Channel it gave polite society in London a frisson of fear of bloody revolution.

The authorities were more sensible, however, and reacted to the mutiny with a moderation equal to that of the mutineers – a moderation in dealing with indiscipline which in fact more often characterised the eighteenth-century navy than the cat-wielding Captain Blighs of the cinema and our imagination. Admiral Howe, over seventy now but still possessed of a great naval reputation as the hero of the First of June, was brought out of retirement to negotiate with the crews. The king was induced to give a royal pardon and Parliament belatedly found the money to pay what the king had promised.

The wars of Revolutionary France dragged on. In 1798 the French essayed an invasion of Ireland and the British captured Minorca. In 1800 the Republic at last brought the insurrection in the Vendée to an end. Everywhere, after seven years of war the will to continue was nearing the point of exhaustion. But fighting continued; in Britain there was talk of French troops massing on the Channel coast, and of barges assembling to carry them to England. Nelson craved, or said he craved, a break from duty and the chance to live quietly in England with his mistress Emma Hamilton. He talked of going into retirement; but the government needed the assurance of his name to satisfy the country that enough was being done to meet the invasion threat. So Nelson was put in command of a 'squadron on a particular service', guarding the coast of England. His writ was to run from Orfordness to Beachy Head; and on the enemy's side of the water from the Scheldt to Dieppe.

The months that Nelson spent on this employment were not his finest nor his happiest. Most of the continent had already made its peace with France. Bonaparte, frustrated of conquests elsewhere, talked of invading England. To the professional naval officer it sounded a hollow threat, but the English people, weary of war and fearful of old Boney, welcomed the reassurance that Nelson, England's idol, was on the job. He spent a week in London studying papers, which suggested that thirty-six gun-sloops and over 200 gunboats were assembling on the enemy coast and that 40,000 French troops awaited the order to invade England. He thought it likely that Napoleon would divide his forces and envisaged two landings of 20,000 men each, one east of Dover, one west, followed by an advance on London. He rode like a whirlwind through Kent, arousing patriotic passions everywhere he went. He mobilised the Sea Fencibles, seamen excused service afloat but bound to shore defence, and made plans to post flotillas of inshore vessels, floating batteries and oar-powered gunboats at various places along the coast, with complex instructions for their movement if the French arrived. 'Whatever plans may be adopted,' he told an enthusiastic audience in Faversham, 'the moment the Enemy touch our Coast, be it where it may, they are to be attacked by every man afloat and on shore; this must be perfectly understood. *Never fear the event.*'[4] All this preparation was a far cry from the war of line-of-battle ships and the Nelson touch, with its concentration of power at a single point of decision, but the great man gave it detailed attention.

He also set out, in the style of St Vaast-La-Hougue and Quiberon, to take the war to the enemy's coast and destroy at their moorings any invasion barges he could find. He looked first into the crowded harbour of Boulogne. 'Nelson speaking to the French,' said the people of Dover when they heard the sound of gunfire rolling across the Channel. Ten days later he looked into Boulogne again, and found twenty-four gunboats assembled, moored end to end to protect the port. He ordered a boat-attack on the enemy line. It took place on the night of 15 August 1801 and was as much a fiasco as so many of his battles had been triumphs. His boats were beaten off, forty-four of his men killed (among them a young officer whom he had made his closest aide). After praising his men he added: 'No person can be blamed for sending them to the attack, but myself . . . All behaved well, and it was their misfortune to be sent on a service which the precautions of the enemy rendered impossible.'[5] In his great *Life of Nelson*, A. T. Mahan is unsparing in his conclusions: 'The affair was an entire failure, except so far as to show that the enemy would be met on their own shores rather than those of Great Britain.'[6]

From Boulogne, Nelson turned his attention to an attack on Flushing, but concluded that sandbanks made an attack impossible there. In any case, what he had seen in Boulogne had convinced him of the impossibility of an invasion fleet of flat-bottomed barges getting to sea and safely across the Channel. 'The craft which I have seen, I do not think it possible to row to England; and sail they cannot.'[7] The wider war seemed deadlocked; the British people were war-weary; the Treasury was empty; peace was in the air. Nelson took himself off into Emma's arms, and in March 1802 peace between Britain and France was signed at Amiens.

Amiens was a dull place to choose for a peace conference, its only merit that it lay midway between Paris and London. France was represented by Bonaparte's elder brother Joseph, Britain by Lord Cornwallis, who had surrendered to the Americans at Yorktown twenty-one years earlier. The discussions were bitter and grudging, Cornwallis's relations with Whitehall as bad as Joseph's with ministers in Paris. Both sides signed resentfully, with fingers crossed and many a mental reservation, but sign they did.

At once, half fashionable London rushed to Paris to taste French style and *douceur de vivre* after eight years of isolation from the continent. The journey might be hard, and in bad weather the traveller might have to spend twenty-four horrible hours on the packet crossing to Calais, but in Paris all the excitement of seeing new ladies' fashions and the faces of old enemies awaited them. The new order in Paris offered a very different glamour from that of the old regime, but for a moment it dazzled British visitors.

Bonaparte however remained ambitious and bellicose. When the Treaty of Amiens was confirmed he said, 'What a beautiful fix we are in now; peace has been declared!' In August he proclaimed himself First Consul and in that autumn of 1802 he annexed several Italian principalities and reoccupied Switzerland. Contrary to treaty commitments, he kept troops in the Netherlands. The London wits dubbed Amiens 'the peace that surpasseth all understanding' and it was manifestly nothing more than an armed truce. Finally, in May 1803, Britain, suspicious of Bonaparte's overseas intentions and resentful of his determination to exclude its trade and influence from the continent, declared a new war against him.

Bonaparte had planned to resume hostilities in 1804 but was incensed by the perfidy of the British in going to war before he was ready for it. He ordered the arrest of all British males in France aged eighteen to sixty, and his agents were able to snap up 10,000 of them – victims of the passion for cross-Channel contacts that had consumed them in the fleeting months of peace. Now he put in hand plans to invade England far more serious than those against which Nelson's talents had been deployed. For a time the initiative in and beside the Channel, so long held by the Royal Navy, passed into his hands. But his action in seizing English civilians had aroused support for the war in Britain as nothing else could have done, and the nation turned its attention to defence against invasion.

As for Bonaparte, 'the First Consul had to turn to the business of making an army... It was to be a real, full-dress, organised, trained fighting machine. Its training-ground was to be on the north-east coast of France, and its objective was England.'[8] The new formation was named the 'Army of the Coasts of the Ocean'; its seven corps, six cavalry divisions and Imperial Guard division were deployed along the whole North Sea and Channel coast from a right wing in Hanover to its left wing in Brest. The three centre corps, based at Bruges, Montreuil and Boulogne, were intended for an attack upon England. The attacking troops encamped around Boulogne, Wimereux and Ambleteuse.

On both sides of the Channel, preparations for invasion and resistance pressed ahead. In Britain the points of maximum danger were thought to be the Solent and the Kent coast opposite Calais and Boulogne. The militia and the Sea Fencibles of Kent and Sussex were called up, but they were a flimsy force to put into battle against the Army of the

Coasts of the Ocean. An effective defence called for fortifications. East Kent, Sussex, Hampshire and the Isle of Wight already had their defences, notably Henry VIII's chain of fortresses guarding the Downs and the Solent. Dover Castle remained 'the key to England'. Twenty years earlier, at the time of the American war, the fortified labyrinth on the Western Heights above Dover had been created to protect the town against attack by troops landed further down the coast, and for splendour and sheer surprise value it still outdoes the castle.

A chain of Martello towers was also built along the Kent and Sussex coast against invasion. They were round, tapering pill-boxes; their massive walls sheltered a section of infantry, and most were equipped with an artillery piece on the roof, capable of all-round defensive fire. They can still be seen at places along the coast, as can the lonely stretches of the Royal Military Canal, dug along the northern fringe of Romney Marsh as a stop-line against invasion. It runs from Rye to Appledore, its waters placid, what was once a gun emplacement still to be discerned at turns in its course, and a military road immediately behind it.

But Britain's first line of defence was its fleet. The Channel fleet was powerful enough to blockade or destroy the French line-of-battle ships, keeping them out of the Straits. Under its protection, frigates and sloops could get in among a French invasion convoy and destroy it piecemeal. The admirals were confident. But the battle fleet had to be kept up-wind and away in the western approaches to the Channel. There was always the danger of the unexpected: of a storm blowing the blockading ships off station, of an east wind, of the French making a dash from their ports, of some disastrous mishandling of the British fleet. 'With three days' east wind I could repeat the exploit of William the Conqueror,' Napoleon was supposed to have said. 'Let us be masters of the Channel for six hours and we are masters of the world.' Six hours would scarcely have been enough; but if for three days all had gone well, a French army could have been put across the Channel in a night or a day and a night. Once ashore, like Parma's men before and Hitler's after them, the French troops would have overwhelmed the land forces Britain could put into the field against them.

Yet on the other side of the Channel, Bonaparte – who crowned himself as the Emperor Napoleon in December 1804 – faced even more daunting problems than the English. He was building invasion barges all over northern France and the southern Netherlands. But like Parma he had to find a way to concentrate them in the invasion ports, and above all at Boulogne. He had to protect them against the sort of British amphibious attack that Nelson had attempted, so he canalised the estuary of the Canche at Étaples, restored the port at Ambleteuse, and dug a new basin at Wimereux. Meanwhile his commanders had to embolden their men to commit themselves to this strange element, the sea, put their trust in the novel protection of naval escorts, and set off on the hazardous crossing of the Channel. And while they waited in the Pas-de-Calais the battalions, regiments, divisions, corps and their commanders had to be moulded into a single force serving a single will – an army.

For more than a year, the seven corps of the Army of the Coasts of the Ocean lined the sea-coast from Germany to Finistère. Their commanders plotted and quarrelled, planned and prepared, worked and swaggered. A balloon had crossed the Channel a few years earlier, and now a visionary charlatan brought them an improved version to put to military use. Another visionary brought them proposals for a Channel tunnel. Their men trained and drank, trained and looted, trained and rioted: 'the camps at Boulogne, Wimereux, and Ostend, began to buzz with manoeuvres, inspections, parades, artillery target-practice . . .'[9] Away to the west in the French naval ports the warships awaited the order to put to sea and challenge the Channel Fleet.

Amid all the demands of the business of empire, Napoleon came to supervise the preparations. He based himself in the Château de St Léonard, in what is now a suburb of Boulogne. Napoleon rode out repeatedly to 'the emperor's barrack' overlooking the sea, where the Royal Navy's frigates prowled just beyond the range of his artillery. On 16 August 1804, some 80,000 soldiers and 20,000 spectators were assembled outside Boulogne to watch the first distribution of the new *Légion d'Honneur*, and Napoleon's generals and admirals dragooned their men into paying for the erection of a great column to mark the event. It is visible today from a great distance, and close up it dominates the park in which it stands. It is topped with a statue of Napoleon himself, placed there long after his time by Louis Philippe. Contrary to rumour he faces not out to sea, towards the old enemy England, but firmly eastwards. For this is a triumphant celebration of Napoleon and of what he and his *Grande Armée* intended to achieve on the continent of Europe, not – as too many British visitors imagine – a symbol of frustration at the defeat of his invasion plans.

In the end it was the presence far away beyond the horizon of the line-of-battle ships of the Channel Fleet that defeated Napoleon. At anchor in Portsmouth and Plymouth or out in the western approaches, they had the capacity to destroy any French fleet that dared to face them. So long as their distant presence ruled the waves French warships could not get among the smaller British ships that patrolled the narrows; and as long as the British controlled the narrows it was suicide to embark the Army of the Coasts of the Ocean. In Mahan's words, 'Those far distant, storm-beaten ships, upon which the Grand Army never looked, stood between it and the dominion of the world.'[10]

Finally, Napoleon gave up. Along the Channel coast he had created and trained a new army but failed to devise a means of launching it at the throats of his English enemies. Now he turned his attention elsewhere. In August 1805 the army struck camp. The Army of the Coasts of the Ocean became the Grande Armée: 'the most superb army in equipment, training, experience, morale, men, officers and Commander-in-Chief, that the world has ever seen, turned its back on the white sails of England's fleet and the white silhouette of England's cliffs, and went swinging across France and Holland and Germany'.[11] It was on its way to destroy Napoleon's continental enemies.

On 14 September 1805, a month after the French army abandoned its camps along the Channel coast, Nelson arrived in Portsmouth to take command of the Channel Fleet. His barge took him from the beach at Southsea, where a crowd of well-wishers almost overwhelmed him, out to *Victory* anchored at St Helen's. The flagship sailed slowly down the

Channel, past Portland, Lyme and Torbay on her way to a rendezvous with the fleet out in the Atlantic. Five weeks later, the British fleet encountered the combined French and Spanish squadrons at Trafalgar. The enemy were defeated, Nelson killed. On 5 December *Victory*, her flag at half mast, brought his body home to Spithead, then on to the Downs on its way to a state funeral of unsurpassable magnificence. By now, Napoleon had defeated the Austrians at Ulm and the combined Russian and Austrian armies at Austerlitz. He had ten more years of active life in him, in which he came close to overwhelming all the monarchies of the continent; but his hopes of invading England were over. In the tiger's long struggle with the shark, it was the shark that had prevailed.

Nine years later, in 1814, the French army came back to France defeated, at the end of the adventures that had taken it all the way across Europe to Moscow and then brought it back, what was left of it, all the way to Paris. The victorious allied armies rode into Paris, and agreed that Napoleon should be shut away in Elba, safely out of harm's way. It was time for the restoration of the Bourbons, and on 24 April 1814, Louis XVIII landed at Calais, tortured as ever by gout, and a column on the quayside claims unconvincingly that he was 'restored to the love of his country'. But when in the spring of 1815 Napoleon, restless as a caged tiger in Elba, escaped and returned to France, he quickly gathered popular support and the support of the army. He marched on Paris, throwing the French monarchy into a panic and the victorious powers assembled at the Congress of Vienna into confusion. The king fled from his capital as Napoleon marched in, and he did not rest until he was safe in the Low Countries. Behind him came Napoleon, his armies growing steadily stronger.

The stage was set for a last great battle in the cockpit of Europe, pitting Napoleon against the armies of his former enemies. The Duke of Wellington had been playing his laconic part in Vienna in shaping the concert of Europe. Now he came to take command of the combined British and Dutch army in the southern Netherlands.

He found 67,000 men awaiting him. Only 21,000 of them were British, and most of these were second-line, inexperienced troops compared with the veterans whom he had led in Spain. Many of the others were fonder of Napoleon than of the British. Somewhere to the east was the Prussian army under the formidable old Marshal Blücher.

Army headquarters at the Horse Guards in London was busy rebuilding a supply line to this little army, suddenly confronted as it was by the finest soldiers of Europe. The line ran down the Old Kent Road from London to Ramsgate, which had once been nothing more than a fishing port but which in the course of the French wars had grown into a supply base for British troops in the Low Countries. The wars – and the Waterloo campaign in particular – put Ramsgate on the map, and serene early-nineteenth-Century terraces and street names like Wellington Crescent and the Plains of Waterloo record the fact.

The campaign of Waterloo was a short one, consummated in one day after not much more than a month's manoeuvring. But it had its complexities, and the Channel played a central role in them. Napoleon's aim was to defeat separately Wellington's army and Blücher's Prussians. His opponents wanted to meet him with the overwhelming force of their united armies. But the Prussians were moving westwards very slowly. Wellington knew that his place was in the centre, shielding Brussels. But his line of communications ran away to the west, to Antwerp and Ostend and across the sea to Ramsgate. His and Blücher's armies combined would be strong enough to defeat Napoleon. But he was unsure of Napoleon's position, still more uncertain of the direction in which he was marching. He feared that if he reached out towards the Prussians while Napoleon thrust north-westwards, he would be cut off from Ostend and his communications with England. Yet if he lingered too far to the west, the French might overwhelm first the Prussian army and then his own.

With his concern for the Channel ports, Wellington picked up a theme that has run throughout British history. Policy has been dictated by it, fleets massed, battles fought, armies assembled around it. Fears for the Channel have shaped the course of most of the country's great naval battles. Now they affected also its greatest single land engagement, the Battle of Waterloo. Far inland as it was fought, seventy miles from the sea, nevertheless it was concern for the Channel ports and his communications with England that deterred Wellington from marching decisively eastwards to join forces with the Prussians and brought him close to defeat at Waterloo.

The Prussians were therefore alone when the French fell on them at Ligny. They retreated north-eastwards – moving at first away from Wellington. He, confident at last that Napoleon's position and intentions were clear, shifted eastwards. A Prussian corps swung round towards him. The two armies were drawing closer together. But when, on 18 June 1815, Wellington joined battle with the French at Waterloo, his army was still alone, and significantly weaker than its opponents. His own deadly coolness and the deadly musket fire of his men checked the unstoppable advance of the Imperial Guard. As the French flinched the British advanced and the Prussians came in on Napoleon's flank to complete the famous victory. The French army broke away first in retreat and then in dissolution. When the battle was over Wellington called it 'a damned near-run thing'. If it had gone the other way, if Napoleon had succeeded in his plan to defeat first the Prussians and then the British, Wellington's concern for his cross-Channel communications would have brought him not safety but disaster.

The great banker Nathan Rothschild was famously the first man in London with news of the victory. A messenger from Ostend brought him a Dutch newspaper containing a garbled account of allied victory, anticipating by a day Wellington's own despatch. But it was one of Wellington's dashing aides de camp, Henry Percy, who got the glory of bringing the official account of the victory. He set off from Brussels for Ostend in the blood-stained uniform he had worn in battle, Wellington's despatch in his hand, protected by a folder he had been given at the Duchess of Richmond's ball in Brussels. Off the Kent coast his ship became becalmed and he had to have himself rowed ashore. From Broadstairs he set off in a chaise-and-four up the old London road, captured French banners fluttering from the window. He drove first to Downing Street, and from there he was taken first to a Cabinet dinner party in Grosvenor Square and then on to the Prince Regent. It was an age of balls and the Prince was holding one. It was exactly four nights since Percy had danced in Brussels at another on the eve of the battle. Now he told London society its outcome.

Though none of the participants knew it, Waterloo looks like being history's last battle between those historic enemies, Britain and France. It stands at the end of 600 years of cross-Channel armed conflict, if not yet of animosity. In describing the battle, Victor Hugo penned a long sentence about the qualities which the two sides brought to it. Few Frenchmen and Britons may recognise the national characteristics Hugo described, but it is one man's marvellous summary of the contrasting styles that the old cross-Channel enemies brought to the last battle in their centuries of conflict.

> On one side [Wellington's] precision, foresight, geometry, prudence, all assured retreat, reserves spaced with an obstinate coolness, an impenetrable method, strategy which takes advantage of the ground, tactics which preserve the equilibrium of battalions, carnage executed according to rule, war regulated, watch in hand, nothing voluntarily left to chance, the ancient classic courage, absolute regularity; on the other [Napoleon's], intuition, divination, military strangeness, superhuman instinct, a flaming glance, an indescribable something which gazes like an eagle and strikes like lightning, a prodigious act of disdainful impetuosity, all the mystery of a profound soul, association with destiny.[12]

For the British, Waterloo became as significant an event as the defeat of the Armada in the long process of their national myth-making. Wellington was honoured as the man who had so soundly drubbed a vulgar foreign mountebank. His aura of the cool, laconic gentleman became a model for Victorian behaviour. In the same way, the nation he had served became a model of the qualities that could bring nineteenth-century success. The flamboyant Europe, the reshaped Europe, perhaps even the united Europe, of which Napoleon had dreamed went down to defeat when the French guard flinched at Waterloo. With the success of cool, disciplined British musket fire the cool, commercially minded islanders who had fought the French for the best part of a quarter of a century entered into their peacetime inheritance.

When the French guard flinched, Napoleon's hopes were done for. He hastened to Paris, failed to rally his faltering ministers, abdicated and fled to Rochefort on the Atlantic coast. There French frigates waited to take him to a new life in the United States. But as he was to say to an Englishman in St Helena, 'Wherever there is water to float a ship, we are sure to find you in the way.' At Rochefort he found a British blockading squadron. Behind him were the vengeful Bourbons and the Prussians who talked of hanging him. He surrendered himself to the captain of HMS *Bellerophon*. The Royal Navy, Napoleon's most enduring opponent, took him as a prisoner to the only major country in Europe he had failed to enter as an invader.

Bellerophon brought him first into Torbay, where in 1688 William and Mary had landed. Soon she was ordered to Plymouth. There was then played out a strange little tragi-comedy. Napoleon convinced himself that if he could set foot on land his problems would be at an end. He even talked of setting up as a country gentleman somewhere in the English shires and winning over the hearts of ordinary Englishmen. After a few days' exposure to his magic, the crew of the *Bellerophon* had told their captain that 'if the people of England knew him as well as we do, they would not touch a hair of his head'.[13] Now, while in Paris the people were baying for his blood, in Plymouth the people of England came out in their thousands to get a glimpse of the great man. Tradesmen set up shop on the breakwater to sell refreshments to the crowds; two ladies fell to their deaths in the water; every day a thousand small boats set out to circle *Bellerophon* in the hope of a sight of Napoleon; and the *Morning Post* reported with regret that, 'a large portion of the spectators not only took off their hats, but cheered him'.

Napoleon thought the Prince Regent would welcome him as a royal equal or that Whig sympathisers in England would work the magic of *habeas corpus* for him. But there was to be no more mercy, no opportunity for him to come back a second time from exile and again set Europe in flames. For a few days *Bellerophon* was sent to take him cruising in the Channel out of harm's way while a better ship was prepared for the voyage into exile. Finally, in early August, *Northumberland* sailed out of Plymouth Sound on her long voyage to St Helena.

CHAPTER 11

ONE
HUNDRED
YEARS OF
PEACE

So in 1815, the great master of war sailed for ever out of the jaws of the Channel into exile. The warfare that had consumed the last quarter century vanished with him. The years of peace take its place, bringing very different concerns to the Channel and its ports. Its stages now are dominated by shipbuilders, businessmen, railway builders, middle-class travellers and working-class trippers, artists attracted by seaside sunsets, writers seeking bucolic peace in which to work. The thread that holds the whole story together is the impact on the life of the nineteenth-century Channel of the industrial, economic and technical revolution which in the course of those hundred years so fundamentally changed Britain, France and the whole western world. Any of the Channel's ports and resorts can illustrate an aspect of the changes that came to both coasts in the course of the nineteenth century, but Southampton offers as good a place to start as any. It is a story of a town recovering its vocation after centuries in eclipse.

Southampton's history dates back to before the Romans. To the Anglo-Saxons it was the flourishing port for Winchester and all Wessex. But in the fourteenth century its trade faltered, and in the sixteenth the Royal Navy removed its business to Portsmouth. In the early eighteenth century Defoe dismissed it as a place in its death throes for want of commercial lifeblood. So Southampton stumbled through the eighteenth century, with its deeply conservative town corporation at odds with groups of citizens with plans for its revival, and often insolvent. The story of its rescue begins not with ships, imports and exports but with the new-fangled cult of spas and bathing.

It succeeded in attracting royal attention. George III favoured Weymouth, but the Royal Dukes of York, Gloucester and Cumberland turned their backs on him and brought their patronage to Southampton. The aristocracy and gentry followed, a Royal Society of Southampton Archers was formed for the special delectation of female visitors, and a building boom produced elegant Georgian terraces. Soon traffic jams assumed twenty-first-century proportions, and the town constable was instructed to remove unattended carriages and chain them to a tree in a lane that acquired the name of Pound Tree Road.

With the nineteenth century came the stirrings of commercial and maritime revival, based first on steamships and then on steam trains. In 1820 a first steam packet, *Prince Coburg*, was introduced on the Isle of Wight run, and three years later a regular service to Le Havre. The town proclaimed itself the 'gateway to the continent' and in 1838 the building of new docks was started. In 1840 the first train came puffing down the line from London, and soon the railway company was running day excursions to Southampton with a boat trip round the Isle of Wight thrown in. Ten years later the London morning newspapers were on sale in Cowes by 11.30 in the morning. By mid-century Southampton had re-established itself as a major port, Britain's fifth.

As the world turned ever redder on the map, Southampton grew in importance as a great port of empire, and the terminus for much of Britain's oceanic traffic. In turn Peninsular and Orient, Royal Mail Lines, Union Castle, White Star and Cunard based their liner business here, and not even two visitations of cholera checked its growth for long.

There was no question of its winning back the Royal Navy from Portsmouth, but it made itself indispensable to the army. Regiments sailed out of Southampton Water on their way to the Crimean War, the Zulu War and the South African War and so in 1914 did the British Expeditionary Force. Between 1914 and 1918 Southampton docks were shut to civilian traffic while they shipped abroad eight million soldiers, 859,000 horses, 180,000 vehicles and 15,000 guns. The wounded, and particularly the shell-shocked, came home to Southampton and its great gaunt Victorian hospital at Netley, to be swallowed up in the wards of a building of which Nikolaus Pevsner wrote: 'It would be difficult to find a more extreme example of a building where outward grandeur and rigid planning came first, convenience and "amenity" a very poor second.'[1]. So war set a coping-stone on the town's long peacetime recovery of importance and prosperity. Along the way, it acquired its general hospital, its newspaper, and eventually its university.

Boulogne tells a similar story on the other side of the water. In the course of the nineteenth century its population grew sixfold. It remained heavily dependent on its fishing fleet, and when its railway to Amiens was completed in 1848 and then extended to Paris, the market for its freshly landed fish expanded dramatically. The port grew, and industry and modern shipbuilding arrived. So did holidaymakers, the English prominent among them. In 1840, however, the people of Boulogne saw the arrival of a very different kind of visitor from England. The story of his brief adventures in the town is one-third drama, one-third tragedy and one-third farce.

Louis Napoleon saw himself as the legitimate successor of his uncle, the great Emperor, on the throne of France. The restored French monarchy saw matters differently, and sent him to live out his life in frustrated exile in England. There he conceived the idea of a descent on the coasts of France, rallying supporters there, and a victorious advance on Paris. He hired a paddle steamer, the *Edinburgh Castle*, and took it down the Thames with a crew of adventurers and serving men – fifty-five in all – a cargo of a few weapons, and a comic opera's worth of uniforms and military insignia.

On a dark August night he landed at Wimereux, marched on Boulogne, and exchanged speeches, fisticuffs and the odd shot with the forces of royalist law and order. But there was no enthusiasm about joining his escapade, and eventually he retreated to the foot of the old Emperor's monument, the great column of the *Grande Armée* on its hill above the town. Here he saw himself mounting a last heroic stand, but police and the National Guard quickly put his men to flight. Back to Wimereux he trudged with his little band of ineffectual desperadoes, and on the beach there most of them surrendered. He and a few close supporters took to a boat to reach the *Edinburgh Castle*, but they were hit by fire from their pursuers on the shore. The boat sank and 'by a supreme humiliation the survivors were rescued rather than arrested'.[2]

It seemed the inglorious end of the story of Louis Napoleon. But the idea that straight lines rule history can lead us astray. At the trial that followed his assault on the French monarchy in Boulogne, Louis Napoleon started the process of making himself a national hero. Eight years later he became President of the French Republic, and four years after that Emperor Napoleon III. Soon he came back to Boulogne on an imperial pilgrimage to the column where his fortunes had so spectacularly faltered in 1840. He came again to inspect regiments about to leave for the Crimea, and then, in 1855, to host a grand reception for the kings of the Belgians and of Portugal, for Prince Albert and for Queen Victoria herself. These imperial visits added to Boulogne's stature and self-importance. By the time war came in 1914 it had grown into a place big enough to serve as a major Channel base for the British army in France.

Dover had always provided Britain's shortest crossing to the continent, and the contact was not broken even during the Revolutionary and Napoleonic wars. By 1818 it had a regular steam packet connection with Calais, making the crossing in three or four hours. But it was the coming of the railway in 1844, tunnelled through the high downs to the west, bursting out of a portal like a cathedral's under Shakespeare Cliff on its way to the foreshore, which put the place on the nineteenth-century map. Almost at once the railway company was reaching out to exploit Dover's cross-Channel links, using posters advertising excursion trips to the town, with the option thrown in of a weekend visit to France as well. Soon Dover acquired its Lord Warden Hotel for the accommodation of travellers to the continent.

Dunkirk had been favoured over Calais by eighteenth-century France. Now, however, Calais prospered with Dover, but it was becoming much more than just a cross-Channel terminus. It far outstripped Boulogne in size. Now its heavy industries developed along the coast towards Belgium; its port grew to meet the demands of ocean traffic; and the English families who in 1817 brought lace-making here, risking a death sentence if the authorities caught them taking the secrets of their craft out of England, gave Calais a special trade of its own that it has never lost.

Cherbourg also entered into its inheritance at last. For centuries its natural harbour had gone largely unexploited by anyone except fishermen. British raiders had pre-empted invasion preparations there in 1758 and devastated its little port. Then Louis XVI, in his last years before his fall, conceived a grand plan to turn it into a naval base. Napoleon I took it up where Louis had left it, but it was only in Napoleon III's time that the French navy achieved its long-cherished ambition of a great naval base half-way up the Channel. At last it could look its historic enemy in Portsmouth in the eye just at a time when, had it but known it, that enemy was about to become France's friend.

Brighton took another route to fame. Most of the place and all its fishing fleet were swept away by the great storm of 1703, but within half a century it was building its reputation on seawater cures for the aristocracy and gentry. In the 1780s 'Prinny', the Prince of Wales who was to become the Prince Regent, transferred his fickle allegiance from Southampton to Brighton and became the presiding genius of the place. He brought Maria Fitzherbert, who was to become his morganatic wife; he bought property in Brighton; and he built the most splendid of all Channel coast palaces, the Royal Pavilion. With the attention he attracted, Brighton attained fame, and with it the reputation for fashion, sleaze, discreet adultery, whelks and knees-up beside the seaside which it has never lost.

Forty years later, but still a hundred years before the coming of the *Brighton Belle*, the traveller and essayist William Cobbett detected the presence of a different kind of resident, and the beginnings of long-distance commuting between the town and London: 'Brighton . . . fifty miles from the wen, is on the seaside, and is thought by the stock-jobbers to afford a salubrious air. It is so situated that a coach which leaves it not very early in the morning, reaches London by noon . . . Great parcels of stock-jobbers stay at Brighton, with the women and children. They skip backwards and forwards on the coaches and actually carry on stock-jobbing in Change Alley though they reside in Brighton.'[3]

Though the coming of the railways promoted the importance of the major Channel ports, it undermined the position of the small ones that had always served limited local markets. The Cinque Ports had long been in decline. Now little places on the coast of Devon, Dorset and Hampshire went the same way. So did little ports in Normandy and the Pas-de-Calais. The vogue for seaside holidaymaking came to their rescue, but here too the crowds were attracted to the new resorts that they could easily reach by rail. The really small places had to await the coming of the motor car.

Gradually, Brighton and other Channel resorts of the upper and middle classes were overrun by the new phenomenon of the excursion-ists. From the early years of passenger services, the railways offered cut-price excursions to special events, such as the Great Exhibition of 1851, or to the everyday pleasures of the seaside. They brought people to the Channel who had never travelled more than five miles from home. For them a day beside the seaside was a heady experience, enjoyed in the company of hundreds of fellow excursionists. It brought enormous pleasure, and often great excess, which overwhelmed places used to more decorous visitors. Friction between native, excursionist and middle-class holiday-maker became a feature of the Channel resorts. Gradually each of them asserted its own character: Margate for the masses, Broadstairs for the refined, Bournemouth for the seriously old. The character of many coastal towns altered with the seasons. For example, wrote one rather over-nice observer: 'Hastings itself in the winter months, with its mild grey air, its quiet sea, is the home of the silent invalid, the invalid of the bathchair and the grey muffler... But the summer months see it filled by the noisy Cockney... This usually trying individual grows here very pathetic, very pleasant to contemplate.'[4]

Trade, railways, sea bathing, fashion, excursions to the seaside all came to the French side of the Channel in the same way as to the British, usually a matter of a decade or so later. The railways that ran inland from Boulogne and Calais opened up the whole continent to Cook's first foreign tourists.[5] Le Havre became the French terminus for liners from New York. In the 1860s Napoleon III did for Trouville what Prinny had done for Brighton half a century earlier. The beach at Trouville attracted painters like Eugène Boudin, and at Honfleur he gathered around him others such as Courbet and Daubigny, capturing the sun, light and shadow of the Normandy coast as Turner and Frith had aroused an English taste for the seaside with their paintings of Margate and Ramsgate sands.

The nineteenth century saw an unprecedented explosion in Britain's overseas trade. In the single decade of the 1850s, exports grew faster than ever before or since. It was London and the northern cities that did best from this industrial dynamism, but the Channel ports blossomed also. So did traffic down-Channel and up. And gradually, steam came to take its place beside sail. The slow decline in the importance of the sailing ship and the steady rise in the numbers of steamships in time altered the face of Channel navigation. But it took the whole century to see the more or less complete displacement of sail by steam.

It was an American, Robert Fulton, who brought the first working steamboats to Europe. In 1803 he demonstrated one of his own design, towing two other boats against the current on the Seine at a speed of three miles per hour. Steamships were at work in sheltered British waters before the end of the Napoleonic wars, and in the summer of 1815 the first steamship to sail in Channel waters, the *Margery*, made the passage from Land's End to the Port of London, convincing onlookers on shore that she was on fire. Steam-packets came into service very quickly, but steam came to cross-Channel freight business only in the 1820s, when the *Aaron Manby* took a first cargo of iron and linseed to Le Havre.

Its use grew rapidly. Sail fought back. The nineteenth century saw the triumphs of the great sailing clippers, most of them American, on the long ocean routes. Diminutive 200-ton packets continued to ply out of Falmouth on the Atlantic run. And all over Europe sailing ships with a two-man crew continued into the 1920s to handle much river and coastal traffic. But the long-term trend was of course to steam, and not just on the cross-Channel and transatlantic services. Paddle steamer coasting became a popular diversion of the Victorian summer, with ships plying between Southampton, Weymouth and Lyme, between Brighton and Worthing, and between Hastings and Eastbourne, in imitation of the Cockneys' excursions from London to the North Kent and Essex resorts. Piers were built to accommodate them, and paddle steamers continued to operate after the First World War. Indeed, one or two went to the Dunkirk evacuation in 1944, and another to the Normandy landings in 1944.

Meanwhile the Channel saw Englishmen in increasing numbers take to pleasure sailing. The man who documented the process best was Richard McMullen, who between 1850 and 1890 owned a series of yachts of increasing size, which he sailed, single-handed or in company, from one end of the Channel to the other and once, to mark the Queen's Jubilee, right round the United Kingdom. He describes his voyages in *Down Channel*, the first and some would say still the best bible for small-boat sailors; and though he makes a very Victorian story of the discipline and search for effectiveness he brought to the business, the pleasure he also found in it shines out of every chapter. In the end he died at sea, alone under a moonlit sky, and French fishermen came upon him a day later, still upright at the helm of his little ship.

He exercised an unselfconscious discipline over his hired crews: 'It was time for the hands' dinner and my luncheon,' he writes; and he did not hesitate to send another crew home by steamer from Cherbourg when they turned surly. He is impressed by the newly completed harbour works and fortifications there, but disgusted by French sanitary manners, which make a stinking mess of quays and harbour steps. Having paid off his crew, he brings his boat home single-handed, sustaining himself on his twenty-seven-hour passage to Dover with 'brandy, champagne, granular magnesia, or claret – the last two to quench extreme thirst'.[6]

On another cruise he happens upon regattas at Torquay and Dover, and records disobliging thoughts about men to whom small-boat sailing is not a serious business but mere ostentatious quayside posturing. In a storm off the Lizard he falls in with the crew of a cutter, who lead him to safer waters. It turns out to be a 'tailor's cutter', which meets homeward bound ships out of the Atlantic and offers a new suit, to be cut and sewn during the voyage up-Channel, to those who prefer not to walk ashore 'in sea-stained garments'.[7] Repeatedly he condemns the dangers brought by new-fangled and badly handled screw-driven steamers, which the Channel fishermen call 'silent deaths'. And once, passing Deal Pier, he records a telegraphic description of the Victorian seashore: 'Band playing – boys fishing – boats sailing – paterfamilias, and the whole tribe, out for a row – the beach alive with ramblers in search of "precious stones" and other treasures cast up by the sea – a scene of peaceful enjoyment which never ceases to interest . . .'[8]

That yachtsmen like McMullen could enjoy life on the Channel waves in reasonable safety was in part due to the formation of the Coast Guard, the development of a chain of lighthouses along the coast, and the growth of the lifeboat service. The Coast Guard was introduced in 1820, initially to draw together all the forces of the Crown engaged in combating smuggling. That old trade persisted well into the nineteenth century, but the abolition of tariffs on most imports deprived the smuggler of much of the incentive to risk his life to avoid the Revenue men. In the first quarter of the nineteenth century, Trinity House took further the work that Winstanley had begun at Eddystone, marking all the points of serious danger on the English Channel coast. And in 1824 the Royal National Lifeboat Institution was founded, privately funded, and grew as rapidly as so many other Victorian institutions, from ninety boats by 1850, 200 by 1870, to 300 by the end of the century. Soon lifeboats were stationed all along the Channel coast.

Between them the Coast Guard, the lighthouse keepers and the lifeboatmen formed part of the process of domesticating the Channel. The men of the Coast Guard turned from fighting smugglers to spotting ships in danger. The lighthousemen operated where once only wreckers had shown lights to seaward. And the coxswain and crew of the lifeboats, all of them volunteers and normally found from the ranks of local fishermen, were often descended from families that not so long before had made a more ample living from the smuggling that demanded a different kind of inshore seamanship.

Not even the deep peace of the mid-nineteenth century Channel was entirely free from rumours of war. They came and went episodically, and some left a physical mark on the Channel coastline.

The Duke of Wellington, ice-cold in real battle, began to exercise his elderly imagination on the peacetime possibility of invasion. For him as for all England, France was the traditional enemy, whose menace had been scotched but not killed at Waterloo. The coming of the steamship in particular troubled Wellington. A grateful nation had made him Lord Warden of the Cinque Ports and given him Walmer Castle, from whose terrace he looked out across the Straits towards France. Now, in old age, he imagined a steamship-borne invasion emerging from the Channel mists: 'I see exactly what the danger is; I am as certain of it as if it was passing under my view!'[9] Throughout the age of sail, the Royal Navy had kept Britain safe, but could it be relied on to sink a French army embarked in steamships for the short passage to the English coast? Wellington's prestige fed the fears of lesser Englishmen. If the Duke was anxious, so should all England be, and not all the assurances of the admirals could put an end to his disquiet.

In the year Wellington died, 1852, the threat seemed to become yet more real. Louis Napoleon made himself Emperor of the French. He was determined to reassert France's centrality in European affairs; to the British his very name was a potent reminder of old fears of France; and that threatening naval base at Cherbourg was approaching completion. An invasion scare ensued. It led in the 1850s and 1860s to the biggest investment in Channel defences since the time of Henry VIII. His castle at Hurst in the western Solent was encased in a great half moon of iron-grey granite. A chain of defences was built across the Isle of Wight, and Portsmouth was ringed with defences designed on the best modern principles. Portland was fortified; and out in the Solent were established those great man-made island fortresses visible from the deck of a ferry en route to Cherbourg or Le Havre.

All this investment in land fortifications provoked criticism in naval quarters. Britain's true defence from invasion, it was argued, depended on the Royal Navy. Steam had altered all that, was the reply. In any case the French were building steam-powered armoured battleships. Britain's own steam-powered leviathan, the *Warrior*, was the response, and her armour plate was hung on an iron frame, not a wooden one like those of the French ironclads. She can be seen in Portsmouth today, the most formidable warship of the mid-nineteenth century, restoring Britain's naval predominance at a stroke. And before Dover and Portland extend the great harbours of refuge that were created at the same time to permit the Royal Navy to fight a steamship battle for control of the Channel not, as in the past, out in the Western Approaches to capture the weather gauge but in the narrow seas themselves. At Dover, the works completed then serve a proper modern purpose, sheltering the terminus of the cross-Channel ferries. That at Portland seems more at a loss, a great expanse of sheltered water beneath the bulk of Portland itself, 'England's strange Gibraltar', and the sailing craft that anchor there seem lonely orphans by contrast with the great flocks of boats that crowd the moorings of neighbouring Weymouth.

In the middle of this invasion scare, however, in February 1854, the old antagonists went to war in the Crimea not as enemies but as allies. Alliance demanded at least a show of good feeling, and an era of cross-Channel royal visits began. Napoleon came to Windsor and Queen Victoria went to Paris, the first English monarch to enter the city since the infant Henry VI in 1422. But suspicions remained, and when in 1857 the queen travelled to Cherbourg for a meeting with the Emperor, the inclusion in her suite of an officer of the Royal Engineers aroused

French suspicions that Albion's perfidy would stop at nothing, not even a state visit. His real role, they were sure, was to sketch the fortifications that defended their proud new base. A year later Napoleon III officiated at its opening. Old cross-Channel animosities died hard.

After rumours of war in the Channel comes an isolated act of war itself. It involved not the old antagonists but two American ships, far from home. Their engagement was a matter of entertainment for Europeans who had forgotten the experience of war, and on 12 June 1864 the people of Cherbourg and thousands of excursionists who had come from Paris in special trains for the event watched in fascination as a ship of the United States Navy, the *Kearsarge*, pounded to destruction a Confederate ship, the *Alabama*.

The *Alabama* was a commerce raider which, having preyed successfully on Union shipping, had put into Cherbourg to refit. The *Kearsarge*, despatched across the wide Atlantic to hunt her down, found her there. *Alabama*'s captain was a fine Southern gentleman, and he put to sea expecting a fair fight between equals. He discovered too late that the *Kearsarge*'s hull was protected by concealed armour. *Alabama*'s fire made no impression on her and finally the Confederate ship went down. An English yachtsman who had come across the Channel to see the fight picked up captain and crew and took them to Southampton, where honest Englishmen who loved a loser acclaimed them as 'a set of first-rate fellows'.

Six years later, war on a more ample scale approached the Channel coast but did not quite reach it. In 1870 France went to war with Prussia, expecting to promenade gloriously into southern Germany. Instead the Prussian army turned European expectations on their head. Across eastern and northern France it outmanoeuvred and outmarched the French, besieged some of their armies and shattered others. Finally it trapped the emperor himself in Sedan on the Belgian frontier. Napoleon surrendered and he and his army passed into captivity.

His empress, Eugénie, fled from Trouville in an Englishman's yacht on her way to exile in Chislehurst in Kent. Paris, besieged, fought on. So did French armies south of the Loire and in the industrial north; and

France kept command of the sea. From time to time the French tried unsuccessfully to drive a passage up the coast to reach their forces in the north, and from time to time the Prussians struck out equally unsuccessfully towards the Channel. But the French were weak, the Prussians over-extended. So the towns of France's Channel coast were spared the fighting, occupation and devastation that consumed so much of the country just inland. In 1871 Prussia imposed its victors' peace on the French and proclaimed the German Empire. It was a victory whose consequences took decades to mature. Among them were a bitter eagerness for revenge among Frenchmen, a new suspicion of German might among Englishmen, and a slowly developing conviction that Britain and France would have to stand together against this great new continental power. The seeds of cross-Channel entente had been planted.

Between 1850 and 1900, western Europe grew rich. The aristocracy had always enjoyed their broad acres and rent rolls, early industrialists their profits, the professional classes their comfortable prosperity. Now the triumph of capitalist development added new depth to their wealth and began to extend prosperity to the ordinary middle, even lower-middle, classes. The position of the rural poor may have changed little and the new urban proletariat lived in wretched deprivation, but society as a whole saw unprecedented opportunities. Among them was the chance of foreign travel. In 1851 the Great Exhibition brought thousands of foreign visitors to London, and the long years of Victorian peace gave the British the possibility of continental travel that the Franco-Prussian war only briefly interrupted.

The effect on cross-Channel travel was dramatic. Now quite ordinary people joined the small numbers of those who had crossed it in the past for business, pleasure and edification. Frenchmen came to wonder at British industry, Englishmen went to Paris to admire French art, eat French food, enjoy the charms of French women. Cross-Channel travel became a business. It demanded new railway links, new port facilities, hotels for the weary traveller, porters and travel agents, tour organisers and money changers, new steamships on the Channel routes. In 1851, the year of the Great Exhibition, an undersea telegraph cable was laid between Dover and Calais. One of the first messages transmitted to Paris contained London Stock Exchange prices. The link so changed the logistics of business news gathering that Paul Julius Reuter, father of the Reuters agency, at once moved his base of operations from Belgium to London. And in 1860 Britain and France signed the Cobden Treaty, giving each other most favoured nation status and abolishing British protective duties. The effect was to stimulate cross-Channel trade still further, and alter for good the profit and loss calculus of many a cross-Channel smuggling business.

In the 1870s an American and an Englishman set themselves to cross the Channel under their own power alone. The American was a publicist and adventurer called Paul Boyton, eager to promote himself and a life-saving suit made of black vulcanised rubber with buoyancy tanks in legs, arms and shoulders. His announcement that in this device he would paddle his way from England to France caught the attention of Queen Victoria at Osborne. He scrambled his way across the Channel, some of the way afloat in his suit, more of it in the vessel that escorted him. He presented messy failure as triumphant success, and the queen and the Prince of Wales sent him their congratulations. His chicanery infuriated the Englishman, who proposed to cross the Channel quite unaided, in a red silk swimming costume.

Matthew Webb, the first human being to swim the English Channel, was all that Boyton was not. He was a powerful swimmer dedicated to overcoming the challenge of the Channel. He was a real sea captain, where Boyton merely called himself 'captain'. At least at the time of his attempt upon the Channel he seems to have been an obsessively honest man. He brought to his obsession the passionate simplicity of the Victorian man of action. And in August 1875 he swam a 40-mile, tide-dictated, dogleg course from Dover to the French coast in twenty-two hours of agonised endeavour.

Webb suffered the fate of too many men who achieve a great and singular triumph. For some reason he never got a telegram from Osborne. He felt himself cheated of fame by Boyton's ludicrous expedition and public relations skills. He cast around restlessly for ways of replicating his own great achievement. Finally he came to a dreadful end, persuading himself that he could swim through the Niagara rapids and live. Yet he had his hour when he swam the Channel in 1875, briefly making himself the most famous man in the world, achieving the same kind of fame as Hillary and Tensing would win on Everest three-quarters of a century later. He set a standard of Victorian physical endurance: 500 men and women have swum the Channel since, but it was to be more than thirty years before his achievement was repeated. He swam the Channel with little knowledge of physiology and nutrition, with the most primitive of equipment and support. He swam breast-stroke all the way, with his head held back, clear of the water, like a tyro in a swimming-pool today. He did more than conquer that supremely unfriendly stretch of water between Dover and Calais; he made it the goal of every kind of record-breaker.

While Webb was swimming and Boyton blustering his way across the Channel, other minds were engaged in the idea of a tunnel under it. The great Napoleon had looked at plans for this novel way of getting his Grande Armée to England. By the 1830s a French engineer, Thomé de Gamond, had started surveying a route and in the 1850s the project attracted the favourable interest of Robert Stephenson, Isambard Kingdom Brunel and Napoleon III. A committee of French scientific experts decided that a tunnel was technically feasible, and just before the Franco-Prussian war turned its attentions elsewhere, the French government sought the British government's reaction to the idea.

The queen's first reaction had been girlishly favourable, for the horrors of sea-sickness were on her mind: 'You may tell the French engineer,' she told Prince Albert, who was himself all in favour, 'that if he can accomplish it, I will give him my blessing in my own name and in the name of all the ladies of England.'[10] Her statesmen were more sceptical and now, in the 1870s and bereaved of Albert, she turned hostile to the scheme: 'She hopes,' she wrote to Disraeli, 'that the government will do nothing to encourage the proposed tunnel under the Channel, which she thinks very objectionable.' But a Channel Tunnel Company had been formed, private capital raised; and in 1880 experimental tunnelling was begun. Within two years, 4,000 yards of tunnel were dug, 2,000 each at the English and French ends. Meanwhile Sir Edward Watkin, the Chairman of the company and an enthusiast who had donned Gamond's mantle, took to inviting celebrities, Members of Parliament and the Prince and Princess of Wales to underground luncheon parties in the workings. Direct train journeys between London and Paris began to seem a possibility.

In the end, of course, British reaction triumphed, with arguments as hysterical as we have seen deployed in the last half century against other projects to bind Britain closer to the continent. Gladstone had talked about a wise dispensation of providence that cut England off from its neighbours behind 'a streak of silver sea'. 'Will it be possible for us so to guard the English end of the passage that it can never fall into any other hands?' asked *The Times*. Lieutenant General Sir Garnet Wolseley, Britain's greatest military guru of the age, was only fifty, but his military judgement of the proposal was as eccentric as had been the dying Wellington's fears of steamboat invasion: 20,000 troops could be poured through the tunnel into Dover in four hours, he believed. Far fewer could do the job: 2,500 men 'ably led by a daring, young commander, might . . . some dark night . . . easily make themselves masters of the works at our end of the tunnel, and then England would be at the mercy of the invader'.[11] The military calculations were all nonsense, but the Channel Tunnel Company was instructed to stop work, the diggings abandoned.

Twenty years later it was aviation's turn to link France and England. In 1785 the pioneer French balloonist, Jean-Pierre-François Blanchard, and his American passenger, John Jeffries, had drifted across the Channel from Dover, taking with them the first packet of airmail in history. More than a hundred years later, in 1903, the Wright brothers' *Kitty Hawk* took to the air. Six years after that the London *Daily Mail* offered a prize of £1,000 to the first man to fly the English Channel. Louis Blériot, a wealthy French enthusiast, had sunk a fortune in aviation experiments, most of them unsuccessful, but he was prepared to put more into the pursuit of the Channel prize. A little-remembered

Englishman, Hubert Latham, got into the air over the Channel before him, but his engine cut out half-way across. Making his own preparations, Blériot secured the services of a French destroyer to escort him, and brought his latest machine, a 28-horsepower monoplane known as Model XI, to the French Channel coast. Very early in the morning on Sunday, 25 July 1909, he drove to the field beside the Channel near Calais where the plane was parked. At 4.35 he took off for England from what is now Blériot Plage. What follows comes from his own breathless account of his flight.

> In an instant, I am in the air. My engine is making 1,200 revolutions – almost its highest speed . . . As soon as I am over the cliff I reduce my speed. There is now no need to force my engine . . . I have no apprehensions, no sensations, none at all. The *Escopette* [his escorting destroyer] has seen me. She is driving ahead across the Channel. She makes perhaps 26 miles per hour. So what! I am making over 40 miles per hour! Rapidly I overtake her.

Blériot loses sight of *Escopette*, of France, of England:

> I am alone. I am lost. Then I see the cliffs of Dover! Away to the west was the spot where I had intended to land. The wind had taken me out of my course. I turn, and now I am in difficulties . . . I see an opening and find myself over dry land. I attempt a landing, but then the wind catches me and whirls me around . . . At once I stop my motor, and instantly my machine falls to the ground. I am safe on the English shore . . .[12]

Blériot had landed in a steep field high above the Channel beside Dover Castle, symbol of so many centuries' resistance to French intrusion on English soil. The first Englishmen he meets are soldiers and a policeman. Then His Majesty's Customs arrive. Their official forms contain no provision for arrival by air and, at a loss, they record that Blériot has arrived 'by yacht'. The French are not far behind them: 'Two of my compatriots are on the spot. They kiss my cheeks. I am overwhelmed.'

Blériot had covered 24 miles in 40 minutes, 250 feet above the sea. He collects his prize from the *Daily Mail* and 120,000 Britons flock to see his aeroplane. 'I am the happiest Frenchwoman alive,' says his wife. 'Ah, *la gloire.*'

'Britain's impregnability has passed away,' says a less elated London newspaper; and then, anticipating the desperate battle that will be fought in the skies above Dover Castle thirty years hence: 'Airpower will become as vital as seapower.' And Hilaire Belloc, bringing his little boat the *Nona* into Dover harbour fifteen years later, makes something highfalutin and mystical, almost hysterical, of the whole affair: 'the first man (and he a Frenchman), having flown the Channel, landed upon the sacred island, without leave of the sea'. It was 'something which cannot be undone and which has subtly stolen their meaning not only from old Dover, but from the great keels of the fleet and its guns'.[13]

Already in 1909 there were fears that the peace of the old century could not be indefinitely prolonged into the new one. The power of Germany, which had so nearly reached the French Channel coast in 1870, now loomed over all Europe. In 1897, at Queen Victoria's Golden Jubilee, the Royal Navy had gathered 173 of its ships, fifty of them battleships, for a great display of peaceful power. Foreign dignitaries were taken down the seven-mile-long lines of warships to join in this celebration of British seapower, and their hosts reminded them that no ships had been brought back from foreign stations to add to the display. The show was designed to overwhelm the spectator, particularly the foreigner.

Yet within a year of the Diamond Jubilee, the old queen's nephew, Emperor Wilhelm of Germany, was setting out to disturb what for more than a century had seemed the natural order of things by challenging British naval supremacy and building his own battlefleet. By the turn of the century, along with most of continental Europe, he was rejoicing at British defeats at the hands of the Boers. The British responded. In April 1904 they put away for good their historical animosities with the French and concluded the entente cordiale that bound the two countries together against German attack. Portsmouth dockyard was put to work on the *Dreadnought*, building within twelve months the first of this new class of super-battleship designed to render older warships obsolete.

After the years of Victorian peace came a last few, golden years under Edward VII and George V. But the clouds of European war were massing, and British thinking about the Channel was changing. It was no longer a barrier to French invasion. It became instead the water across which a British Expeditionary Force might be sent into battle, to stand beside the French army in defending Belgium against invasion. In 1909 the Channel Fleet was absorbed into a Home Fleet. New bases were developed in Scotland from which the Grand Fleet might watch and contain the growing German navy. The importance of the Channel bases declined.

Nevertheless, it was at Portsmouth that in the summer of 1914 the Home Fleet assembled for the naval review, an event which, like the Jubilee Review, was a political demonstration of naval power as well as a decoration of the summer season. But the Archduke died at Sarajevo and Europe went sleep-walking towards war. Winston Churchill was at the Admiralty, consumed by the excitement of it all. Without consulting the cabinet he ordered naval mobilisation. Hilaire Belloc was at sea off Start Point in *Nona* when he saw ships of the Atlantic squadron steaming up the Channel: 'Like ghosts, like things themselves made of mist, there passed between me and the newly risen sun, a procession of great forms, all in line, hastening eastward. It was the Fleet recalled.'[14] All the navy's capital ships were ordered out of the narrow seas to their wartime stations in Scapa Flow and Rosyth. They steamed at full speed through the Straits of Dover on their passage to the north, bow-waves biting silver into the dark sea, smoke streaming black across the face of the summer clouds. Their departure was a last sign that the years of peace were over and that war was returning to the Channel.

CHAPTER 12

FOREIGN
FIELD

I n the fifteen years leading up to the First World War, the British
were again assailed by anxiety about invasion. Now the threat
came from the Germans, but it unleashed the same old arguments
between generals and admirals as earlier fears of the French. The official
conclusion was that invasion was impossible if Britain retained command of the sea. But the press and pressure groups continued to stir the
pot of popular agitation. Finally the War Minister, Lord Haldane,
concluded that the point on which to concentrate was 'the continued
occupation by a friendly nation like the French of Dunkirk, Calais and
Boulogne, the vital northern ports of the Continent'. And that 'implied
that we should have an Expeditionary Force sufficient in size and also in
rapidity of mobilising power to be able to go to the assistance of the
French . . .'[1]

In 1904 the old cross-Channel antagonists at last reached an understanding. The entente cordiale reflected the fact that Britain and France
had long since ceased to threaten one another and that the ambitions
of Germany, which had so humiliated France in 1870, increasingly
threatened Britain as well. Over the next ten years the entente bred
naval and military understandings. The Royal Navy would guard
France's Channel and Atlantic coasts, setting the French free to
concentrate their fleet in the Mediterranean, and if Germany ever
violated Belgian neutrality Britain would despatch an army to the

continent. It would support the French army, and keep those 'vital northern ports' out of German hands.

In 1914, all these British commitments were called in. On 3 August Germany invaded Belgium and on the following day, after hesitations that tested France's faith in her ally, Britain declared war. Two days later the Cabinet decided to despatch four of the six infantry divisions of Britain's little army, and one cavalry division, to France. With absurd over-confidence, the German admirals offered to try to intercept the ships taking the British Expeditionary Force across the Channel. The Chief of the General Staff patronisingly replied: 'This is not necessary, and it will even be of advantage if the Armies of the West can settle with the 160,000 English at the same time as the French and Belgians.'[2]

In the event the transports made the crossing unharmed. They sailed unescorted, but covering squadrons had sealed each end of the Channel and the Grand Fleet moved south to tackle any heavy German units which tried to intervene. On 12 August the first troops sailed from Southampton. Over the next ten days 120,000 men were transported to Le Havre, Rouen and Boulogne. For many there was an outing-on-the-ocean-wave atmosphere about their first crossing of the Channel, but a piece of doggerel tossed off by a young officer who made the journey later in the war does not quite succeed in concealing anxiety about what lay ahead:

> At last the time has come for
> Which we always used to pine,
> We're all aboard the *Viper* and we
> Lounge and smoke and dine,
> And watch the wheeling seagulls
> And the distant shores of France,
> And the sunlight on the water and
> The waves which gaily dance.
> For we're all off together
> We're making for the War,
> We don't need to worry
> Or grumble any more.[3]

None of the 120,000 was lost at sea; such was the secrecy of the operation that for days the Germans were unaware that a British army was at large upon the continent. And the battalions arrived to heroes' welcomes: 'Our journey was a sort of triumphal progress, and wherever we stopped the whole population appeared to be there, offering us bouquets, chocolate, bread, fruit . . . every sort of thing!'[4] 'Home before Christmas' was the mood, until the shells began to fly.

The Expeditionary Force was soon in action. In staff talks in 1911 the British had agreed that it would fight on the left of the vastly larger French armies. In terms of size at least, it really was the 'contemptible little army' that British propaganda claimed the Kaiser had called it. Nevertheless, for a month in August and September it fought and marched and fought again beside the French, conforming 'to its disgust and disappointment', said *The Times* in full jingoistic flow, 'with the movements of the French in retreat'.[5] That retreat took the British army all the way from Mons in southern Belgium, past Le Cateau and St Quentin in Picardy, into the Île de France around Paris. In these weeks it was operating further from the Channel and deeper into France than any British troops would again until the very last weeks of the war. For commanders and men alike, the campaign was a shattering experience, and twice the commander in chief, Sir John French, talked of detaching his exhausted army from the French, retreating across the Seine for rest and recuperation, fortifying a base on the French Atlantic coast, even withdrawing to the United Kingdom. Kitchener, the Minister for War, had to take a destroyer across the Channel to order him to go on fighting beside his allies.

French's fears for his army were overdone. The Germans had exhausted themselves as they marched so far into France. At last came the French counter-attack on the Marne. Now the Germans drew back to the Aisne. They would remain deep inside France until the very end of the war, but there was to be no repetition of the French catastrophe of 1870, no anticipation of the French disaster of 1940.

Yet these first weeks of the war could have panned out very differently. In their assault on France the German armies followed the plan laid down by General Alfred von Schlieffen in 1905. With all the assurance of the General Staff he prescribed the strategy and logistics of an invasion of France. Thirty army corps – nine-tenths of the German army's total strength – would be deployed on the western front. The main attack would be launched on the right, crossing Belgium and swinging down through northern France to envelop Paris from the west. To Schlieffen, blind to political considerations, it was unimportant that this violation of Belgian neutrality would bring Britain into the war, for his infallible projections showed that by Day 31 after mobilisation the German army would be on the Somme and by Day 42 victorious before Paris.

In that advance, Schlieffen had ordained, the right-hand man of the right-hand company of the right-hand division of the German attack must 'brush the coast with his sleeve'. 'Should the English land and advance, the Germans will halt . . . defeat the English and continue the operations against the French.'[6] But in 1914 the stubborn Belgian defence of Antwerp blocked the German right wing's way to the sea. In consequence it turned towards Paris and moved south not along the coast but 100 miles inland. Without that Belgian obstinacy, the Germans would have taken the Channel ports. If they had, Britain would once again have faced an enemy within 25 miles of Dover. All those hundreds of thousands of British soldiers would have died in the years that followed not in Flanders and Picardy but south of the Somme, perhaps south of the Seine. As it was, the scene was being set for a massive 'British military presence in northern France and the Channel ports that was to last as long as the war.

Before the conflict settled down into trench warfare, there came the 'race to the Channel'. After the French victory on the Marne the two armies glared at each other for a while. Then each side set out to look for a way round the other's flank. In doing so, they despatched divisions, corps and armies northward, always seeking to reach out beyond the enemy into undefended country. The Belgians sallied out from Antwerp in the hope of joining forces with the French and British. They were forced back into the fortress and Britain sent them seaborne reinforcements. Beside himself with excitement, Winston Churchill, then First Lord of the Admiralty, plunged into the affair. He led a personal striking force of Rolls Royce limousines converted into armoured cars and a scratch force of sailors, grandly entitled for the occasion the Royal Naval Division, in a fleet of London buses along the coast road from Ostend to Antwerp. There, he busied himself with plans for the defence of the city. But Antwerp fell, Churchill went home, the British were re-embarked, and the Belgians were left to fight their way along the coast to join hands with Allied forces coming up from the south. 'German Dash for Calais Stopped by the Allies', announced the *Daily Sketch*.

But the Germans were still determined to fight their way into the Channel ports. The Belgians had flooded the coast road, so the Germans shifted inland and at the very end of October 1914 they attacked at Ypres. It was only 25 miles from Dunkirk, only 50 miles from Calais and Boulogne. The British were clinging to the salient around the little Flanders city only by their fingernails and a breakthrough here would open up the way to the sea. The new German commander in chief, Falkenhayn, launched new divisions into the assault, replacing the old formations that had been consumed by the advance to the Marne. The German ranks at Ypres were filled with the cream of young civilian manhood, university students and schoolboys, more often than not led by their teachers. They were shot down in their thousands by the uneducated, cynical professional soldiers of what was left of the British Expeditionary Force. Slum kids from the Gorbals saw off the finest students of Heidelberg and Tübingen. The Germans called it a *Kindermord*, a massacre of the innocents. At the end of it, the British army still held the Ypres salient and the Germans were as far as ever from capturing the Channel ports.

After that defensive success, the line stabilised. It ran pretty well due south from Nieuport on the North Sea coast. The end of the line here was held by what was left of the Belgian army, hanging on to a last small corner of Belgium, and in Nieuport a huge and very moving monument commemorates King Albert and his gallant little army. It towers over the sluice gates which, opened to admit the waters of the

North Sea and the Channel, spread a wilderness of flood water in front of the advancing Germans. From Nieuport the line looped round Ypres in the famous salient. The line continues past Givenchy, Vimy Ridge and Arras, past the great monument to the Allied dead at Thiepval and on to the Somme. The war cemeteries along it mark its course, still cherished more than eighty years after the killing ended. Then, beyond the Somme, it turns away to run south-eastwards across France all the way to the Swiss frontier.

Between the Belgians and the Somme, the British Expeditionary Force held most of the line. It was always a lightweight beside the French and against the German armies, and it had been terribly mauled in the battles of those early months of the war. It held a 70-mile front, roughly 50 miles inland from the sea. For thousands of British soldiers, the quadrilateral of French soil behind it became synonymous with France itself, its towns and villages part of the English scenery, their names mangled into English approximations. For the living it became a part of Britain, a home away from home across the water. For the dead it became 'forever England'.

The area's character was shaped by the demands of the firing line. In the words of Malcolm Brown of the Imperial War Museum, that front:

> was a monster, it was a Hydra, a thing with many heads, and also with innumerable limbs. Over the years the Western Front grew and developed until it became a society, a world on its own, a temporary alternative civilisation . . . Its ramifications stretched far behind the fire-step and the machine-gun post, to the artillery lines, the billet villages, the supply dumps, the training-grounds, the casualty clearing stations, the base hospitals, the veterinary establishments, not to mention the baths (often brewery vats) to which the troops came from time to time to be deloused. And the estaminets and brothels, one might add, and the towns and cities away from the war zone into which men could occasionally escape for a taste of quasi-normal life. It also had its postal and transport systems, its own labour organization, its canteens, its concerts, its burial force.[7]

Seen otherwise, however, the character of this quadrilateral of French soil was shaped not by the front line but by the fact that it lay so close to England. Its base ran along the French shore of the English Channel. From the English coast you could see the French cliffs, in Kent you could hear the great bombardments that preceded an offensive, and when the mine under Messines Ridge was detonated the explosion could be heard in London itself. Officers and men released from the demands of the Hydra could be home on leave in England within a day. The headquarters, the depots, the training camps and the hospitals that sprawled along the French Channel coast lay within a couple of hours' journey from England. And yet people at home, protected by the era's stiff-upper-lip discretion about the horrors of the front line, never really understood what was going on in this new piece of England just across the water. The establishments along the coast that supported the war proved inadequate interpreters of England to the front-line fighters, and of the front line to England.

Today the tourist trade has named this Channel shore the 'Opal Coast', whose gentle beaches seem to stretch to eternity. The country inland is welcoming, a far cry from Flanders further north. It is dotted with old towns – Amiens, Abbeville, Arras, St Omer – their medieval charms long since recovered from the devastation of war.

Yet everywhere there are reminders of the support services that settled down in this area behind the fighting lines. The Channel ports – Boulogne, Le Havre, Dieppe, Calais – are the places from which the leave ships and hospital ships departed and where new drafts arrived. The railways that linked the ports and the front are mostly neglected now and overgrown with weeds, but their traces are still there. The sand dunes at Étaples are the same ones in which the great training camp was established, the 'bull ring', devoted to hardening new arrivals before they were despatched to the trenches. There were base hospitals beside the sea also, marked now by the cemeteries in which lie buried the surgeons' and doctors' failures to work medical miracles on the gravely wounded. And in the later years of the war Montreuil housed the general headquarters of the British armies in France. Here Sir Douglas Haig gave his 'backs-to-the-wall' order in March 1918, when it looked as if the German assault might sweep the British armies in France into the sea, and here he still sits heavy in bronze on his bronze horse.

What went on in these headquarters, supply dumps, bases, training camps and hospitals simultaneously served and angered the men of the front line. They served them with orders and purposes, food and military supplies, reinforcements and medical care. They inflamed them with the anger of fighting men of any era against those who seem not to share their hardships and yet expect of them the respect due to superiors and fellow men-at-arms. The front-line soldiers looked at the generals, far back in their châteaux; at the disembarkation officers, the rail transport officers, the administration officers and quartermasters, at the doctors making their Olympian life-or-death decisions, at the staff officers and aides-de-camp drawn from elegant regiments, at anything that wore red tabs and did not seem to share their dangers – and they did not like what they saw.

As its last old soldiers go to join their comrades who died eighty-five years before them, the words of the poets among them survive. They sang many different songs, of exultation, courage, grief and blind terror; but to our ears they are at their most convincing when they sing of disillusion. They hated in particular the men in the rear. Three examples catch the tone.

A company sergeant major, with only fleeting poetic ambitions, composed a jingle:

> Haig and his mob keep well to the Rear,
> Living in luxury, safe in old St Omer,
> Flashing Red Tabs, Brass and Ribbons Galore,
> What the hell do they know about fighting a War?[8]

In *Goodbye to All That* Robert Graves takes aim at the staff, with a throwaway line about Paul the Pimp, a staff-officer who 'wore red tabs upon his chest/And even on his undervest'.[9]

But it was Siegfried Sassoon's poem 'Base Details' that most success-fully skewered for posterity the 'London Clubmen dressed as Colonels,

Majors and Captains with a conscientious objection to physical discomfort'[10] who sat at comfortable desks in the Channel ports:

> If I were fierce, and bald, and short of breath,
> I'd live with scarlet Majors at the Base,
> And speed glum heroes up the line to death.
> You'd see me with my puffy petulant face,
> Guzzling and gulping in the best hotel,
> Reading the Roll of Honour. 'Poor young chap',
> I'd say – 'I used to know his father well;
> Yes, we've lost heavily in this last scrap.'
> And when the war is done and youth stone dead,
> I'd toddle safely home and die – in bed.

So much for poets. For more ordinary men it was the training camps,
the 'bull rings', which most angered the front-line soldiers. At Harfleur
near Le Havre and at Étaples on the coast below Montreuil enormous
tented camps were established. Through them passed new drafts on
their way to the front, to be initiated into something of the hardships
which awaited them there. The process of conditioning started with a
20-mile route march to Étaples from Boulogne: 'The whole approach
from Boulogne was depressing, with hospitals and cemeteries lining the
whole route. When we got to Étaples it was new kit and rifles and more
abuse until we got to our quarters.'[11]

Some took the training cheerfully enough: 'The instructors gave us a
lively time of it with bayonet fighting – "Gnash-your-teeth-show-the-
whites-of-your-eyes-and-look-as-if-you-mean-it!" We spent a charming
day killing straw Germans . . .'[12] But units pulled out of the line for rest
and recuperation were also put through the bull-ring; and so were men
who had been wounded and now were returning to the front. They
found the training irrelevant to the conditions of real war that they
already knew at first hand; and they resented the mindless brutality of
the drill sergeants and the remoteness of the officers in command.

For the Canadians and Australians, there were few constraints of
discipline or deference. When they found their commanders wanting,

they told them so. The British troops endured longer, but in the end they too rebelled. For one soldier the camp at Étaples was 'a hellish dump without a single redeeming feature'. For another, 'One PT sergeant was so maltreating the soldiers in the Bull Ring that I had a dust-up with him and laid a complaint, but I was just rapidly posted away to the front.'[13] In the summer of 1917, resentment of conditions at Étaples led to mutiny. Hundreds of soldiers broke out of camp, defied their officers, manhandled troops sent to contain them, and went rampaging, looting and raping down the road toward Le Touquet. Some of them joined forces with a small army of deserters who were camped out among the sand dunes, living a life of brigandage almost as ferocious as the warfare in the trenches from which they had fled. In the end, authority reasserted itself, but it hushed up the outbreak, and when order was restored it handled the mutineers far more gently than the French army handled the vastly more dangerous mutinies in its own ranks. The worst abuses were attended to, but the bull-rings, like the ports, hospitals, railway stations and supply dumps, went on serving the destructive gods of the front line.

The base hospitals along the Channel coast represented the last stage or the last stage but one in a long process of evacuation of the wounded. Men in the trenches longed for a 'Blighty' wound that would take them home, but even a base hospital in France was something to be desired. Siegfried Sassoon, suffering nothing more heroic than severe enteritis, utters a 'spontaneous Magnificat' when a doctor orders him down the line: 'Now, with any luck, I thought, I'll get a couple of weeks at one of those hospitals on the coast, at Étretat or Le Tréport, probably. The idea of reading a book by the seaside was blissful.'[14] In the hospitals and convalescent camps, the wounded soldier saw another, gentler army face, a show of that old-world innocence that adds such poignancy to so many First World War stories:

I got wounded during the Somme. We went down to St Valéry, near the coast and that was absolutely wonderful down there ... They tried to nurse us back to good health, those of us who weren't wounded badly enough to go to England. They marched us down every day down to the beach with a smashing band . . . and we had to do country dancing to try to take our minds off the war . . . my partner was a bricklayer with three kids, and there would be this chap, 'Bow to your partner. Hold hands. Advance three paces'. Just imagine me with a bricklayer going backwards and forwards. He said, 'If my kids could see me now, they'd never speak to me again.'[15]

For most of the wounded, the journey away from the war had been a way of the cross, as stretcher bearers took them down the communication trench to an advanced dressing station, lurching motor ambulances bore them further back to field hospitals, and crowded hospital trains carried them to base hospitals in France. Those with 'Blighty' wounds were taken to the ship for England. Suffering and death followed these casualties back to the Channel coast, as all those war cemeteries beside the sea testify. Those who survived long enough could escape the war on the ship for home: 'The Hospital Ship left Rouen about midday. While we steamed down the Seine in fine weather I lay watching the landscape through a porthole with a sense of thankfulness which differed from any I had ever known before.'[16]

The Channel ports spelt another kind of escape as well, escape without the pain of wounds, the leave ships to England. 'A week's leave! The ship steamed out of Boulogne crowded with officers and men. The escorting destroyers picked her up on her twenty-knot dash for Folkestone. England again!'[17] Once the front line set him free, a man could be aboard a ship within hours, in Dover or Southampton soon afterwards, dancing at the Café Royal the following day. But what the system released the system recalled. Every ship departing passed another bound for France, with its load of men returning to serve the Hydra of the trenches.

The war at sea was the navy's business. The Royal Navy's big ships were deployed in the north, at Scapa Flow and at Rosyth. But there was always a danger of German warships getting loose in the North Sea, as the bombardments of Hartlepool and Scarborough in December 1914 testified. It was the submarine flotillas, however, which were to develop into the greatest threat to British superiority at sea.

At first they operated from bases on the German coast. British patrols had the whole of the North Sea in which to intercept them before they broke through into the Atlantic or the Channel. But once the German army had occupied the Belgian coast, the navy set about developing submarine bases at Ostend and Zeebrugge. The submarine threat came 300 miles nearer to its targets.

The Dover Patrol had been established at the outbreak of war, with four cruisers, twenty-four destroyers, thirteen submarines and a mass of armed trawlers and other light craft, and with its headquarters in Dover Castle. Rear Admiral Horace Hood, scion of a family of Hoods who had made great names for themselves in battle against the French in eighteenth-century wars, commanded the Patrol. Some French warships were attached to the Dover Patrol, and on one occasion Hood went into action flying his flag in a French destroyer. It was, said the French, the first occasion on which an officer of the Royal Navy had ever flown his flag in a French warship. As such, it was an occasion to be noted in the ancient story of cross-Channel love, hatred and restless rivalry.

To contain the submarine threat, the Dover Patrol laid a minefield along the Belgian coast. It tried to reinforce it with a barrage of nets and mines stretching from England to France, just east of the route from Dover to Calais. In October 1916 the Germans launched an attack in force on the light forces patrolling the barrage. They did great damage, and there was no guarantee they could not repeat the exploit: 'It is as easy to stop a raid of express engines with all lights out at night, at Clapham Junction,' wrote the officer who had by now succeeded Hood in command of the Dover Patrol, 'as to stop a raid of 33-knot destroyers on a night as black as Erebus, in waters as wide as the Channel.'[18] Yet to illuminate the barrage spelt suicide for the small ships that patrolled it.

Fifty-seven British and Allied merchantmen had been at sea in the Straits that night, protected by the same darkness which gave the Germans their advantage. If the attackers had got among them it would have been a great Channel tragedy. In fact, more often than not the Dover Patrol succeeded in keeping the Germans out of the waters of the Channel, and the army's cross-Channel supply lines were never broken.

But submarines, minelayers and fast surface craft did break through, and in 1917 Edward Evans, a British destroyer commander who had won fame by marching to within 150 miles of the South Pole with Captain Scott five years earlier, engaged, rammed and sank a German destroyer off Dover itself. With his action he won yet more fame, the DSO, promotion and the lasting sobriquet 'Evans of the *Broke*'.

A year later, in the last January of the war, the Royal Navy went over to the offensive. Germany was preparing for its last throw, as much at sea as on land. Its submarine fleet was still increasing, operating aggressively from its bases at Ostend and Zeebrugge. By now Vice-Admiral Roger Keyes commanded the Dover Patrol, and he determined to take decisive action to block both ports. On St George's Day, 23 April 1918, he led a force of destroyers and block ships against the entrance to the Germans' submarine base at Zeebrugge on the Belgian coast. The concept was bold, the execution heroic, but the moon was full and the German defences prepared. The ships came alongside Zeebrugge's great mole and marines and soldiers stormed ashore. They fought off German counter-attacks and sank their block ships in the throat of the harbour. It was the kind of dashing, sea-borne attack that the British thought was their kind of warfare, and it shone by contrast with the disasters that were descending on the army 100 miles away in northern France at just that time. Keyes got a knighthood, eleven men Victoria Crosses.

But the attack achieved little of lasting value. A parallel attack on the base at Ostend was a complete failure, and the canal network which linked both ports to Bruges enabled the Germans to shift their sub-marines between them. They still threatened Allied shipping, and the 170 men who lost their lives and the 400 wounded at Zeebrugge died and suffered for little real purpose.

The military presence in northern France had a profound effect on the attitudes of the British at every level towards their French allies. Initial enthusiasm for gallant partners-in-arms faded as quickly as euphoria about the war itself. General Sir John French was at odds with his allies within the first month of the war, and even after Douglas Haig replaced him the relationship at the very top remained crabbed and suspicious. Lower down, enjoyment of the food and wine and kisses that greeted the troops in the first days of the war soon gave way to resentment of the people among whom they lived. To the troops the French peasant was dirty, suspicious, avaricious, the French soldier a selfish and unreliable ally. Resentments flourished. When prices rose in the roadside cafes that brought the soldiers some fleeting comfort, they became convinced that the French were profiteers. When French whores hustled their clients, they decided that Frenchwomen were unfeeling monsters. When plans for the great offensives leaked to the enemy, Frenchmen were spies.

Yet at the same time the soldiers knew the fighting quality of the French army; the efficiency of its artillery, which frequently came to the rescue of nearby British divisions in difficulties; the very size of France's commitment to the war and the length of the front it held all the way from the Somme to the Swiss border. Respect, even affection, mingled with soldierly disdain. There was respect too for the civilian population, for peasants and miners who remained at work within a mile or so of the front line, for the endurance of Frenchwomen left to farm on the edge of a British battlefield while their menfolk were fighting at Verdun or in Champagne. The British armies in France saw a people in extremis, a countryside ravaged by war. In their own sufferings they often had little compassion to spare for their allies, but in their better moments they knew that they owed it to them.

Attitudes to the Channel itself were affected too. For centuries it had been seen as marking a divide between ancient enemies. The French Channel ports had always been potential threats to England's security, the waters of the Channel its ultimate security. Suddenly the Channel became a thoroughfare, a highway to the war. The French Channel ports were absorbed into the most complex military organisation that Britain had ever established overseas, their operations supervised by British officers. So Harfleur, into the breach in whose walls Henry V had so famously stormed, became a British military base. Calais became once again almost a part of England, as it had been for 200 years before Bloody Mary lost it. Boulogne, where Napoleon had massed his invasion barges, became the place where home leave began. And Cap Blanc Nez, from which Frenchmen had always looked across the water towards the most obstinate of their enemies, became like Dover a lookout point for the Dover Patrol.

In these years something changed in the quality of the cross-Channel relationship. Happy ignorance of one another gave place to a wry and cautious intimacy. To know one another did not mean liking one another, and too often intimacy bred dislike and even contempt. But with intimacy came some degree of knowledge, a few words of French, a kind of military domestication of French towns and villages. Millions came to know the broken French villages of the war zone, the poor French towns of the rear areas, the modest luxury to be had in the Channel ports themselves. Later, more millions came to know the war memorials and cemeteries of northern France and Belgium. Corners of French fields became forever England.

The French made similar if less intense discoveries about the British. They haggled with British billeting officers in the rear areas, they watched the British battalions march by on their way to battle, they saw the Hydra of the front line spread its tentacles throughout northern France. There was much for them to resent, but it took a very blinkered Frenchman or woman not to appreciate that the purpose of this great military machine, with all the clumsy damage it did to those around it, was to defend French soil. It was the indispensable instrument of an ally who, for all Sir John French's early waverings, remained steadfast to the last. The Great War, in short, leached some of the ignorance and bitterness from the old cross-Channel relationship.

For four years the trench line in Flanders and Picardy held fast. Attempts to drive it eastwards at Loos, the Somme and Passchendaele all failed. The tank attack at Cambrai promised better things and the Germans pulled back to the Hindenburg Line, but the essential character of the Western Front remained unchanged from the winter of 1914 to the spring of 1918. It was an almost immobile war, fought by unseen thousands on each side, hidden in their underground burrows, raiding one another, undermining one another, bombarding and gassing one another.

Then suddenly, in March 1918, the static assumptions of trench warfare gave way to a war of movement. Russia had been driven out of the war, the Italians forced back from Caporetto. Once again the Germans could concentrate the bulk of their armies on the Western Front. They had a second chance to carry the Schlieffen plan to success, to capture Paris or drive the British Expeditionary Force into the sea before the trickle of American troops arriving in France through the Atlantic ports increased to a flood.

The Allies expected an all-out German attack but were uncertain where it would fall. Haig thought that the Flanders front at the north end of his line, where the First, Second and Third Armies guarded Dunkirk, Calais and Boulogne, was the most vulnerable. A breakthrough here and an advance of under 50 miles would bring the Germans to the Channel coast. Haig, seeking French reinforcements, argued that the French, by contrast, had depth behind them. They could ride out an attack, retreating if necessary to the Seine. In the event, the Germans chose to attack not the French nor the extreme north of the line but the southern end of the British sector, where the Fifth Army held a 30-mile front astride the Somme. Behind the Fifth Army lay Amiens and Abbeville, Rouen and Le Havre. Here the Germans had further to go to reach the Channel ports than in the north. But the Fifth Army was fully stretched, numerically weak, its positions exposed, its morale shaky, its leadership uncertain. On 21 March the Germans fell upon it.

Some Fifth Army brigades fought bravely, some broke, some were blown away by the German whirlwind. 'By the end of the ten days, the Fifth Army had gone back fifty miles, and we kept doing counter-attacks, take that wood, lose it, take it again, and so on. But it was always one step forward and three back . . .'[19] After four years of war, moral resources were close on exhausted: 'there were young boys, young men who'd just come out and hadn't got the esprit de corps, and they were running away'. 'I must confess', wrote a British officer afterwards, 'that the German breakthrough of 21 March, 1918 should never have occurred. There was no cohesion of command, no determination, no will to fight, and no unity of companies or battalions.'[20]

The Germans' immediate goal was Amiens. 'It is quite evident that the Boche means to get to Amiens,' a British general wrote in his diary, 'and if he does he will cut the British army off from the ports of Rouen and Havre, as well as separating us from the French Army.'[21] The Fifth Army reeled under the attack. French and British reinforcements were moved to its support but there was an immediate danger that the Allies would be driven apart. Haig issued his 'last man, last round' order. Engineers, cooks and cavalrymen were brought into the line. Half-trained new recruits were rushed across the Channel. 'What have you got there?' one eighteen-year-old records an English-speaking French-woman asking. 'Men, soldiers come to fight for their country,' replies the sergeant major. 'No, them's piccaninnies,' she replies, 'they should get home with their mother.' 'They've got to fight,' he replies. 'Ah! It's not right,' she says.[22]

The French commander, Foch, was given overall command of all the Allied armies. Gradually, the British army recovered its courage and resistance stiffened. The German attackers took terrible losses and their discipline began to crack. 'Well, we have won the war,' says a British divisional commander as he assesses a battle in which he has lost most of his men, for the Germans have suffered even greater losses than he.[23] There is the same kind of wry confidence lower down in the British ranks. 'More prisoners are coming back in bunches now,' records a German soldier. 'Our lieutenant talks with a wounded enemy officer who has been hit in the eye and arm by a shell fragment. We are astounded that he has the guts to talk to us. The lieutenant tells him that we are on way to the English Channel. But he replies with pride, "There are trenches over trenches all along the way!" '[24]

The attack, a week ago apparently unstoppable, grinds to a stop: 'the troops will not attack, despite orders', a German officer reports. 'The offensive has come to a halt.'[25] It reaches its furthest point at Moreuil near Amiens, only 30 miles from the Channel. The Germans abandon their hope of reaching the coast and turn south instead, towards Paris.

American troops move up to the line and Vera Brittain, then a nurse, later a writer, sees them swing past her field hospital. 'They looked taller than ordinary men,' she wrote, 'their tall, straight figures were in vivid contrast to the under-sized armies of pale recruits to which we were grown accustomed.' They looked, she thought, like 'Tommies in heaven'.[26]

A fortnight after the first attack, the Germans try again, this time in the north on the line of the little river Lys. Again, they are unable to carry their initial success to decisive victory and again their attacks grind to a halt. The German armies facing the British are exhausted and the threat to the Channel ports is over. But in the early summer of 1918 the Germans try yet again to break the Allied line, this time on the French front on the Marne. Here too they are ground down, and now they lose their last chance of victory. The Allies go over to the offensive, buoyed up by the incoming tide of Americans. Through the late summer and into the autumn the British and French armies surge eastwards, reinforced by the inexperienced but undaunted Americans. On 11 November the firing ceases. The war that for four years had made part of France British is over. It has turned old enemies into allies, and altered the significance of the Channel that lies between them.

CHAPTER 13

SEA, SAND AND SUNSHINE

The twenty years of peace that separated the First World War from the Second took further the process of domesticating the Channel. There was not much that man could do about seas, skies, tides and weather, and he was still at the mercy of Channel storms. But after centuries of settlement, exploitation and development, he had put his imprint nearly everywhere along the Channel coast, tamed most of the shoreline and classified the vagaries of geology, meteorology and the sea itself. In 1918 human violence had been banished from the Channel by the war to end war. Like Europe, it thought it could look forward to another century of peace.

Domestication bit deeply on the English coast. In the 1920s and 1930s Poole, Bournemouth and Christchurch were linked by unbroken urban development. The same happened between Worthing and Brighton, Margate and Ramsgate. Torquay extended its reach around Torbay. Taken all together, there are 50 miles of coastline submerged beneath houses, hotels and holiday camps. Add in the expansion of ancient fishing villages and nineteenth-century seaside resorts, and the figure doubles.

On the coast east of Brighton, development took a more considered form. There C. W. Neville founded Peacehaven, a vast seaside bungalow colony at the very point where the Greenwich meridian crosses the Channel coast. He endowed the place with its own garden city ethos and style, even its own logo. At Peacehaven and places like it, the lower-middle classes entered into their Channel inheritance: patriotic, deferential but essentially self-sufficient. It is still a place for house-improvers, dog walkers and deep-breathers when the November wind whips up the waves on the foreshore.

Elsewhere, ancient and modern rubbed against one another. Martello towers, lighthouses and coastguard cottages became desirable marine residences. Even places with ancient origins such as Pegwell Bay and Hengistbury Head got their own golf courses, links in a chain that seemed to fill the rural gaps between every brick and tarmac development the length of the Channel coast. The Isle of Wight, once withdrawn into itself and punctuated only occasionally by history, surrendered to the demands of ordinary holidaymakers. Education came to the coast, prep schools took over old Victorian mansions, and Dover College, Lancing and Roedean evolved instant traditions of their own.

Old Mr McMullen's taste for pleasure sailing attracted imitators, whose boats began to crowd the river at Dartmouth, the estuary at Salcombe and the harbour at Barfleur. One of them was Hilaire Belloc, who built a whole book – *The Voyage of the Nona* – around a voyage from the Welsh coast, round Land's End, and up the Channel. Amid all his prejudice, bombast and whimsy, he paints a picture of the English Channel coast as it was soon after the First World War, the best part of 100 years ago now, as seen from the cockpit of a little ship sailed by a man who knew and loved these waters.

Belloc starts with a tribute not to opinion but to fact. Put your faith in the Admiralty's Channel Pilot: 'There is no theorising, no mumbo-jumbo . . . The "Channel Pilot" tells you the truth. You stick blindly to its text and you are saved.'[1] But whimsical opinion follows close on the heels of fact. Fowey, to Belloc, 'is the harbour of harbours, and the last port town left without any admixture of the modern evil. It ought to be a kingdom of its own. In Fowey all is courtesy, and good reason for the chance sailing man.' Plymouth on the other hand is a place he prefers to pass by, 'what with Drake and the Armada, and the Bowls and the Rock upon the other side of the sea'. But up-Channel lies 'a heavenly piece of coast, all this southern bulge of Devon, with its little secret rivers and untainted towns'. Portland is another matter, for the Chesil Bank, with its 'rough and tumble shingle of great stones' and a bottom on which the anchor drags in any burst of wind, is enough to put the fear of God into any little-ship sailor. So is Portland Race, which swallowed a 14,000-ton merchantmen and its load of machinery, truly 'the master terror of our world'.

Poole is a famous harbour, used by Romans and Vikings and Saxons, and yet impossible to get into. As for Southampton Water, Spithead and the Solent, 'this patch of water is packed with history as no other in Britain, except London River' – and Belloc gallops off on a five-page excursion into the great London dock strike of 1890 whose only effect was to divert trade from London to Southampton. The small harbours of Sussex put him into better humour. Rye for example is neat and beautiful, but its harbour with its shifting sands is a cruel place. As for Dover, great port as it is, it is too big for Belloc. He finds its regulations bewildering and he shies away from a wreck of a munitions ship in which lie 'the bodies of men entombed'. In any case, in Dover 'one never knows that some great death-ship, on its way to Calais or Ostend, will not leap out suddenly upon one as one opens the harbour'.

The southern counties had long appealed to the modestly prosperous and the comfortably off. Now their numbers expanded. Little towns such as Lyme Regis and Rye attracted war widows, pensioners and the retired middle classes, living on their War Loan dividends. So, on a more expansive scale, did Bournemouth, Eastbourne and St Leonards. The rentier class took over Sussex and Kent, and to a lesser extent Hampshire and Dorset.

Writers and artists made a mark of their own. Sussex in particular became a kind of rural Bloomsbury. Intellectuals and aesthetes tended to keep away from the coast and settle in the South Downs' exquisite villages and little towns. So the writer Virginia Woolf settled at Rodmell near Lewes. Her sister Vanessa Bell set up a ménage a trois with husband and lover not far away, and it was from the well-loved route over the Downs to visit her sister that, in 1941, Virginia turned aside, loaded her pockets with stones, and drowned herself in the little river Ouse. Nearby at Ditchling lived Eric Gill the sculptor, who founded a community of artistic and religious enthusiasts and who practised yet more errant sexual behaviour than Vanessa and her ménage. Another artist, Walter Sickert the impressionist painter, spent four years in the 1930s teaching at Thanet School of Art in Kent. More improbably, T. S. Eliot took an attack of nervous exhaustion to Margate and there wrote much of *The Waste Land*.

Others found a particular local inspiration. Thomas Hardy was born and died within three miles of Dorchester, and his genius made Dorset his own. Daphne du Maurier did the same for the wild coasts of the West Country with *Jamaica Inn* and *Rebecca*. E. F. Benson, living and writing in a house that had once been owned by Henry James, succeeded in skewering Rye with his *Lucia* novels about the loves, hates, excitements and social distinctions of any introverted small town in the south of England. Graham Greene captured the viciousness of a different kind of Sussex resort in *Brighton Rock*. And in the years of his prosperity Rudyard Kipling made up for the six miserable childhood years he had spent in a boarding school in Southsea by setting himself up in a grand Jacobean manor house. He lived till his death in 1936 at Bateman's in East Sussex, writing, strolling proprietorially in his garden, entertaining ever more distinguished visitors, and having himself driven in state around the south country in his Rolls Royce limousine.

Ordinary people increasingly got in on the act as well. For the middle classes and even for the workers, holidays now were longer, and holidaymakers flocked to bed-and-breakfast resorts and the establishments which, after 1945, were to burst into full flower as holiday camps. A better class of visitor patronised places like Torquay (which is supposed to have promoted itself with the slogan 'Where every prospect pleases', forgetting that in the second half of the couplet 'only man is vile'). Ramblers came in pursuit of fresh air and exercise. They walked along the edge of the cliffs at the Seven Sisters and goggled at the sheer drop beneath their feet. Another kind of traveller took a single ticket from Victoria to Eastbourne, and cast himself upon the rocks at the foot of Beachy Head. And still the day-trippers came, as they had started to come in Victoria's golden days. *Brighton Rock* captures the flavour of their excursions:

> They had stood all the way from Victoria in crowded carriages, they would have to wait in queues for lunch, at midnight half asleep they would rock back in trains an hour late to the cramped streets and the closed pubs and the weary walk home. With immense labour and immense patience they extricated from the long day the grain of pleasure: this sun, this music, the rattle of the miniature cars, the ghost train diving between the grinning skeletons under the Aquarium promenade, the sticks of Brighton rock, the paper sailors' caps.[2]

This being Brighton, there was brassy pretension being played out in parallel to these simple pleasures of the poor, and again Greene has an eye for it:

> Young men kept on arriving in huge motoring coats accompanied by small tinted creatures, who rang like expensive glass when they were touched but who conveyed an impression of being as sharp and as tough as tin. They looked at nobody, sweeping through the lounge as they had swept in racing models down the Brighton Road, ending on high stools in the American Bar.[3]

Similar developments were taking place on the other side of the Channel. Holiday resorts stretched themselves around the Bay of the Seine in an unbroken line all the way from Deauville to Bernières. Le Touquet-Paris-Plage turned its back on war cemeteries and abandoned wartime hospitals and training camps. It flourished as a peacetime holiday resort, to which Parisians came down for the day or the week as Londoners went down to Brighton. Along the Belgian coast, resorts gradually recovered from wartime destruction. They joined hands, till the whole 40-mile coastline became one. Most of the places along this Belgian coast were dedicated to the working-class holiday pleasures of sand castles, moules and chips and beer, but one or two were defiantly up-market, here with stylish casinos and there with beaches catering, like England's Frinton, to the particular needs of the delicately nurtured upper-class child.

Cross-Channel travel grew. Millions of Englishmen had spent four years crouching in the mud of northern France; now they crouched beside their children to build sandcastles on French beaches, then wandered off, duty done, to have a drink and practise their wartime recollections of the French language upon the natives. Other English-men and women came on more grievous errands, in the great exploration of the world war battlefields for memories of lost sons, husbands and brothers. Kipling was one of them, driving around the fields of Flanders in his Rolls Royce, first pursuing some trace of his dead son and then researching his campaign history of the son's regiment, the Irish Guards.

The Imperial War Graves Commission did its best to assuage the grief of these thousands of cross-Channel travellers. It gathered the dead into its military cemeteries, making something simultaneously glorious and domesticated of their tragedy. Equality was one of its principles, the same headstone for every one of its residents, from Guards officer to Chinese labourer. So was the simplicity and discipline of the lines of headstones. Infinite care was devoted to maintaining the cemeteries, which can still be seen to this day. For the remains of those, like his son, whose very identity had died with them, Kipling coined the consolation 'Known unto God'. The architect Reginald Blomfield conceived the 'Sword of Sacrifice', a monument depicting sword superimposed on cross which forms the focal point of every cemetery. The largest of these vast empires of the dead are inland, at Tyne Cot in the Ypres salient and on the Somme. But the French coast has its own war cemeteries, hidden away behind the dunes or high on a cliff top, each of them filled with the bones of men who died of wounds or disease in the hospitals beside the sea.

With faster communications, quite frivolous reasons to cross the Channel came into their own. Food and wine were part of the attraction; so was the glamour of continental casinos and horse racing; so was the allure and fabled availability of French women. More and more British people could afford a gay weekend in a French Channel resort; a favoured dashing few took to flying over for lunch and a flutter on the horses or at the tables.

A different kind of Briton chose to settle in France. Paris and the Riviera were the greatest lures, but some of the Channel towns had established Anglo-Saxon colonies. Some refugees from Britain came in search of French style, some in pursuit of French prices. English families escaped embarrassment by letting the house in Kensington and taking temporary refuge in a resort like Ambleteuse, while strict economy gradually restored their balances with Barclays Bank.

Others had even more pressing reasons to get away from home. There was an established tradition of fleeing to the continent from one's creditors, and the French Channel ports attracted many of the defaulters. On his release from Reading Gaol Oscar Wilde had taken refuge in exile just outside Dieppe. Now, in the 1920s and 1930s, Anglo-Saxon writers, artists and aesthetes came again to the French Channel coast, and some of them could not tear themselves away when times changed. So P. G. Wodehouse lingered too long at Le Touquet in the summer of 1940 until the advancing Germans took him prisoner. They took him to Berlin, and there he made his naïve, ill-judged broadcasts on the German radio beamed to Britain. They looked, or could be made to look, like German propaganda, and malice in ministerial offices in London interpreted them as such. In the end it took victory and the magnanimity that goes with it to restore the nation's best-loved comic writer to the nation's favour.

The pressure on cross-Channel ferries and their terminals grew. There were travellers who wanted to get away from the vulgar scrum of ordinary passengers, and new ferry services were introduced to serve them. Some were luxurious, some specialised. In 1929 came the *Golden Arrow*. A Pullman boat train conveyed first-class passengers from Victoria to Dover. A specially built steamship, the *Canterbury*, took them across the Channel. In Calais they cleared French customs in their own customs shed. From there, the service became the *Flèche d'Or*, belting across the north French plain on its way to Paris.

In June 1940, Evelyn Waugh's Guy Crouchback is preparing to be sent to his death in the defence of Calais. His mind's eye turns not to the coming drama of war but to the luxurious routine of peace. He sees the town as if from the window of the Golden Arrow:

> No secret was made of their destination. Maps of that terra incognita were issued and Guy studied the street names, the approaches, the surrounding topography of the town he had crossed countless times, settling down to an aperitif in the Gare Maritime, glancing idly at the passing roofs from the windows of the restaurant-car; windy town of Mary Tudor, and Beau Brummell, and Rodin's Burghers; the most frequented, least known town in all the continent of Europe. There, perhaps, he would leave his bones.[3]

In its early days, the *Golden Arrow* offered the traveller a very special brand of exclusively first-class travel, with a cachet that Eurostar has yet to equal. In 1938 a night ferry was added to the amenities of travel to the continent, so passengers could sleep their way from London to Paris. Other well-off travellers wanted to take their cars across the Channel, and in 1931 the first specially designed car-carriers appeared on the crossing. In that year Southern Railway introduced its *Autocarrier*, built to outdo Townsend's competing ship, *Artificer*. With a carrying capacity of 300 passengers and a grand total of twenty-six cars, *Autocarrier* was the first of a long line of cross-Channel car ferries, each of them bigger and faster than its predecessor.

* * *

Southampton, Cherbourg and Le Havre were the home ports of ships of a grander kind, the transatlantic liners. By the 1920s steamers had been in service between Southampton and New York for the best part of a century and had become a part of the life of both cities. When she set sail on her one-way voyage into the history books the White Star Line's *Titanic* was Southampton-based and Southampton-crewed. Cunard, which also operated out of Southampton, was White Star's main competitor. The Cunarder *Lusitania* was torpedoed in 1915, but her sister-ship, the *Mauritania*, sailed on into the inter-war years, the best loved of all the transatlantic liners. She was joined by many others, French, American and British, three of them seized from Germany as post-war reparations. And between the wars came new ships, *Ile de France* and *Normandie*, *Queen Mary* and *Queen Elizabeth*, bigger and ever more luxurious. The new ships were faster too, *Normandie* fastest of all, winning the Blue Riband in 1937 with a crossing time of three days, twenty-two hours and seven minutes.

These great liners storming down the Channel at almost 30 knots were the Concorde of the inter-war years. When they steamed out of Southampton or Le Havre their first-class passengers epitomised fashion, glamour and importance. But in tourist class they carried a different kind of passenger. The great days of American immigration were over, but the liners still carried emigrants to Canada and the United States, excited by the new lives that lay ahead of them. Parting remained a sweet sorrow and the quayside ceremonies – the band playing, gangways removed, the breaking of the streamers between ship and shore as the tugs nudged the liner away from the quay – were all calculated to heighten emotion. So although one of the great ships left port every other day or so, each departure generated a new and insistent excitement among those who stayed behind, and those who saw them make their way into the ocean. Their passenger-lists, their attempts at record-breaking, their very passage down-Channel, all formed an integral part of life on the south coast of England in the 1920s and 1930s, as they continued to do in the early years after the Second World War.

Though it would have taken genius to recognise it, the writing was on the wall for the ocean liner quite early in the inter-war years. On 18 August 1919 'the first flying boat service in the world' came to the Channel. On that day an amphibian – a flying boat with a retractable undercarriage – took off from Southampton Water. She was a converted wartime machine, carrying four passengers in an open cockpit, and flew no further than Bournemouth. But soon the rare intrepid passenger was undertaking the five-hour flight to Paris in these primitive machines. In 1923 regular flights to the Channel Islands were introduced. So were more comfortable seven-seaters, in which the passenger sat in an enclosed cabin.

In 1924 a new company was formed, Imperial Airways. It brought together four companies that had pioneered post-war passenger aviation. It was government-inspired and government-subsidised, its prime purpose being to quicken imperial communications and bind the Empire together, and it raised the ambitions of aviation between the wars to a new and quite different level.

Imperial Airways operated from Southampton Water, with its maintenance base at Hythe. A fleet of twenty-eight four-engined Short flying boats was ordered, each of them capable of carrying twenty-four passengers and mail to the furthest reaches of the Empire at a speed of 150 miles per hour. Operations started late in 1936, and within two years Southampton was linked by air to Australia, Asia and South Africa. At each staging point handwritten cards were delivered to each passenger. They notified him of the name of the company's representative at that station and of the hour at which he would be called; they told him when the machine would take off; that lunch and tea would be served in flight; and that dinner awaited his arrival when the aircraft alighted for the night at Alexandria, Khartoum or Colombo.

The first of Southampton's flying boats were built by a little company called Supermarine. In the 1920s it turned its attention to building high-speed aircraft, in pursuit of the Oscar of fast flight, the Schneider Trophy. A gifted chief engineer, Reginald Mitchell, produced an aircraft that in 1921 took the trophy from its Italian holders at a record-breaking speed of 145 miles per hour. Supermarine won it again at Venice in 1927, and prepared to defend it in 1929, on a course laid out over its home waters in the Solent. One and a half million people came to watch; there was a last-minute crisis over a new cylinder block in the Super-marine's Rolls Royce engine; but come the day it stormed to victory at 328 miles per hour. To hold the Schneider Trophy for good Supermarine needed only to defeat the Italians again, in 1931. But the government withdrew its financial support; Supermarine was out of its depth in debt. A private donation saved the day, and in 1931 the Supermarine S6B completed the course at a triumphant 407 miles per hour.

From the winning design Supermarine developed the Spitfire fighter, which flew for the first time at Southampton in 1936. War clouds were gathering, and the aircraft was hurried into production, with the first Spitfires joining front-line squadrons early in 1939. Meanwhile, mysteri-ous secret establishments began to appear along the South Downs overlooking the Channel. Rumours about them abounded, and people talked of car engines mysteriously cutting out in their vicinity on dark nights. They were the first radar stations, part of the Chain Home system rushed into service in 1938 to guard the south and east coasts of Britain against intruding enemies. Radar and the Spitfire came into service just in time, for the years of the Channel's domestication were ending. Before long radar operators and fighter pilots would be in battle the whole length of the Channel.

But a few last years of peace remained, in which the optimist could believe that the domestication of the Channel might last for ever. That domestication takes its purest forms in the islands of the Channel. They come in many sizes from miniature to intimate, and each offers some-thing different to the visitor.

Brownsea Island in Poole Harbour runs to a mere 500 acres. In 1907 Baden Powell, still basking in Mafeking glory, held his first Boy Scout camp here. Between the wars rich owners barred visitors and preserved it from development, so that nature ran riot on the island. After the Second World War it passed into the hands of the National Trust, who run it still, trying to balance the conflicting needs of visitors and nature, kids on a day out on the one hand and red squirrels, herons and deer on the other.

Burgh Island in Devon is a very different kind of place, only just separated from Bigbury on the mainland alternately by sea and sand as the tide comes and goes. Its crowning glory is the Art Deco, Odeon Cinema architecture and decoration of the island's sole hotel. Better than anywhere else on the Channel coast, Burgh Island Hotel captures a slice of a certain kind of life between the wars, a place offering elegance beside the sea, gentle sea-bathing, golf in plus-fours on a Devon course, motoring in the Devon lanes, then back to tea, tea-dancing, champagne cocktails and dinner, and the shrill excitement of the flappers at the next table.

Mont-St-Michel on the frontier of Normandy and Brittany represents an earthier, more vigorous world. Its famous profile derives from the work of the medieval monks who built a monastery on this strange rock, just off the coast where Normandy meets Brittany. Over the centuries they piled buildings on top of one another on its precipitous sides and crowned its 300-foot summit with a glorious thirteenth-century church. Pilgrims came, sometimes perilously across the sands; and ever since the days of the French Revolution, which ended St Michel's religious reign, tourists have been coming in their wake. So now Mont-St-Michel attracts visitors by the raucous hundred thousand, who eat in the restaurants and buy tat and souvenirs in the shops that crowd the steep paths that take them up to the summit. All human life crowds into Mont-St-Michel, and above it the abbey church still sits in religious and architectural splendour, the 'Marvel' that has always been the ultimate goal for visitors to this extraordinary place.

From across the bay from Penzance, the profile of St Michael's Mount looks like that of Mont-St-Michel, but this is a very different kind of place. Its origins too are ecclesiastical, a priory that went the way of all the old religion in England in the sixteenth century and was privatised to the satisfaction of its new owners in the seventeenth. Now the National Trust keeps it in domesticated order, advertising its armoury, a Gothic drawing room and its fourteenth-century church. Where Mont-St-Michel is raucous, popular, infinitely vulgar, St Michael's Mount is infinitely proper; the visitor is advised to wear 'sensible shoes'.

The Isle of Wight represents a steep change in size, for this is no scrap of land or off-shore islet but a real island. It is easy to get at, a twenty-minute ferry ride away across the Solent, and its castles and forts have played occasional bit-parts in English history, yet it has always clutched to itself a certain sense of difference, its own brand of domesticity. Queen Victoria and her Dear Albert settled here in 1851, and in the queen's words Osborne House above Cowes offered 'a place of one's own, quiet and retired'. Here she shut herself away from the world for much of her widowhood and here she died. In the First World War, wounded officers were brought to Osborne to convalesce. Today, painstakingly restored by English Heritage, it displays the blend of royal grandeur with the rather cloying intimacy that Victoria and Albert contrived for themselves a century and a half ago.

Hotels and boarding houses sprang up all over the Isle of Wight in modest imitation of the queen's patronage and the island's main resorts still bear a heavy nineteenth-century imprint. But all around the Victorian centres spread the signs of later development. The Isle of Wight became the place where between the wars working men of discernment brought their families for a week of bed-and-breakfast beside the seaside. Every year in Cowes week a very different kind of visitor came to the island, the Royal Yacht Squadron kind, glossy with wealth, smooth with real or assumed distinction. But in the 1920s and 1930s the Isle of Wight belonged, as it still does, to the modest visitor, whose needs matched the modest hospitality that the islanders offered.

The Channel Islands, nestled between Normandy and Brittany, are different again. They demand rather more effort of their visitors but they offer much more of a change from life at home, with the chance of real sun and a novel, almost continental flavour. And visitors before the war could get there in a few hours from Weymouth, as in our time they can fly there in less than an hour from Heathrow.

There are nine islands in all, the main ones being Guernsey, Jersey, Alderney and Sark. Taken together they amount to no more than 75 square miles of fields, woods, cliffs and houses, a little over half the size of the Isle of Wight, with 150,000 people. Though they lie just off the

French coast, which is within sight on a clear day, they were never French possessions. In the tenth century the Normans annexed them to their new Duchy of Normandy, but after the conquest William I decided to attach them instead to the English Crown. English they remained, though most of the inhabitants went on speaking French. The Tudors vigorously fortified them against French attack, and in the English Civil War, when the islands were at odds with one another, Jersey supporting the king and Guernsey the parliamentarians, they nevertheless remained English possessions.

They withstood occasional French attacks through the eighteenth-century wars. Once, in 1781, the French got ashore, and in the Tate Britain art gallery in London there is a splendidly vivid representation of the fighting in the streets of St Helier that followed. John Singleton Copley was an American artist who left Boston on the last boat before the American Revolution. Stout loyalist and British nationalist, he was entranced by the story of Major Peirson, the twenty-four-year-old commander of the Jersey garrison, and made him a national hero.

The French attack itself was a heroic affair. On 6 January a force of 1,000 men landed in Jersey, unnoticed by a British garrison preoccupied with Twelfth Night celebrations. Six hundred of the attackers climbed a 500-foot cliff, leaving 400 trapped by the incoming tide. The British governor was surprised in his nightgown and promptly surrendered. Peirson rejected the surrender and led a successful counter-attack, only to be killed in Royal Square in the moment of victory. Copley's brave masterpiece shows him dying in the arms of his men. The structure of his picture is all diagonals, its colours martially scarlet, all its sentiments heroic. But the artist took the trouble to get every detail right, of military uniforms and of the town of St Helier alike. He added the poignant touch of Peirson's wife, fleeing with infant and nursemaid out of the bottom right-hand corner of the picture. With one picture he made himself famous and Peirson a hero.

Yet martial splendour is alien to the Channel Islands' traditions. Throughout the nineteenth century and between the twentieth-century wars, they were peaceful places, and when they were occupied in the

Second World War the inhabitants did their best – some say their shameful best – to live their lives in peaceful harmony with the occupiers. They have always enjoyed their own peculiar constitutional arrangements, with their Lieutenant Governors or Dames of Sark answerable to the British crown but in most matters free from direction by the United Kingdom. Throughout the twentieth century they attracted British visitors in increasing numbers, but they had agricultural underpinnings too. Three of them, Guernsey, Jersey and Alderney, have given their names to breeds of cattle and for a time they cornered the British market for new potatoes. Some of the islanders, using Portuguese immigrant labour, began to get into the cut-flower business as well, but its great growth, like that of the financial services industries, came later, after the Second World War. Before it, Jersey and Guernsey were for the British visitor undemanding places for holidays on the beach, pottering around the islands' lanes in a horse-drawn open carriage, or taking a boat ride round the harbour, from Jersey to Herm or from Guernsey to Sark, or even across the water to the real abroad of Mont-St-Michel or a Norman seaside resort.

The Isles of Scilly are by a large measure more diminutive. They lie 25 miles off Land's End and there are 140 of them, and they are almost certainly not the remains of legend's lost land of Lyonesse. Only five of them are inhabited and the population scarcely touches 2,000 – natives, summer residents and all. The Isles are owned by the Duchy of Cornwall, but the main one, Tresco, is pretty well a fiefdom of a single family, the Dorrien-Smiths. Every so often, questions about their rule ruffle the London papers. Some residents admire their businesslike ways, while others question what they see as paternalism and a tendency to monopoly.

But such questions scarcely interest the visitors who find their way to the islands across an often unpleasantly lumpy stretch of sea. Ever since the 1920s they have come to play on the beach, investigate the islands' sub-tropical flora, and nose around in what remains of their sixteenth-century fortifications, with romantic associations of a young Prince of Wales taking refuge there in the Civil War and with two forts known to this day as Cromwell's and King Charles's castles. Visitors' interest in the Scillies built up throughout the 1930s, only to be cut off by the war years in which the islands saw only a little garrison of bored soldiers and the occasional ship torpedoed off-shore. Then, after the war, came a broader interest. A few outsiders settled in the islands. The flow of day-visitors increased, and the introduction of a 20-minute helicopter service spared them the discomforts of the sea crossing from the mainland. When Harold Wilson, most incorrigibly middle-class of all Britain's prime ministers, bought a bungalow here, domestication appeared complete.

But the Scillies have a darker, much less domesticated history. These were the islands where, 250 years earlier, that most unfortunate of British admirals, Sir Cloudesley Shovell, ran his fleet upon the rocks. If he had survived he would have faced court martial and ruin but, as he staggered up the beach from the wreck of his flagship, a woman of the islands intercepted him. She hit him over the head, ripped an emerald ring from his finger, and left his body to the incoming tide among the rocks.

The Scillies have come a long way in the best part of three centuries since, given over since the 1920s to the domestic joys of sandcastles and sunbathing. Better than anywhere else around the Channel coast, they illustrate how far domesticity has succeeded in taming human nature, and on a summer's day, that success seems complete. But when in 1997 a freighter inexplicably ran herself on the rocks on the eastern side of St Mary's, and her cargo of shoes, shirts, golf bags and anoraks came bobbing ashore on the waves, the Scilly islanders gathered in her harvest as thoroughly as their ancestors had dealt with the wreckage of Sir Cloudesley's fleet. These were people whose ancestors had prayed 'not that wrecks should happen, but that if any wreck should happen, Thou wilt guide them into the Scilly Isles'.[4] And the elements play their own inimitable part in challenging domesticity. In winter the westerly gales sweep in from the Atlantic, the storm-clouds race up the Channel, the seas rise and the waves crash upon the rocks. The Scillies seem for a time to be going the way of Lyonesse and drowning beneath the waters.

So much then for domestication, in the Scillies, in the Channel's other islands, along the Channel's coast or on the bosom of its waters. In fair weather it seems to have conquered the Channel, conquered it with pleasure boats and sandcastles and ice-cream cornets. And then nature reasserts itself in all its fury and reminds presumptuous mortals who is boss.

CHAPTER 14

ESCAPE
FROM
DISASTER

On 3 September 1939, Britain again declared war on Germany, and a new British Expeditionary Force was despatched to France. It moved across the Channel with greater deliberation than in 1914. This time it was the Poles, not the Belgians, who were under attack, and there was nothing the Allies could do to help them. Two divisions arrived in France in October, two more in November. They crossed from Southampton to Cherbourg, assembled between Normandy and the Loire and eventually moved northwards towards the Belgian border. Once again the British took up positions on the left flank of a vastly larger French army. The expeditionary force's headquarters was set up near Arras, where its commander, Lord Gort, and his corps and divisional commanders had learned their trade in the last war to end war. Among them was General Sir Alan Brooke, later Lord Alanbrooke, who was to be the Chief of the Imperial General Staff for most of the war. There was no hurry, Brooke noted in his diary: 'I was assured ... that it was quite impossible for the Germans to attack through Belgium before the winter sets in.'[1] The British and the French settled down to wait.

In the months that led up to the war, preparations to fight it came slowly to the Channel coast. For Britain, the 1930s were divided years; divided between on the one hand rejection of the very idea of another war, and on the other reluctant but increasing acceptance of its inevitability. The Oxford Union had resolved: 'In no circumstances will this house fight for King and Country.' Stanley Baldwin had warned Parliament: 'The bomber will always get through.' But he had added words whose logic committed Britain to involvement in the affairs of the continent: 'Since the day of the air, the old frontiers are gone. When you think of the defence of England, you no longer think of the chalk cliffs of Dover; you think of the Rhine. That is where our frontier lies.'[2] In the late 1930s Britain slowly began to rearm. In 1938, at Munich, Chamberlain bought time with dishonour; but after it the pace of rearmament accelerated.

Above all, throughout the 1930s preparations pressed ahead to meet the new threat of attack from the air. Supermarine had been developing the Spitfire in Southampton, and a chain of primitive but top-secret radar stations was being built along the North Sea and Channel coasts. The Royal Observer Corps mobilised men and women with binoculars to supplement the wonders of technology. The aircraft industry was put into what passed in peacetime for overdrive and in 1938 Fighter Command formed its first monoplane squadrons. Gas masks were issued, conscription introduced. There was fear but little surprise when at last war came. Announcing it, Neville Chamberlain's voice came thin over the airwaves, the voice of an old man whose hopes of peace were now dashed; but to the nation it declared an inevitable war.

Chamberlain's broadcast marked the start of a five-year period in which the Channel played a central role in history, starring in a way it rarely had before. Yet its early months were bereft of drama and indeed of action, though its waters became an essential part of the British Expeditionary Force's lines of communication, to be guarded as in the first war against intrusion by German ships and attacks by aircraft. Along their border with Germany the French stood on the defensive and the Germans showed no eagerness to attack. Belgium maintained its neutrality. In France and Britain, with their haunting memories of the last war, the people relapsed into an edgy passivity, hoping that somehow the war could be won without fighting, or at least without fighting in France. By the beginning of 1940, journalists were already writing about a 'Phoney War'.

In the course of the 1930s the French had fortified the length of their border with Germany for defensive war. The shell-proof forts of the Maginot Line were designed for mutual support. They were surrounded with fields of barbed wire, linked to one another with underground railways, their garrisons protected in deep concrete shelters. Visitors from the British Expeditionary Force were impressed, for these were unsinkable 'underground warships' with powerful guns in retractable turrets. But Alanbrooke, visiting one of the largest of the Maginot forts, wrote: 'I am not convinced that it is a marvellous military accomplishment. Millions of money stuck in the ground for a purely static defence . . . Their most dangerous aspect is the psychological one, a sense of . . . sitting behind an impregnable iron fence.'[3]

Maginot had given the French the same sense of impregnability as the Channel had long given the British. But at the Luxembourg border, the Maginot fortifications ended. For a further 200 miles France sheltered behind nothing more robust than Belgian neutrality. Through-out the exceptionally harsh winter of 1939–40, the men of the British Expeditionary Force and the French army put the last war's techniques of defence to work, digging trenches and redoubts and spreading barbed wire entanglements across northern France from the Ardennes to the coast. The British called their works the 'Gort Line'; but they could produce nothing to compare with the apparent impregnability of Maginot's.

In April 1940, the Germans attacked Norway and Denmark. The Royal Navy went into action, troops were landed along the Norwegian coast. Both sides' losses in men, ships and aircraft were heavy, but the Germans took control of the country. Then, on 10 May, the real war began. The Germans attacked Holland, Belgium and Luxemburg, sending dive bombers, parachute and glider forces and shock troops against cities, forts and airfields. At once there was talk of spies signalling from dark farmhouses and parachutists dressed as nuns. The French armies and the British Expeditionary Force, by now ten divisions strong, moved into Belgium to meet the Germans. They advanced 'on a most glorious spring day with all nature looking quite its best'[4] to an enthusiastic welcome from ordinary Belgians.

The Allies' aim was to hold the line of the River Dyle before Brussels, but when they reached it they found it unfortified, and looked back with regret to the prepared positions they had left behind in France. They did not hold it long. On 12 May the Germans switched the focus of their attack further south, through the hills and woods of the Belgian and French Ardennes. In doing so, they turned inside-out the first war's Schlieffen plan of a right hook through the Belgian plain and down the Channel coast. Now the weight of the attack fell on Sedan, where in 1870 the Prussians had trapped the French army. By 13 May, three days after the attack in the west had begun, the first Panzer divisions were across the Meuse.

The French were holding this section of the front lightly, for no one believed that a tank army could fight its way through such close country. For the best part of a day the fighting along the Meuse hung in the balance, and a resolute counter-attack might have cut the attack short. But already the French were showing signs of the defeatism that so quickly consumed them. On 15 May, Churchill's private secretary, John Colville, quotes Churchill's defence adviser, 'Pug' Ismay: 'He says the French are not fighting properly; they are, he points out, a volatile race and it may take them some time to get into a warlike mood. Pray Heaven not too long!'[5]

The Germans steadily pushed forward from the river and out of the wooded Ardennes. Now their tank armies were free to race across northern France towards the Channel. By 17 May, Colville is quoting senior officers just back from a visit to the French government with Churchill: 'the French were not merely retreating but were routed. Their nerves were shattered by this armoured warfare and by the German air superiority, and the French Government were upended by this sudden shattering of their faith in the invincible French army.'[6] British Cabinet minutes record the despair of the French prime minister, Reynaud: 'He said that the counter-attack last night on the Germans who had broken through south of Sedan had failed and the road to Paris was open and the battle was lost. He even talked about giving up the struggle.'[7] Within a week, the Germans were on the Somme battlefields.

By 20 May, they were beyond them. German tanks had reached Amiens and were advancing towards Abbeville and the Channel coast itself. They were past the point at which the British had finally stopped them in 1918. Now they broke through to the sea. On 21 May their tanks reached the little resort of Le Crotoy on the estuary of the Somme, where 600 years earlier Edward III had only just escaped being trapped with his back to the Channel. Now there were hundreds of thousands of French, British and Belgian troops north of the Germans' line of advance, cut off from the rest of France. The British divisions streaming westwards across Belgium and northern France to the coast faced encirclement. 'It looks like the retreat from Mons beginning all over again,' said Colville to a fellow private secretary. 'It is awful the way history repeats itself.' 'I wish history would repeat itself,' is the reply, 'but I am afraid it is not going to. There seems to be no proper liaison or co-operation between the French, British and Belgian Staffs and the whole thing is dropping to pieces through sheer ineptitude.'[8]

The British mounted an armoured counter-attack at Arras. They briefly succeeded in rattling a Panzer division led by Erwin Rommel and came as near to success as anything the Allies attempted in those terrible weeks. But an SS division came to Rommel's rescue and the British tanks were beaten back. The German advance continued, now swinging northwards up the coast. By 22 May they were attacking Boulogne. The British Expeditionary Force and its French and Belgian allies, still holding places as far to the east as Lille, were forced back into a steadily narrowing corridor. It led to Calais and Dunkirk.

As the Germans reached the sea the French and British governments ordered a concerted attack on them from north and south to break through the wall of the corridor. To men far from the fighting, a counter-attack must have seemed to have a good chance of extricating the northern armies from the German trap. The Panzer divisions had advanced 120 miles in a week and exhausted themselves. They were still outnumbered by the French army. But the Germans dominated the air; their armoured forces were full of confidence; great gaps had opened between the British, French and Belgian armies; many French units had lost all will to fight. Erwin Rommel wrote to his wife on 24 May: 'On the go all day of course. But by my estimate the war will be won in a fortnight.'[9] To Lord Gort, unable to shift his forces to the south, the idea of a break-out there was fantasy. The concerted attack came to nothing, and Gort told London that his only hope of salvaging something from the wreck was evacuation by sea. The Cabinet authorised him to retreat on Dunkirk, defend a 25-mile long strip of land along the coast from there northwards into Belgium, and get away to Britain what forces the navy could rescue. Gort himself believed that he would be lucky if he could get 50,000 men away, leaving their equipment on the beaches.

The focus now shifts to Dover Castle. There, on the evening of 26 May, Vice-Admiral Sir Bertram Ramsay, Flag Officer Dover since the outbreak of war, received the order to mount Operation Dynamo to rescue the British Expeditionary Force from Dunkirk. He had known these narrow waters as an officer of the Dover Patrol in the first war and taken part in Keyes's assault on Zeebrugge in April 1918. But even in the blackest days of the German assault that spring there had been no thought of a naval evacuation from the French coast. Now Operation Dynamo required the Royal Navy to execute the hitherto inconceivable.

The visitor can explore today the tunnel complex below Dover Castle, dug by French prisoners of the Napoleonic Wars. In these tunnels Ramsay and his staff laboured for the eight days of the evacuation. 'No bed for any of us last night and probably not for many nights,' Ramsay wrote; and again, 'Days and nights are all one.'[10] They called in destroyers, merchantmen, tugs, ferry boats, medical supplies, specialist personnel. Pleasure steamers that had never tasted salt water, lifeboats, even private yachts were enrolled. All these ships converged on Dover, crowding the docks and desperately vulnerable to air attack. Ramsay decided that the ships of the rescue armada should be collected at

Sheerness on the Thames, and brought forward to Ramsgate only to be armed, fuelled and supplied, before going off in convoy to Dunkirk.

Constant air cover over the beaches was needed – the cover whose apparent absence so angered the men in the long lines waiting for evacuation under incessant Luftwaffe attack. It was needed too to protect the evacuation ships as they crossed to the English coast. In the Kent ports, reception arrangements were needed, nurses and doctors to care for the wounded, trains to get the troops away from the coast. The scene in the tunnels under Dover Castle was one of protracted, unwearying, organised chaos.

The Germans were closing in on Dunkirk from south as well as east. The armoured forces that had reached the Channel at Le Crotoy and turned north had first to deal with the defenders of Boulogne and Calais. Boulogne fell quickly, but Calais was held by a small, scratch force of determined British troops. Confusion was rampant. Order succeeded order, coming in succession from the French area commander, from the War Office in London, from Gort up the coast, from the War Office relaying fresh orders from the French commander on the spot. There was talk of evacuating the wounded to Dover, of evacuating French coastal gunners to Cherbourg, of reinforcing the garrison, even of counter-attacks towards St Omer and Boulogne.

The garrison of Calais was composed of case-hardened regulars, raw recruits and half-trained territorials of the Green Jackets and the Rifle Brigade, the Queen Victoria's Rifles and the Royal Tank Regiment. They fought in the outskirts of the town, on the roads to St Omer and Gravelines, in Vauban's bastions around the port and all the way back to the harbour. Small numbers of determined French soldiers fought beside them. It was an epic defence, which has been overshadowed ever since by the far larger numbers involved in the evacuation going on up the coast at Dunkirk. 'The men of Calais,' Churchill said two months later in one of his many outbursts of historical analogy, 'were the bit of grit that saved us by stopping [the Germans] as Sidney Smith stopped Napoleon at Acre.'[11]

In the end, however, the Panzers fought their way into the town, and at last reached the great crumbling Citadel where the British had their headquarters. The Citadel, which the French built around Henry VIII's castle when they took the place from the English in 1558 and beside which the Armada anchored thirty years later, still crouches at the western end of Calais, midway between the ferry port and the cross-Channel shopping centre. Here at last the British commander surrendered, and the road to Dunkirk lay open.

There, the Allies were creating a kind of entrenched camp on the French and Belgian coast. It extended from La Panne, just inside Belgium, almost to Gravelines, west of Dunkirk. Five miles inland one of Flanders's great artificial waterways, the Bergues-Furnes Canal, presented a last obstacle to the German armoured advance. Dunkirk was a major port, properly equipped to handle an embarkation if German aircraft could be kept at bay. Its beaches were less favourable for evacuation, particularly at low tide, since they shelved so gently as to keep even small boats far offshore, while the soldiers waiting on the grey sands were horribly exposed to air attack.

In terms of numbers, the Dunkirk garrison was strong. Its French defenders were under orders to hold it, as a bastion in the continuing battle for France; for them there was no thought yet of evacuation, and unlike so many French troops in the summer of 1940 they fought with resolution. As the British divisions made their way to the coast they added to the numbers within the entrenched camp, and something to its defences. The first British troops were got away from the port of Dunkirk relatively easily.

Ever since the miraculous week of the evacuation, commentators have disagreed about the Germans' failure to complete their victory by storming Dunkirk and the beaches. Some detect a political motive, with Hitler dreaming of making the British his accomplice by letting them keep their empire if they would leave the continent to him; or perhaps, with his suspicions of his generals, he may have wanted Goering's Luftwaffe to get the credit for victory at Dunkirk. Others say that it was his generals who held back, obsessed with keeping their tank forces fit to turn against the main French armies. Some stress the physical and material exhaustion of the attackers, who had come so far in ten days of

Blitzkrieg. Yet others argue that here in Flanders the German armoured columns had at last run up against real water obstacles, which culminated in the major obstacle of the Bergues–Furnes canal. Each argument in part explains the check in the German advance; whatever the truth, the consequence was that the evacuation planners across the water in the tunnels beneath Dover Castle got a breathing space in which to organise the impossible. Over the last days of May and the first days of June, the numbers evacuated steadily increased, from thousands, to tens of thousands, to hundreds of thousands.

There is a second Dunkirk controversy that commentators have picked over ever since. In 1940 the French and British blamed one another for defeat, plumbing depths of bitterness and recrimination. The evacuation from Dunkirk generated animosities that were to damage British–French relations for years afterwards. The British had seen French units break and flee in panic; they had little respect for their comrades-in-arms in May 1940. But over Dunkirk the French could take their revenge. The British, the French said, lied to them, promised them support, promised them evacuation, then took to their ships and abandoned their allies, leaving them fighting doggedly to cover their flight. For evidence the French drew on many things that were said, done and left undone in those desperate days.

On 31 May Gort handed over command of the British Expeditionary Force to Major General Harold Alexander. Gort himself had been ordered home; other arrangements for the Dunkirk command had gone awry; Alexander – an unflappable and perhaps blessedly unimaginative Guardsman – was the right man to salvage what he could from the disaster. In handing over command, Gort gave Alexander fatefully ambiguous orders about the evacuation of French units along with British ones. Meanwhile, Winston Churchill was locked in one of a series of highly wrought meetings with the French Prime Minister, Paul Reynaud. Asked about evacuation from Dunkirk, Churchill, desperate to keep the French in the war, talked emotionally of evacuating the two armies on equal terms, a Frenchman for every Englishman, arm in arm. '*Bras-Dessus, Bras-Dessous*,' he shouted. Yet in Dunkirk Admiral Abrial, commanding the French garrison, was still under orders to hold the place, not evacuate it. Gort had never understood him; he had never understood Gort. Now he faced another laconic British commander, Alexander. The scene was set for confusion to be seen as perfidy, chaos as treachery.

Meanwhile, British ships came night after night to Dunkirk and the beaches to its east. They steered towards the columns of smoke from the port's oil tanks. 'The westerly wind,' recalled an articulate French soldier, 'beats down the immense column of grim black smoke from the flaming oil tanks. Truly this is the suffocating breath of the last judgement.'[12] Naval shore parties scrambled the waiting troops aboard. In some units, discipline shamefully broke, in others, it was gloriously maintained. Often men had lost their units or units had broken up. After hours in the water trying to co-ordinate the loading of men into boats, Brian Horrocks, who had been newly appointed to command a brigade, found that his brigade had been ordered away down the beach, to Dunkirk itself. He set off down the beach to find them, 'a very wet, very tired and very temporary brigadier with no staff and no troops'.[13]

Under constant air attack, the ships got away to sea on course for England. Many were sunk, many more crippled; some escaping soldiers had ships twice sunk under them. But a June calm such as the Channel had never seen before helped the escape. So did sortie after sortie of British fighters. With British command of the sea the Channel, so often a barrier, became a kind of thoroughfare, signposted by sinking ships, to safety in England. The navy plotted three routes back to Dover and Ramsgate from Dunkirk, two of them north of the Goodwins, one south. In the end, 338,226 men were taken off, almost a third of them Frenchmen. Despite constant air attack, almost all of them eventually reached safety. Many of the ships came back again and again to Dunkirk. Only one civilian crew, aboard a Channel ferry, refused to go back and their captain sailed her away, against orders, down Channel.

When the last British troops had been taken off and before he himself left Dunkirk, Alexander took a boat around the port and along the beaches looking for men still waiting for evacuation, French as much as British. He found none; port and beaches were empty. Yet further inland many thousands of French soldiers were still fighting desperately to hold the contracting Dunkirk perimeter. Already the French, in anguish at their inability to save their country, were arguing that the British had failed them when they refused to commit yet more fighter squadrons to the battle of France. Now, here in Dunkirk, they found another example of betrayal. The British themselves were haunted by the feeling that they had let the French down. To get more French troops away, they sent ships back into the Dunkirk maelstrom for one more night than they had planned. They rescued many, including Admiral Abrial himself. But 40,000 of the French defenders were left to surrender to the Germans. In Dunkirk today, the memories and the guide books tell two quite different stories about what happened there in the early summer of 1940. For the French it is a story of a gallant defence – a last round, last man kind of story. For the British it is a story of miraculous salvation – almost as miraculous as England's salvation from the Armada on this coast 350 years earlier.

On his return to London after the Dunkirk evacuation, Alexander reported to Anthony Eden, the Secretary of State for War. Summing up the conditions in which the evacuation had been conducted, he concluded: 'We were not pressed, you know.'[14] Self-effacement and calm understatement were the qualities on which Alexander's reputation was to rest ever afterwards. To the Frenchmen who fought and were left behind when the British withdrew from the fight for Dunkirk, that week in 1940 cannot have seemed quite like that.

The Battle of France was not yet over. The French still had whole armies physically untouched by war. There were thousands of British troops south of the Somme and Seine, and more were still being despatched to France. Churchill and Reynaud argued that the Allies could still make a fight of things, fight before Paris, stabilise the situation, fight on until the Americans came in as they had done in 1917. Other French political leaders and most French commanders lacked their conviction and moral courage. France was rotten with defeatism, its soldiers shattered by the experiences of the last month. Churchill urged them to fight in Paris, to fight beyond the Loire. They begged him to throw more Royal Air Force fighter squadrons into the battle, and he could only tell them that an irreducible minimum must be kept at home, to fight the Battle of Britain if the Battle of France were lost.

There was still talk of holding the line of the Somme, even of counter-attacking across it. But the Germans were there in force far stronger than anything the disorganised and divided Allies could send against them. The story now straggles down the Channel coast. There were several French divisions close to it between the Somme and the Seine. Two British divisions joined them: the 51st Highlanders, which had been on detachment under French command in the Maginot Line, and the 1st Armoured Division, newly landed in France. As at Calais, order clashed with counter-order, purpose with cross-purpose. Meanwhile, the Germans were advancing towards the mouth of the Seine as they had advanced to the mouth of the Somme. Erwin Rommel led his armoured division to the coast and wrote home: 'The sight of the sea with the cliffs on either side thrilled and stirred every man of us; also the thought that we had reached the coast of France. We climbed out of our vehicles and walked down the shingle beach to the water's edge until the water lapped over our boots.'[15] The Germans reached Rouen. For a second time British and French troops were trapped between the Germans and the Channel, this time in the Havre peninsula and lower Normandy.

It was decided to attempt an evacuation through the little port of St Valéry-en-Caux. But the defence was weakened by cross-purposes between French and British. A few of the 51st Division's wounded were waiting to be got away to safety. In the first war the destroyer *Broke* did great things in the Channel under a captain who had trekked to within 150 miles of the Pole with Captain Scott. Now a new *Broke* came inshore to take them off. Her commander was Peter Scott, son of Scott of the South Pole. But the *Broke* was alone, and when she was gone fog came down to delay the ships that followed her. The Germans got so close that their guns commanded the port and beaches. The British were for fighting, the French for surrender. Finally 46,000 men laid down their arms, 8,000 of them British. 'No less than twelve generals were brought in as prisoners,'[16] Rommel wrote. At St Valéry the Germans achieved what they had failed to achieve at Dunkirk.

Still there were plans to reconstitute a British Expeditionary Force to continue the fight in western France. Alanbrooke was ordered to return to France and take command: 'This was certainly one of my blackest moments. I knew only too well the state of affairs that would prevail in France from now onwards. I had seen my hope in the French army gradually shattered...'[17] But troops were landed through the western French Channel ports. There was talk of attacking the Germans, of holding a redoubt in Brittany. None of this had any chance of success. In the chaos Alanbrooke came to the same conclusion as Gort had reached three weeks earlier. What was left of the British army must be evacuated to fight another day. He got men away from Le Havre and Cherbourg, Brest and Nantes and ports the length of the French Atlantic coast. In the end a further 200,000 men were saved, 140,000 of them British; 18,000 Frenchmen came with them, 25,000 Poles and 5,000 Czechs.

In the throes of the Allies' agony, a small group of Englishmen and Frenchmen conceived a last desperate move. Over lunch at the Carlton Club in London they proposed that the British government should offer France an indissoluble Franco-British union of governments, states and nations. The idea's symbolism was dramatic, and in other circumstances its potential would have been enormous. The following day, Sunday, 16 June, it came before the War Cabinet. Churchill, prosaic for once, said that he had been instinctively against the idea but that they must not let themselves be accused of lack of imagination. So 'with remarkably little detailed consideration, the offer was evolved: common citizenship, a single united War Cabinet, amalgamated armed forces, and maybe, although nothing was specifically said about this, a single polyglot parliament'.

The proposal was, wrote Roy Jenkins sixty years afterwards, 'an amazing confection. In retrospect it is difficult to decide which was the more staggering: the presumption of the view that the disparate and complex mechanisms of the British and French states could be successfully put together by a document of barely 300 words; or the utterly heterogeneous nature of those who assisted at its hasty creation.'[18] For among them were three men who after the war took widely differing positions on projects to make Europe whole: Jean Monnet, the architect of the European Common Market, Charles de Gaulle and Churchill himself.

If the French government had accepted the idea of union, it would not have saved France from an occupation more complete and terrible than the one that actually occurred. But it would have bound the French Empire and France in exile closely to the continuing Allied cause and altered the face of the war. In the longer run such a union would have created an entirely new kind of cross-Channel relationship and changed the face of post-war Europe. On 22 June, however, the French government, defeated, defeatist, suspicious, turned the offer down. They were bound to do so, and by almost any practical measure they were right. Yet one observer thought it came only a day too late: 'If only the Declaration had been approved twenty-four hours earlier,' John Colville wrote in his diary, '. . . the terms of the Declaration "against subjection to a system which reduces mankind to a life of robots and slaves" would have assuredly found response in France and the US. There would have been difficulties to surmount, but we had before us the bridge to a new world, the first elements of European or even World Federation.'[19] To which, sixty years afterwards, one can only say 'Maybe'.

John Colville wrote those words in June 1940. The French chose instead the road that led to capitulation. The armistice provided for German occupation of two-thirds of France, including the whole of the Channel and Atlantic coast, and the establishment in the other third of a puppet regime based in Vichy. Some French colonies followed de Gaulle, others stayed with the Vichy government. The Battle of France was over, Churchill told the British; the Battle of Britain was about to begin.

CHAPTER 15

THERE'LL BE
SPITFIRES
OVER...

W hen the 340,000 men of the British Expeditionary Force came home in the early summer of 1940 they joined many thousands more stationed at home. The manpower was there for a formidable new army. But the men who came back were exhausted, obsessed by German military superiority and demoralised by the often shameful circumstances of their own defeat. Some – not many – brought their personal weapons with them, but all the army's heavy equipment had been lost during the retreat or destroyed at the evacuation ports. The generals had men who had experienced war, and in particular trained officers and NCOs, but little else with which to defend the United Kingdom and conjure a new army out of the wreckage.

The Royal Navy too had suffered serious losses, first in the Norwegian campaign and then in getting the army in France away to safety. Nine destroyers had been lost in the evacuation from Dunkirk alone and more ships off the western French ports. But whereas the army now had next to no strength to put into battle, the navy remained the most powerful in the world, still vastly outweighing any force the German navy could send against it. Before any invasion could be launched the German air force would have to drive British ships out of the North Sea and the Channel.

To do so it would first have to master the Royal Air Force, which like army and navy had lost heavily in the Battle of France. The squadrons based on French airfields had been in constant combat. Repeatedly they were reinforced from Britain and, when the German advance approached the Channel coast, aircraft from British bases were thrown into the battle too. The air defence of Dunkirk above all had absorbed British fighter resources. In total, the Royal Air Force lost 900 aircraft in the Belgian and French campaign, 450 of them Hurricanes and Spitfires; and on 15 June 120 machines had to be burnt on French airfields for lack of enough fuel to fly them back to England.

But the British had held back from committing the bulk of the Royal Air Force's fighter strength to the Battle of France. As things went badly for the Allies and as the French government begged for more air cover for their shattered divisions, Winston Churchill and his Cabinet had faced agonising decisions. On the one hand, every military principle argued for the concentration of force where the decisive battle was being fought: in France. It was agonising to deny relief to an army and an ally in extremis. On the other hand, it was manifest that if the Battle of France were lost, a Battle of Britain would follow. If the country's air defences had been reduced below an indispensable minimum, that battle would be lost as surely as the Battle of France.

Winston Churchill flew to France, desperate to keep the French in the war. They begged for more British squadrons. Repeatedly the British increased their commitment to the Battle of France. Repeatedly the French, and the situation, demanded more. 'If we send the fighters and lose them,' John Colville, Churchill's private secretary, wrote in his diary as early as 18 May, 'then this country will be left at the mercy of concentrated German attack and can hardly avoid destruction. It would be a terrifying gamble, but I am afraid it is one we ought to take.'[1] Others drew different conclusions. The commander of Fighter Command, Air Marshal Hugh Dowding, begged the Cabinet to hold the fighters back. The Air Council had taken the considered view that a minimum of fifty-two fighter squadrons was necessary for the defence of the United Kingdom; now he was down to thirty-six. Sending more aircraft to France was like pouring 'water in the desert sand'.

Supporting Dowding, Sir Cyril Newall, the Chief of Air Staff, wrote: 'I do not believe that to throw in a few more squadrons whose loss might vitally weaken the fighter line at home would make the difference between victory and defeat in France ... It can, however, be said with absolute certainty that while the collapse of France would not necessarily mean the ultimate victory of Germany, the collapse of Great Britain would inevitably do so.'[2]

Finally Churchill drained the bitter cup that the logic of his air marshals forced on him. He told the French Prime Minister, Paul Reynaud, that no more squadrons could be spared from the defence of the United Kingdom. In doing so he added another item to France's long catalogue of cross-Channel complaints against its ally. He also presented yet another reason for despair to all those French ministers and generals who wanted to come to terms with the enemy. Finally Reynaud yielded to them. On 15 June he asked the Germans for an armistice and a week later he accepted their surrender terms.

For Churchill, who had put such faith in the French army and had fought desperately to keep France in the war, the French surrender was pure tragedy. It marked the end of hopes of engaging the enemy anywhere on the continent and brought the German army to the whole Channel coast, and within sight of England. But in that overwrought summer of 1940 it brought a kind of relief to other islanders. It was simpler, clearer-cut, to stand alone, and proud insularity had a field-day. The king himself captured the mood with the kind of brutal banality that the House of Windsor has made its own. He wrote to his mother, 'Personally I feel happier now that we have no more allies to be polite to or pamper.'[3] David Low the cartoonist drew a soldier on the cliffs of Dover shaking his fist at a German plane: 'Very well, alone.' To comfort Churchill, Colville found two sentences from Shakespeare's *Henry VI*:

'Tis better using France than trusting France.
Let us be back'd with God, and with the seas.

And in her poem 'The English War', the writer Dorothy Sayers gave new wings to the thought 'Praise God now for an English war . . .' she wrote:

> When no allies are left, no help
> To count upon from alien hands,
> No waverers remain to woo,
> No more advice to listen to,
> And only England stands.

As for Dowding, hoarding his fighters for the battle to come, he had more substantial reasons to rejoice that France was out of the war. When he heard the news of the armistice and knew that French demands no longer threatened his irreducible minimum of fighter squadrons, he told Lord Halifax, 'I went on my knees and thanked God.'[4]

The Germans had so far given little serious thought to how to follow up their conquest of France. The army and air force were astounded by the speed of that success. The navy's commanders, asked almost casually to turn their minds to the problem of invading Britain, found themselves appalled by its difficulty. Hitler remained ambivalent. As long as France stayed in the war he was obsessed with fear of a military reverse. After the armistice he still hoped for a political settlement with the British. He was at least subconsciously aware of the risks of an invasion, and his mind was already turning to settling accounts with his true enemy, the Soviet Union. The golden days of late June saw a kind of hiatus along the Channel coast between war in France and battle over Britain.

For the British, there was no time for sunbathing. The army was redeployed. Brooke took command of home forces, Alexander was sent off with 1 Corps to guard the coast of Yorkshire and Lincolnshire while Montgomery was given the most critical command of all, south-east England. All along the Channel coast the troops were set to work to reinforce the historical coastal defences. They dug trenches, laid barbed wire and strung devilish devices along the beaches. The concrete pill boxes with which they lined the south coast of England are still visible, many of them in curious places, such as the camouflaged strongpoints built into the Roman remains of Pevensey Castle. They were supplemented by the Local Defence Volunteers, quickly renamed the Home Guard. Weapons were scraped together from every source. Depots were cleaned out, ancient rifles and machine-guns refurbished. The arms factories laboured to make good something of the loss in France. Shipments came from the United States. But the Chiefs of Staff concluded that 'should the Germans succeed in establishing a force with its vehicles in this country, our army forces have not got the offensive power to drive it out'.[5]

Yet the Germans had much to do before they could hope to establish such a force in Britain. For the British, with command of the sea, the Channel had offered a clear if hazardous way of escape from destruction at Dunkirk. To the Germans it presented an almost insuperable obstacle. These might be the narrow seas, but their distances, tides, currents and unpredictable weather made them an obstacle quite different in kind from the rivers and canals that they had forced so easily in the Polish and French campaigns. Airborne attack, such as they had used in Holland, could be effective only if it were quickly reinforced by heavier units. But serious reinforcements could be got to Britain only by sea, and the German navy, fearing the striking superiority of its opponents, could see no way of securing the Channel on its own.

The British feared that the French fleet, the world's fourth most powerful, might fall under German control. Had it done so, its ships might have given the Royal Navy the fight of its life in the narrow seas. But the British moved fast, with resolution, some said with brutality, against their fallen ally. They seized French ships in the English Channel ports and at Alexandria, and attacked and destroyed them in the ports of French North Africa. Italy came into the war on the side of the Germans, but its admirals had no thought of bringing their ships out of the Mediterranean. The German admirals would have to fight the Royal Navy on their own, and knew that they could not do so successfully. It was up to the Luftwaffe to drive the Royal Navy out of the Channel, and it could only do that if it could first overwhelm the Royal Air Force.

So only the Luftwaffe could open the English oyster. Triumphant as it had been over Poland and France, it now faced a serious challenge. The fighting over France had shown a rough equality between British and Germans in terms of men and machines. Now, if it went on the offensive to destroy the British air bases, the Luftwaffe would be at the disadvantage of operating away from its own. To offset that it would have to look to numerical superiority. The shape of the Battle of Britain was being formed.

Against the Poles and the French the Luftwaffe had tasted one victory after another, and its pilots had gained vital experience in air combat which most of its British opponents as yet lacked. Yet in many ways the German air force was as ill-prepared for an onslaught on Britain as the German navy. Its earlier triumphs had been won in close support of an advancing army. Its dive bombers had been used like artillery, softening up resistance ahead of the army's tank columns, while its fighters overhead blocked interference by the enemy. The fighter pilots' experience, therefore, was of dogfights engaged almost as close to their own bases as the enemy's. The strategic framework was set by the advance of the German forces on the ground. As the German air bases were moved steadily forward behind the army, the enemy's bases had to be pulled back or be overrun, their equipment seized or destroyed.

The campaign against Britain, by contrast, would require German pilots to cross the Channel to penetrate the enemy's air space. They would be engaging the defenders relatively far from home, with an eye as much to their own fuel gauges as to enemy aircraft. If British airfields and aircraft factories were to be destroyed, German fighters would have to protect bombers on flights deep into British airspace, and in defending them against British attack the German fighter pilots' hands would be tied. Even geography was against them: if they came down over England they would be taken prisoner; if they crashed into the Channel they would drown.

Though the Germans did not at first know it, they also faced the world's most sophisticated air defence system. In May, at the height of the Battle for France, the code-crackers at Bletchley Park had broken the Luftwaffe's most secret cipher; soon they were reading 1,000 messages a day. Radar was still theoretically a secret; but fifteen radar stations were at work along the Channel coast, capable of identifying the strength and direction of German attack before it crossed the English coast. Their reports were fed into an elaborate and highly efficient plotting system at Fighter Command and at the headquarters of the fighter groups. The system enabled the fighter controllers to commit squadrons to action against identified threats rather than keep them wastefully airborne on patrol. Anti-aircraft batteries, balloon barrages and ground observer stations rounded out the defences.

Against all this the Germans could throw the experience of their pilots, their unbroken record of victory, and their superior numbers. But although the strength of the German airfleets engaged could appear overwhelming on the radar screens as they formed up over northern France or to the observer stations as they came streaming in across the Channel coast, they never enjoyed the huge advantage of numbers with which British propaganda credited them. In combat the aircraft that really mattered were the single-seater fighters, and at the beginning of the battle the Royal Air Force had 700 Hurricanes and Spitfires to put into battle against a slightly larger number of serviceable German ME 109s.

And so to the aircraft that fought the Battle of Britain. The Germans deployed bombers by the hundred, most of them Junkers. The JU 87, the Stuka dive bomber, had terrified soldiers and refugees in Poland and France when it came howling down upon them. When it found itself up against modern fighters, however, it was a sitting duck. Fairly early in the Battle of Britain it was withdrawn from front-line service. The JU 88, by contrast, was a more conventional bomber, handicapped in the main by its slow speed and limited bomb load. Delivered safely to its target by its fighter escort, the JU 88 was intended to destroy radar stations and airfields, terrorise cities and pulverise aircraft factories, in short to clinch the Battle of Britain. In all this it failed.

To escort the bombers, the German airfleets deployed two Messerschmitt fighters. The ME 110 was a two-seater fighter, formidably well armed. The Germans expected great things of their ME 110 squadrons, based mainly in western France, but in the Battle of Britain they proved incapable of looking after themselves, let alone the bombers they escorted. Like the Stuka, they too were soon withdrawn from the battle.

This left German hopes riding on the single-seater ME 109, an aircraft in most respects fully the match of its British opponents. In the end it was the ME 109 that bore the brunt of the Battle of Britain for the Germans, and went on to spearhead German air campaigns almost to the end of the war. Like the Hurricane, the Messerschmitt never acquired the Spitfire's glamour, but it was its all-round equal. Its great weakness in the Battle of Britain was its lack of endurance, which compelled its pilots to break off the fight and turn for home if they were to get back to their bases on the other side of the Channel.

Against these aircraft the British fielded four fighters or fighter bombers: the Blenheim, Defiant, Hurricane and Spitfire. Of these, the twin-engined Blenheim lacked the agility for dog-fighting. In the end it found its *métier* as a night-fighter and short-range bomber.

In contrast, the Defiant had more pretensions and more faults. It was conceived as a single-engined fighter with the particular hitting-power of a four-gun, electrically powered turret behind the pilot's seat. In favourable conditions it could surprise its enemy and then shatter him with gunfire. Occasionally, in the early days of the Battle of Britain, it did just that. But like the ME 110 it lacked survivability in dogfighting, and soon it was withdrawn from the Royal Air Force's front line.

The front line remained throughout the battle the preserve of the Spitfire and Hurricane. Each was the equal of the ME 109, its superior in some respects, its inferior in others. The Spitfire's speed, manoeuvrability and sheer beauty gave it a unique reputation that it never lost. But the Hurricane was more versatile and robust; it outnumbered the Spitfire in the battle by a factor of four to one. It was the British workhorse of the Battle of Britain and the eventual victory was its victory over the ME 109.

In many respects the German pilots resembled their British opponents. Many on both sides were the model of fighter pilots: courageous, devil-may-care individualists. But there were differences too. The Germans, for one thing, were rather older and usually more experienced. They brought to the battle experience over Poland and France and, many of them, in the Spanish Civil War. The typical British pilot, by contrast, came straight out of school, through a terrifyingly short period of flight training, to take his place in the front line. This was a fight of the 23-year-old against the 18-year-old. Both believed in their cause. One wanted to see his country triumph, complete its long run of success and re-establish itself among the great nations. The other wanted to save his country from the most deadly assault ever launched across the Channel. Both wanted beer, cigarettes, girls, glamour and glory.

When the Battle of Britain started is a matter of interpretation. To a degree the wars in France and over Britain ran into one another. Seen otherwise, 10 July marked an intensification of air combat into a continuing battle. Others put the real onset of the battle in early August. All see its culmination in the middle of September.

The battle began in a contest of wills about the use of the English Channel. At first the British, instinctively reluctant to surrender a sovereignty over the narrow seas that went back centuries, were determined to continue to put convoys through the Straits of Dover. They faced attack by German aircraft and fast attack boats, the E-boats. The navy was told to escort the merchantmen and the Royal Air Force to provide the necessary air cover. The convoys, it was argued, were bait that would bring the Germans to battle. But repeatedly the Germans penetrated the defences and sank ship after merchant ship in the Channel. Churchill fumed at the services' failure to provide effective cover: 'And the British navy let them sink those poor little ships in broad daylight,' he said to his private secretary.[6]

To the air marshals, Churchill was falling into a trap in his determination to persist with these convoys. The need to cover them was forcing the country's precious fighters to go out to meet the Germans half-way between their bases and Britain's. Losses on both sides were heavy, but the Germans could accept them more easily than the British. Finally, London looked reality in the eye and abandoned its instinctive claim to rule the waters of the Channel. Precious aircraft and pilots should be reserved for more vital business; the passage of convoys through the Channel was limited, well nigh abandoned. First blood to the Germans.

Still Hitler seemed to hope for a negotiated settlement. On 19 July in a speech to the Reichstag he delivered what sounded like an offer of peace. Churchill refused to respond: 'We are not on speaking terms.' But the Foreign Secretary, Lord Halifax, did respond, in a speech in which 'he spoke more of God than of Hitler'. He ignored Hitler's peace feelers and, coming from a member of the Cabinet who in 1938 had argued for appeasement when Churchill was urging war, his speech had more resonance than a more bellicose response from Churchill would have had.

Perhaps in consequence, on 1 August Hitler gave his air force new orders, reflecting a new determination to settle accounts with Britain. He wrote:

In order to create the conditions for the final overthrow of England, I intend to wage the air and sea war against the English homeland in a more intensified form than before . . . The German air force is to beat down the English air force with all available forces as quickly as possible. Attacks in the first instance are to be directed against airborne formations, their ground bases . . . furthermore against the air armaments industry . . . After a temporary or local air superiority has been achieved, the air war is to be continued against the ports . . . Compared with this, the battle against enemy warships and merchant ships from the air can be postponed . . . I reserve the right to order terror attacks as a form of reprisal . . . The increase in the air war may begin from 5/8.[7]

Meanwhile, the army and navy were ordered to prepare to launch an invasion in mid-September, by which time, it was assumed, the Royal Air Force would have been driven out of the skies.

The commanders of the two airfleets deployed in France fixed on 13 August as 'Eagle Day' for the first great onslaught on Royal Air Force bases in the south of England. Goering sent them the most bombastically vacuous of all orders of the day: 'From Reichsmarschall Goering to all units of Air Fleets 2, 3 and 5. Operation Eagle. Within a short period you will wipe the British Air Force from the sky. Heil Hitler.'[8] On the day before Eagle Day the Germans had struck with only limited success at four radar stations along the Channel coast: Dunkirk in Kent, Dover and Rye, and Ventnor in the Isle of Wight. Now, on the great day itself, they launched 1,500 sorties. Two days later a third airfleet joined in, flying long range and inordinately costly attacks against north-eastern England from its bases in Scandinavia. But the heart of the matter was in the south-east, and there the battle continued through one perfect summer's day after another during the rest of August and into early September. By 6 September the Germans had lost 670 aircraft. Fighter Command had lost fewer, some 400, but its men and systems were close to breaking point. Then on 7 September the Germans, convinced that an attack on the capital would force the Royal Air Force to throw in its last reserves, switched their attention to London. Taking the pressure off the British fighter airfields was a fundamental strategic error that lost them the Battle of Britain.

Throughout August, the Germans went ahead with preparations for 'Sealion', a seaborne invasion of England. The navy, which had lost half its ships in the Norwegian campaign, remained convinced that a seaborne attack could succeed only when the Royal Air Force had been destroyed and the Royal Navy driven out of the Channel. The Luftwaffe commanders were equally sceptical, convinced at first that they could bring the British to their knees by air attack alone and later uneasily afraid that they were failing to win the battle of attrition with the Royal Air Force. But the German army took planning seriously, and fleets of barges, tugs and steamships were assembled in the Channel and North Sea ports. Army units themselves were exercised in the new arts of cross-sea invasion, discovering everything from the difficulties of embarkation and of assault on the enemy's beaches to the vagaries of the Channel's tides.

Hitler, in private never convinced of its feasibility, in public continued to forecast invasion: 'In England they're filled with curiosity and keep asking, "Why doesn't he come?"' he told a wildly applauding audience on 4 September. 'Be calm. Be calm. He's coming! He's coming!'[9] Meanwhile, the army was squabbling with the navy about the width of the bridgehead to be established on the English Channel coast. Finally it was agreed that invasion convoys from the Dutch and Belgian ports and from Dunkirk, Calais, Boulogne and Le Havre should transport nine divisions to landing areas on the coast of Kent and Sussex between Folkestone and Brighton. Once established, the beachheads would be expanded to a line across the Weald. Thereafter, the advance would be carried forward to a line running roughly south-westwards from Chatham to Chichester. 'Everything looks like an invasion starting tomorrow from the Thames to Plymouth!' wrote Alanbrooke on 13 September. 'I wonder whether we shall be hard at it by this time tomorrow?'[10]

Against this threat the British army was steadily improving its capacity. By now the Channel coast had been turned into a death trap for the invader. The commanders created mobile forces, to strike where the enemy landed rather than hold a static line. Morale recovered from the shock of Dunkirk. Weapons flowed from the armament factories to the units. Even the Home Guard was at last issued with rifles. But the British army remained no match for a strong German invasion force that got ashore in England.

Fighter Command continued its duel with the Luftwaffe, but the Royal Navy and Bomber Command went over to the offensive. Air attack on the German concentration ports sank invasion barges and damaged tugs and steamships. The navy looked into every French and Belgian Channel and North Sea port, finding German preparations incomplete and devastating those they found. Churchill rejoiced when the battle was thus taken to the enemy. 'How wonderful it would be,' he wrote as early as 3 June, when the Dunkirk evacuation was still continuing, 'if the Germans could be made to wonder where they were going to be struck next instead of forcing us to try to wall in the Island and roof it over.'[11] He was to continue for years to come demanding offensive action in the Channel, more often than not unwisely. But this assault on the German invasion ports made as good defensive as aggressive sense.

Of course, despite repeated alarms, the invasion never came. If it had, events in the Channel would have changed the course of history, and not to Germany's advantage. No one at the time could afford complacency, but in retrospect it is clear that a seaborne attack on England launched in that late summer of 1940 must have ended in fiasco. In a broadcast to the French people, Churchill promised this at the time. *'Nous attendons l'invasion promise de longue date,'* he said in that extraordinary French of his. *'Les poissons aussi.'* ('We await the long-promised invasion. So do the fishes.') The German navy was weak, the German army unprepared for a cross-sea operation and the Luftwaffe, powerful as it was, had still not mastered the skies. Formidable as they seemed at the time, the Germans' preparations to invade England in 1940 were pathetically feeble, even amateurish. German invasion convoys, launched with this manifestly inadequate preparation and without control of the air, would have been torn to pieces by the ships of the Royal Navy. Defeat in the Channel would have ended at a stroke the myth of German invincibility. The Germans would have lost perhaps 100,000 men and their capacity to wage war against Russia. Europe would have been spared five more terrible years of war.

Instead it was left to the airmen to fight the duel to the end. The German switch from targeting British bases to the assault on the cities had saved Fighter Command. Now, in the shortening September days, the British won one air battle after another over the Luftwaffe. The Germans were being engaged not over the Channel, equidistant between British and German bases, but deep inland over London and the towns of southern England. The need to escort the bomber squadrons inhibited the German fighter pilots. Neither side suffered anything like the losses that their opponents routinely claimed, but the Germans repeatedly lost more than the British. Crippled German aircraft faced a long crawl home under fighter attack all the way and their crews dreaded being brought down in the sea.

The Germans used flying boats and seaplanes to pick up airmen who came down in the sea, and when the British government announced that it would no longer recognise the immunity that the aircrafts' Red Cross markings demanded, they put experienced air-gunners aboard them.

British arrangements to rescue pilots who came down in the sea were amateurish by contrast. Captains of merchantmen in the Channel were urged to keep a sharp look-out, a few Admiralty and Air Force launches were stationed in South Coast ports, and RNLI lifeboats also went out in search of pilots in the sea. But 'it remained a tragic fact . . . that many a fighter pilot, who had survived combat and escape by parachute, died of hypothermia, his body washed ashore sometimes weeks later'.[12]

In the end it was German bomber morale that cracked first. The German air attacks were scaled down, invasion plans repeatedly postponed. The Battle of Britain petered out, and gradually the Germans switched the emphasis of their campaign to night attacks on Britain's industrial cities. The British had won the Battle of Britain, bringing down 1,733 German aircraft for the loss of 915 of their own. Now they faced the even greater problem of moving successfully to the offensive. Soon the Channel would see small-scale British offensive action, which some saw as promising bigger things to come. But it took the Allies three and a half years to mount the cross-Channel invasion that had proved so manifestly beyond the Germans' powers. That is a measure of how far the Germans were from repeating on British soil the triumph they had so easily won in France in May and June 1940. It is a measure too of the Channel's ability to frustrate those who do not approach it with sufficient seriousness.

CHAPTER 16

SCRAPPING
IN THE
CHANNEL

I n the autumn of 1940 the Germans abandoned the daylight bomber
raids around which the Battle of Britain had been fought. They
persisted with the night attacks that became a constant feature of
the war, and night raids did more damage to London and the industrial
cities than attacks in daylight had ever done. They were directed also
against the Channel ports. In one raid, Plymouth was heavily attacked,
and its modern city centre, re-created after the war, is a continuing
testimony to the destruction done there. Another raid killed more than
a thousand people in Portsmouth. Royal Air Force attacks on the French
ports increased too, and by 1943 outweighed the German raids in the
opposite direction. Dover and Calais suffered additionally the attentions
of long-range artillery. Civilian nerve never came near breaking point,
but night after night the inhabitants of the Channel coastal towns were
subjected to hardship and danger, punctuated by regular tragedy.

There remained at least the theoretical possibility of an invasion of
England. In January 1941 Alanbrooke conducted major home defence
exercises, and army and navy both went on record as considering an
attempt 'probable'. There was talk of using oil as a 'means of lighting

up the sea as part of the defence against invasion'.[1] In the spring the danger seemed to grow. In May the Germans mounted an attack on Crete. While the Royal Navy sank their ships the Germans succeeded in capturing the island with airborne troops alone. The fanciful feared their attempting a similar stroke in Britain. 'We have to contemplate the descent from the air of perhaps a quarter of a million parachutists, glider-borne or crash-landed aeroplane troops,' Winston Churchill wrote.[2] Even at the time, others saw how extravagantly wrong he was. But just as the aged Duke of Wellington had descried the threat of steamship-borne invaders, Churchill was haunted by the idea that a sudden airborne coup could achieve what conventional enemy action could not.

Another British warhorse, and one of Churchill's cronies, Maurice Hankey, even feared subterranean attack. He suggested that the Germans might put to use what remained on the French side of the nineteenth-century Channel tunnel workings, complete them, and debouch unannounced into the fields of Kent. It was agreed to keep an eye on the possibility, with regular air reconnaissance over the French diggings and the stationing of underground listeners in the English ones. Later, when the German invasion of Russia seemed for a time to be succeeding, so releasing forces to send against Britain, Churchill returned to the danger of invasion. But airborne landings, tunnelling, an improbable evasion of the Royal Navy on the way to the English coast – all remained outside the bounds of reasonable calculation.

Nevertheless, the army, so ill-prepared in 1940, went on developing its capacity to repel the invasion that would not come. Seaward defences were still further improved, with the erection of underwater steel barriers on vulnerable beaches. Great numbers of men were under arms in Britain, almost a million of them designated for home defence. Their equipment steadily improved, and their leaders' minds were steadily shifting from defence to the prospect of cross-Channel attack. By 1943, American troops were flooding in to join them. The Home Guard still aided and abetted the full-timers, growing in numbers to one and a half million, receiving into its ranks conscripts as well as over-age volunteers, equipped increasingly with weapons that could do real damage to an enemy. But theirs was a war of waiting, as phoney in some ways as the war in 1939.

At sea, real battle was engaged. The Royal Navy kept its capital ships well away from the narrow seas, at Scapa Flow in the Orkneys and Rosyth in Scotland, but its destroyers continued to escort the occasional convoy through the Channel. The Germans brought their E-boat squadrons of fast torpedo boats and gun boats into the Channel to attack them and the British sent out their own light craft to hunt them down. The battle was fought mostly at night, and finding the enemy was as difficult as it was for the night-fighters of the air. When contact was made, the fighting was sudden, fragmentary and bloody. And when the Germans found a convoy (or, as occasionally happened, the British attacked a bold German-controlled merchant ship in the Channel) the consequences could be devastating. Add attack from the air, and attack by the submarines that penetrated the minefields at the ends of the Channel, and the life of a merchant seaman was lived on a knife-edge of fear and danger.

Once, in February 1942, the Channel saw bigger ships engaged, in an action that was for the British one of the blackest of the war. In 1941 the Germans had sent some of their major warships commerce-raiding in the North Atlantic, doing serious damage until the *Bismarck* was brought to battle and sunk by the Royal Navy. Other German big ships, the pocket battleships *Scharnhorst* and *Gneisenau* and the cruiser *Prinz Eugen*, had taken refuge at Brest, where the Royal Air Force regularly tried to cripple them. Hitler decided that they must be withdrawn from this exposed forward position and brought north to join in the attacks on Allied Arctic convoys to the Soviet Union. To get to the north they must risk the Royal Navy's guns in the Atlantic – or attempt a dash through the Channel.

By now it was established doctrine that without air cover capital ships could not withstand air attack at sea. E-boats could protect the big German ships against British torpedo boat and destroyer attack, and minesweepers could clear a passage for them through the minefields. But they could hope to get up the Channel only if surprise, fighter cover or fog could protect them from effective air attack. And even then, in the Straits themselves, they would be exposed to fire from the big gun batteries at Dover. So the Germans would be undertaking an inordinately risky operation if they tried to get their three big ships through the Channel.

They therefore looked for weather conditions that would keep British aircraft grounded, but which were clear enough in the Channel to enable the escapers to storm the Straits at their full speed of more than 30 knots. 'Now the weather god had to be consulted,' commented Adolph Galland, commander of the fighter squadrons assigned to protecting the German ships, 'for he played an important if not decisive part.'[3] Three submarines off the coast of Iceland were charged to provide advance warning of the weather coming out of the Atlantic. The meteorologists were in charge. On 12 February they were satisfied that conditions were favourable. The German navy launched the Channel dash.

Nothing went right for the British. By the time they had established that the German ships had left Brest they were already well up-Channel. The navy could not find them and low clouds blinded high-level bomber attack. At first, the same bad visibility prevented torpedo-attack aircraft from landing on the airfields where their torpedoes awaited them, and when at last they got into position to attack the German ships the aircraft themselves, slow-moving, string-and-sealing-wax Swordfish biplanes of the Fleet Air Arm, were terribly vulnerable to defensive fire. All six were shot down, and the award of a posthumous Victoria Cross to the man who led them, Lieutenant-Commander Eugene Esmonde, symbolises the hopeless gallantry of the attack. Even Dover's great guns were ineffective. In the end, the German ships escaped into the protection of the North Sea's impenetrable winter weather, and made their way to their north German home ports.

Two months earlier, Britain had lost *Prince of Wales* and *Repulse* to Japanese torpedo-bombers off Malaya. The Japanese attackers were 3,000 miles from home, yet the combined might of the Royal Air Force and Royal Navy could not sink *Scharnhorst*, *Gneisenau* and *Prinz Eugen* 15 miles off the coast of Kent. Government and public consternation was terrible. *The Times* cast its mind back to the victories of the Dutch admirals Ruyter and van Tromp. 'Nothing more mortifying to the pride of our seapower has happened since the seventeenth century,' it thundered. At the heart of government, Alanbrooke brought the whole story together in a blizzard of exclamation marks: 'News of Singapore getting worse, and that of Burma beginning to deteriorate! Added to that the *Gneisenau, Scharnhorst* and *Prinz Eugen* succeeded in running the gauntlet of the Channel without being destroyed, whilst we lost 40 aircraft to the 20 enemy planes brought down! These are black days! Even Russia is not doing as well as she was.'[4]

In fact the German ships had been badly damaged by mines in the North Sea and they played no further effective part in the war. The German Admiralty recognised privately that the Channel dash had been a flight away from the war, not towards it, a tactical success that masked a strategic retreat. But for the British this was a terrible defeat suffered precisely where they had proclaimed themselves supreme for 700 years – in the throat of the Channel. February 1942 was a bad month for Britain.

Almost as soon as British forces were driven from the continent in 1940, Churchill started to demand offensive action to resume the battle there. He had sent Alanbrooke back to France after Dunkirk in the hope of shoring up a new battle front in the west, only to see the British army forced out again in the second great cross-Channel evacuation of the summer of 1940. At the same time, Britain abandoned the Channel Islands, evacuating more than 20,000 islanders. Soon there was talk of 'raiding companies', which would land on the French coast in the darkness of a Channel night, pull down a radio mast, slit German throats, wreck German morale and put heart back into the French, then slip away to their boats offshore. There was even talk, later on, of re-taking the Channel Islands.

This was the British way of war, grounded in British maritime history. It recalled Sluys, Nelson's 'squadron on a particular service', and Keyes's attack on Zeebrugge in 1918. It gave a psychological fillip to forces that had grown defensive-minded, served some propaganda purpose, and gathered some intelligence. It had its enthusiasts all the way from Churchill at the top to adventurous irregulars looking for an escape from regimental soldiering. Keyes himself was appointed the first director of 'combined operations', as this kind of activity was named, and followed by Lord Louis Mountbatten. Both men had a highly developed taste for publicity and self-promotion, and they frequently made more of their operations than the facts justified. So the British public greeted as major successes an attack on the German garrison of a Channel Islands lighthouse and a parachute and commando attack on a German radar station near Le Havre early in 1942.

In March, however, the commandos struck harder, on a larger scale, and to more purpose. This time their target was the dry dock at St Nazaire on the Loire, the only one on the French Atlantic coast capable of accommodating Germany's last modern battleship, *Tirpitz*. They rammed an ancient destroyer into the dock gates and blew her up. They killed most of the defenders, knocked the dry dock out of the war, suffered heavy casualties themselves and won four Victoria Crosses. But St Nazaire was an exception among commando raids. More usually this war of pinpricks, the old game of 'breaking windows with guineas', had little effect on the bigger scheme of things. And when Mountbatten's private war was pushed too far, as it was at Dieppe in the summer of that year, it produced tragically costly failure.

No historian has ever succeeded in making complete sense of the decision to make an attack in force on Dieppe in August 1942, but the context is clear enough. In Russia the Germans had reached the Crimea and were on their way to Stalingrad. The Russians were clamouring for a 'second front'. Churchill wanted to show his American allies what Britain could do. The western allies needed to establish whether a port could be captured by frontal assault. Alanbrooke pronounced himself in favour of an experiment, arguing that 'if it was ever intended to invade France it was essential to launch a preliminary offensive on a divisional scale'.[5] The Canadians were restless for action and playing merry hell in half the pubs in the south of England. It was decided to attempt a 'reconnaissance in force'. So 5,000 Canadians and 1,000 British soldiers were despatched to a frontal attack on the French fishing port and resort of Dieppe.

Dieppe lies crowded by the seaside, flanked by cliffs and shut in by steep hills. It is the nearest French port to Paris and has always attracted Parisian holidaymakers and travellers. By 1850 a railway linked it to Paris and a daily packet service to Newhaven. It became a favourite of the English, their first taste of France on their way to Paris and one of their best-loved French resorts. An entry in Alanbrooke's diary captures the way many felt about it: 'Main interest of morning's COS [Chiefs of Staff meeting] was examination of proposed large scale raid in the vicinity of Dieppe. Little did I ever think in the old days of my regular journeys of Newhaven–Dieppe that I should have been planning as I was this morning!'[6] Dieppe had Canadian connections too, for French seamen had sailed from here to colonise Quebec. For Canadians and British alike, it was familiar, at least by affectionate reputation. It was to become a death-trap for the attackers.

A dress rehearsal for the Dieppe assault was held at Bridport on the Dorset coast. It was a fiasco. A second rehearsal was more encouraging, but then the weather turned against the operation. Doubt and muddle persisted. The navy declined Mountbatten's request that they bring the firepower of big ships into the Channel to soften up the Germans: 'Battleships by daylight off the French coast? You must be mad, Dickie.'[7] When Churchill asked if success could be guaranteed, Alanbrooke, with uncharacteristic fatalism, is quoted as saying 'If he, or anyone else, could guarantee success, there would indeed be no object in doing the operation. It is just because no one has the slightest idea of what the outcome will be that the operation is necessary.'[8]

Dieppe stretches for some 2,000 yards along the shore. The entrance to the fishing port and ferry terminal marks the eastern end of the town centre, the medieval château the western. Between them, the attackers in the centre had to cross a broad esplanade. The Germans were strongly entrenched in a row of hotels that fronted it, and had blocked the roads that led into the town. From positions on the château cliff they could rake the esplanade with flanking fire. Away from the centre, the attackers could escape from the German guns only by fighting their way up steep chines through the town's suburbs. The massacre that resulted was graced only by three Victoria Crosses, awarded to a Canadian colonel, a British commando and a Canadian chaplain.

German propaganda talked about the British fighting to the last Canadian, and the affair elicited Hitler's only recorded joke: 'This is the first time,' he said, 'that the British have had the courtesy to cross the sea to offer the enemy a complete sample of their weapons.'[9] The German army was mystified, and its interrogators asked a prisoner, ' . . . it was too big for a raid and too small for an invasion. What was it?' 'If you can tell me,' was the answer, 'I would be very grateful.'[10] The real purpose of the raid lay deeply hidden. Lessons were learned at Dieppe, apologists said ever afterwards, that were put to good use in the Normandy landings two years afterwards. The most important was that you could not hope to take a port by direct attack from the sea.

Throughout these years in which the Channel balance steadily shifted from German to Allied advantage, the artillery duel between the guns at Dover and those on Cap Gris Nez continued. Neither side's guns were ever used to break up an invasion force, and neither quite succeeded in closing the Straits to the passage of the other's ships. What either side achieved by exchanges of shellfire is difficult to estimate; but neither was prepared to end it unilaterally.

It started on 22 August 1940, when the German guns fired first on a Channel convoy and then on Dover. Churchill had been demanding big guns for Dover for some time and now old battleship guns were emplaced there. Inevitably, one was christened 'Winnie'. Equally inevitably, its partner became 'Pooh'. The Germans deployed many more guns along the cliffs between Calais and Boulogne, giving their batteries more Teutonically serious names such as 'Siegfried' and 'Prinz Heinrich'. With them they heavily outgunned the British and turned Dover into 'Shellfire Corner'. Artillery bombardment brought a particular horror to total war, and the civilian population of Dover largely removed themselves to places of greater safety inland.

But the Germans had bombardment of a different order of magnitude in preparation. By the end of 1943 they had completed a number of V1 'flying bomb' bases close to the French Channel coast. Slave labourers from all over Europe were put to work on the job, and at Éperlecques, between Calais and St Omer, visitors today can see what their labour wrought. 'Le Blockhaus' there, the tourist attraction that has been created out of a gigantic concrete bastion from which V1s and later V2 rockets were despatched against Britain, is as awe-inspiring as any of the fortifications, ancient and modern, to be seen on either side of the English Channel.

On 13 June, a week after D-Day, the first V1s were fired towards England. Of the first batch of ten, five crashed almost immediately after launching, only four reached England, and only one caused casualties, in London's Bethnal Green. But faults were corrected, the Germans stuck to their launchers and the V1s kept coming, caused some damage and much alarm. For Londoners they re-created the atmosphere of the Blitz, which they thought they had seen the back of a year earlier. Anti-aircraft gunners and fighter pilots learned to engage the slow-moving pilotless aircraft and their ravages were kept within bounds, but they carried German bombardment all over southern England and far beyond Shellfire Corner. In the end, the Germans launched 2,754 flying bombs in this cross-Channel assault upon England, and Roy Jenkins notes the curious fact that between them they killed 2,752 people.[11]

There was no defensive answer to the supersonic V2 rockets which came into action later in 1944. Bomber pilots pounded Éperlecques and other bases but they failed to put them out of action. The only real solution was to capture the bases, as the Canadian army eventually did when it cleared the French Channel coast. Even then, V2 bases in Holland continued the bombardment of London and Antwerp. In March 1945 the last V2 was fired. It landed at Orpington in Kent and claimed the life of the last civilian to be killed by enemy action in Britain in the course of the Second World War.

In 1943 and the first half of 1944, the history of the English Channel increasingly becomes the story of preparation for the return match, the assault on Hitler's Fortress Europe and the liberation of the continent.

Gradually the Allies achieved first air superiority and later air domination. Fighters were no longer needed to defend English air space against German raiders, and they flew great sweeps deep into northern France instead. American troops by the hundred thousand arrived. The Allied armies trained obsessively hard all over Britain. The British and American ship yards were pouring out everything from aircraft carriers and destroyer escorts to landing craft for tanks and infantry alike. The Dieppe disaster had shown that the invaders would have to take their harbours with them, and the massive concrete and steel components of the prefabricated Mulberry harbours – the very conception still a deadly secret – were being prepared in British dockyards, to be floated across the Channel once Allied forces were re-established on the continent. The Bletchley Park code-breakers interpreted many of the millions of words plucked out of the ether over the French side of the Channel, and schemes of strategic deception were put to work to mislead the German planners. The Germans for their part concentrated on building their Atlantic Wall fortifications the length of the Channel coast.

All this obsessive activity put a deep psychological and physical mark on the Channel and the Channel coasts. In Britain, the beaches had been closed to civilians ever since 1940. Now whole communities were deported from deployment and training areas. American forces were packed into the West Country, British into Kent and Sussex. The preparations consumed the resources of two nations and imposed themselves on every aspect of life in southern England. They demonstrate by very contrast how superficial, almost frivolous had been German preparations for their own attempt at a Channel crossing in 1940.

One element of these preparations produced a very particular tragedy. The long beach in Devon between Start Point and Dartmouth near the village of Slapton offered conditions similar to the Normandy invasion beaches. In April 1944 it was resolved to practise American assault engineers in landings there. A miniature invasion fleet was assembled and set out to put its troops ashore on Slapton Sands. In the darkness of a spring night a squadron of German torpedo boats somehow spotted the Allied ships and attacked what looked like a conventional shipping movement along the Channel coast. They sank two tank landing ships and damaged a third; 639 American soldiers were lost, ten of them officers who knew some part at least of the plans for the coming assault. If one had been picked up alive by a German boat he could have compromised the invasion plans. Every body washed ashore or picked up at sea was carefully examined. All ten American officers were among them. The invasion secrets were safe. Today shore memorials commemorate the men who died at Slapton, and give an account of why they died there. Just over a month later new batches of assault engineers landed on the other side of the Channel to carry out for real the operations that had been rehearsed at Slapton Sands.

CHAPTER 17

THE GREAT INVASION

I n the course of 1942, graffiti started to appear on the walls of British cities. 'Second Front Now', they said; and the slogan, painted by British Communists with a new enthusiasm for the war after Hitler's attack on the Soviet Union in the previous year, fed the widespread British conviction that the heroic Russians were being left to fight Nazi Germany virtually alone.

Britain and Canada attempted the disastrous attack on Dieppe in part to show the Soviet Union and the United States that they were in earnest about getting to grips with the enemy. Soviet suspicions of the western Allies were endemic, engaged one issue after another, and persisted to the end of the war. But United States suspicions that the British were reluctant to commit themselves to an attack in the west also died hard, and they played a bigger role in the shaping of the western Allies' strategy.

The British and Americans had very different memories of the First World War. For the British it had consumed a generation, as well as Britain's world supremacy. They believed that a landing in anything less than overwhelming force would lead straight to the slaughter they had suffered then. 'Memories of the Somme and Passchendaele and many lesser frontal attacks upon the Germans,' Winston Churchill recalled when the fighting was over, 'were not to be blotted out by time or reflection.'[1] For the Americans, entering the war only in 1917, in time to play a relatively small part in the final triumph, it had been a great adventure that at little cost had won them authority in Europe and worldwide. They were determined that the way to beat the Germans was by a straight knock-out punch in the west. When the British maintained that neither their forces nor the Americans' were ready for a cross-Channel attack and proposed Mediterranean adventures instead, the Americans suspected British politicking or empire-building. 'The "Second Front debate" was . . . the crux of the most important of all wartime Anglo-American misunderstandings.'[2] Distrust between the Allies ran deep in 1942 and 1943.

Alanbrooke's diary entries capture the British conviction that at first the Americans had no conception of what an invasion of the continent would entail. He describes a first meeting in London with George Marshall, his American opposite number: 'Started COS at 9 am as Marshall was due at 10.30. He remained with us till 12.30 and gave us a long talk on his views concerning the desirability of starting western front next September [1942] and that the USA forces would take part. However, the total force which they could transport by then only consisted of 2½ divisions!! . . . Furthermore they had not begun to realise what all the implications of their proposed plans were!'[3] A week later Alanbrooke returns to the point. Marshall's 'plan does not go beyond just landing on the far coast!! Whether we are to play baccarat or chemin de fer at Le Touquet, or possibly bathe at Paris Plage is not stipulated! I asked him this afternoon – do we go east, south or west after landing? He had not begun to think of it!!'

But the facts of the military balance in 1942 were clear, and the Americans gradually accepted that an invasion undertaken prematurely would face defeat. That would be politically as well as strategically disastrous, as Hitler knew very well. Perhaps he recalled his own fears about the consequences of failure in an invasion of England in 1940. 'Once defeated,' he told his generals, 'the enemy will never try to invade again . . . they would need months to organise a fresh attempt. And an invasion failure would also deliver a crushing blow to British and American morale . . .'[4]

At one stage, in an attempt to reconcile the American thirst for action with British caution, the Allies toyed – the Americans with more conviction than the British – with the idea of seizing and holding the Cotentin peninsula (at the end of which Cherbourg lies) as a base for a later foray into France proper against the Germans. It was as fanciful as British and French ideas in 1940 of holding a Breton redoubt, and would have thrown away the advantage of strategic surprise offered by command of the Channel (and without that command there could be no thought of invasion). In the end the argument for the long build-up of strike capacity which alone could guarantee success proved irrefutable. After long cross-purposes and horse-trading, the western Allies reached agreement that a thoroughly prepared invasion of France should be launched in May 1944.

The obvious place to land was the Pas-de-Calais. A landing on the coast between Calais and Boulogne, in sight across the water from Kent on a clear day, offered a short sea-crossing, close proximity to fighter bases in southern England, and the shortest land-route into Germany. But this was where the Germans expected attack. They fortified this coast even more thoroughly than elsewhere and deployed their 15th Army with most of their strongest divisions immediately behind it. And the landing beaches here were backed by high ground that favoured the defenders and sometimes by impassable cliffs. Getting ashore anywhere on the French coast would be difficult. Here, the planners concluded, it would be impossible.

They settled instead on a landing in the Bay of the Seine in Normandy, on the stretch of coast between Cherbourg and Le Havre. Here the beaches were backed at worst by low cliffs, more often by a ribbon of development with open country behind it. This coast was still within reasonable range of fighters operating from British bases. Offshore there was room to deploy the naval armada that would bring the invaders to France and pound the enemy's positions to pieces. The Normandy coast was half as far again from the German frontier as the Pas-de-Calais, which would make the eventual exploitation of victory more difficult. But Allied aircraft could make that victory cheaper and more certain by destroying the bridges over the Seine and Loire and so shutting out German reinforcements from the Normandy battle area.

The planners excluded both Cherbourg and Le Havre as goals for the first wave of operations. Dieppe had shown the price of trying to seize a heavily defended port by frontal attack and not even vastly better supported attackers could hope to take Cherbourg or Le Havre head-on. The Allies would have to win their essential port facilities by attack overland, along the coast from their invasion beaches. How to sustain the invaders until a port could be seized? The prefabricated Mulberry harbours were the answer.

How many troops could the Allies put ashore in the first assault? At first, the number of landing craft that could be made available seemed to impose a tight constraint, and the planners thought in terms of a first wave of two divisions. But two divisions could land only on a narrow front, vulnerable to immediate counter-attack and too narrow to be developed into a bridgehead. Eventually it was decided to seize five beaches around the Bay of the Seine, with six divisions landing more or less simultaneously from the sea and three – two American and one British – from the air. The seaborne divisions would fight their way inland, join up with the airborne, move on to seize Caen and Bayeux in the first onslaught and link the beaches into a single bridgehead 50 miles wide. More forces would be poured in behind them. The Allies would destroy the German divisions sent against them in a great Normandy battle, seize Cherbourg and break into Brittany, and then move eastwards towards Germany. The French forces of the interior would rise up in support and another American and French army coming up from landings on the Riviera would join them.

To position, equip and train the forces for this great invasion would take over a year. At the same time a fleet of specialised landing craft must be created. So must special equipment for the invading troops: the tanks that could swim ashore, the flail tanks to thrash through minefields, the bulldozer tanks to hack through earthworks. So must the components of the Mulberry harbours. Air attack on German positions, camps and troop trains steadily increased. So did support for the sabotage and intelligence gathering of the French resistance. Meanwhile, the planners gathered their intelligence about what faced the invaders, with constant electronic snooping, incessant air reconnaissance and the painstaking creation of a great photographic panorama of the whole French coast. To compose it they drew on holidaymakers' snaps, gladly sacrificed to the war effort. The photograph of daddy up to his fetlocks in the shallows, of son buying his ice-cream from a cafe on a street corner, of mother sheltering from the sun beneath a sea wall: all these taken together gave the attacking troops precise images of what would lie before them when the ramps on their landing craft were lowered and they waded ashore to liberate the continent.

It was no secret that an invasion was coming. For the Germans the problem was to decide where. Their commander in the west, Field Marshal von Rundstedt, expected landings on the Pas-de-Calais coast or even further north, in Belgium. Hitler's instinct told him instead that they would come in Normandy. Intelligence found it hard to substantiate either guess, for Allied air superiority shut out German reconnaissance flights against England and Allied air strikes against targets in France ranged so widely that they gave no indication of where the seaborne blow would fall. Nor did radio traffic. The Allies' 'Double Cross' programme created a fictitious 1st American army corps based in southeast England under General George Patton, with misleading radio transmissions and German agents who had been captured and turned conveying the impression that these non-existent divisions would lead an invasion of the continent across the Straits of Dover.

The Germans had used vast quantities of concrete and slave labour in building an 'Atlantic Wall' of fortifications along the Channel coast. And they had strong armies in northern France, far stronger than anything the Allies could get into action ashore in the first weeks of the invasion. But the Germans had a long coast to cover. Rundstedt envisaged holding most of his men back from the coast and throwing them into devastating counter-attacks only when the Allies had committed themselves to the continent. Hitler told himself that the landings would be a great opportunity, to destroy enemies who had to come to him from an island where he had been unable to get at them. His generals must think not in terms of enemy lodgements ashore but of enemy forces to be torn apart and thrown back into the sea.

But the Allies dominated the skies and Erwin Rommel, taking charge of the defence early in 1944 under Rundstedt's overall control, realised that it would be impossible to move forces to the counter-attack over long distances under air bombardment. He therefore reversed Rundstedt's policy and decided to meet, attack and destroy the invaders on the beaches, and meanwhile to invest yet more effort, concrete, barbed wire and explosive devilry in making those very Channel beaches impassable. In doing so he was making the opposite switch from the one that the British had made when in 1940 they prepared for the invasion that never came, when they decided to shift from static defence on the beaches to mobile counter-attack.

In the early months of 1944 the roads, villages and fields of southern England filled with troops and their equipment. The Americans made a particular impression on the war historian John Keegan who was a schoolboy at the time: 'with them they brought a new wave of equipment, half-track scout cars, amphibious trucks and gigantic transporters, laden with tanks and bulldozers . . .'[5] Gradually an armada of ships and landing craft packed every Channel harbour from Cornwall to Sussex. There were aircraft everywhere, the fighters flying great sweeps deep over France, the bombers pounding away equally at German industry and at targets along the French Channel coast. Now gliders and troop-carrying aircraft came to join them. Armies, airfleets and navies were poised for the attack.

Only the Supreme Commander, General Eisenhower, could give the word to go, and he was at the mercy of his weather forecasters. The strike aircraft that would pound the German defences needed clear weather. The troop carriers needed moonlight if they were to find their dropping zones. The landing craft must hit the beaches before the receding tide exposed Rommel's explosive defences and entanglements along the foreshore. The whole enterprise required calm weather, not just on D-Day but for a week at least while the beach landings were still vulnerable. If a window of opportunity was missed in early June, another would not open before the end of the month – and the invasion had been promised originally for May, not July. The Channel, eternally temperamental, would rarely deliver the weather combination on which the Allied commanders depended, and on 4 June it seemed to turn against them.

Then, on 5 June, came a chance of a period of fair weather. In his official report on the campaign in Europe, Eisenhower wrote:

> The latest possible date for the invasion on the present tides was 7 June, but a further 24-hour postponement until then was impracticable as the naval bombardment forces . . . would have had to put back into port to refuel and the whole schedule of the operation would thus have been upset. I was, therefore, faced with the alternatives of taking the risks involved in an assault during what was likely to be only a partial and temporary break in the bad weather, or of putting off the operation until tide and moon should again be favourable.[6]

He wrestled with the decision alone, drafted a press statement for use in the event of failure, in which he took personal responsibility for the attack. Then he gave the order to go. The armada would sail and the first invading forces would land in France at dawn on 6 June.

A British admiral, the same Sir Bertram Ramsay who had organised another cross-Channel armada five years earlier when he extracted the army from Dunkirk, commanded the fleet, and the Royal Navy provided the majority of the warships. Indeed, D-Day marked a great climacteric, as much on land as at sea; for it was the last day, probably in all history, in which Britain went to war on equal terms with, perhaps even as senior partner with, the United States. Eisenhower might have overall command, but his deputy was a Royal Air Force officer. Montgomery commanded the land forces as Ramsay commanded the fleet. So much of the planning, so much of the new technology deployed on D-Day was the fruit of British minds. And British and Canadian troops outnumbered the Americans in the D-Day landings themselves.

So the Allies – British, American, Canadian – set sail for France. The armada's crossing had, Ramsay reported to Eisenhower, 'an air of unreality about it, so completely absent was any sign that the enemy was aware of what was happening. No U-boats were encountered, the bad weather had driven the enemy surface patrol craft into port, the German radar system was upset as a result of our air attack and scientific countermeasures, and no reconnaissance aircraft put in an appearance.'[7]

The first thing to hit the German defenders was aerial attack, and then the great bombardment from the sea. In the early summer of 1944 the Germans had grown used to the bombers pounding them and the ground-attack aircraft screaming in to blast their positions. The naval bombardment was different in kind, as cruisers and destroyers, battle-ships even, laid down the heaviest barrage from the sea that history has ever recorded. 'Off the Normandy coast,' wrote John Colville, a Royal Air Force pilot now that he had temporarily escaped from Churchill's service, ' . . . lay a semi-circle of grey battle-ships. Some, like *Rodney* and *Warspite*, were immediately recognisable, and . . . we could see their huge guns belching flame and smoke as they fired at targets inland.'[8] At the receiving end were second-rate German units, some of them immobile, many of them made up of the recently wounded or the over-age. Like German units everywhere, they took their punishment with extra-ordinary stoicism and then came out to fight the enemy as he landed.

The first troops to land were the men of the airborne divisions: American parachutists of the 82nd and 101st landing at the base of the Cotentin peninsula at the west end of the invasion beaches, British troops of the 6th between the Orne and Dives rivers at the east. They flew south in a great armada of aircraft and gliders, squadron after squadron struggling to keep formation and so deliver their human loads on target. The Channel saw that night the biggest such air armada in history, its commanders serene at least in the knowledge that the German fighters whose guns could tear the troop carriers and gliders apart were kept at bay by Allied air supremacy. It was, John Keegan reminds us, not just the largest such armada, but the last, as obsolete – though its crews and passengers did not know it – as the battle fleets that had joined battle at Jutland.[9]

In the event, the British landed right on target, their gliders bouncing to a halt within a hundred yards of the vital Bénouville bridges over the Orne and the Caen Canal. The aircraft and gliders carrying the much larger American force were thrown into confusion when they hit a sudden bank of cloud. They scattered their passengers across the base of the Cotentin peninsula. More were drowned in inundated fields and in the sea on both sides of the peninsula than were killed by German fire. It took hours for the survivors to assemble into effective fighting units, and they were fortunate that the Germans were equally slow in moving against them. But capture their targets the 'All Americans' and 'Screaming Eagles' eventually did, and they were there to link up at last with seaborne forces coming forward off the beaches.

The seaborne invaders had had a rough Channel crossing. The first wave of infantry divisions embarked at Plymouth, Torquay, Poole, Southampton, Portsmouth and Shoreham. The great armada formed up south of the Isle of Wight, at a point inevitably named Piccadilly Circus, and from there it steamed southwards towards the coast of Normandy. Well offshore in the Bay of the Seine the troops were transhipped into the landing craft, every man crawling, desperately overloaded, down the ship's side to the boats bobbing perilously below. Most got there safely, though some plunged to a quick death by drowning and a few were crushed like flies between the rolling hulls.

The invaders landed at five beaches between the Cotentin and the river Orne. The one codenamed Utah, in the extreme west, lies beyond the estuary that bites into the coastline towards Carentan. Omaha, next, is on the coast of the Bessin, which stretches between Carentan and Bayeux. These two were the Americans' beaches. Next along, just east of Arromanches, came Gold, a British beach, followed by Juno, assaulted by the Canadians, and finally Sword, the other British beach near the mouth of the Orne. They are all there to this day, signposted for the visitor, with their remains of fortifications and gun emplacements, their cemeteries and trophy tanks and museums, their memories of order and confusion, heroism and suffering, victory and death, all waiting to be examined in peaceful tranquillity more than half a century afterwards.

The face they present to the pilgrims who visit them subtly changes from east to west. Sword beach starts in the suburbs of Oustreham, a flourishing little cross-Channel ferry port today. In small places like Riva Bella, Lion, Luc and Langrune-sur-Mer, the coast road is lined almost without a break by shops, restaurants, cafes, little hotels and houses for summer visitors. At Juno things are a little more open and at Gold more open still, with Arromanches a pleasant little seaside resort surrounded by open country, where the remains of a few of Mulberry's great artificial reefs can still to be seen out in the bay. By Omaha, the coast has become almost empty, overlooked only by the occasional wrecked concrete gun emplacement and by the great American war cemetery at Saint-Laurent-sur-Mer, perhaps the most beautiful of all the military cemeteries in France. And at Utah the land behind the beach is flat and deserted, set between a landscape and seascape of huge skies, with the coast road as isolated from the hinterland by marshes as it is from the sea by the waves.

The 4th American Infantry Division's landings at Utah went well, almost unopposed. The suffering here in the extreme west was borne by the airborne divisions, floundering around in the flooded fields and marshes inland, not the men landing from the sea. At Omaha things were very different for the 1st and 29th Divisions, for this was the one place where the sea landings on that first day went badly wrong. The attackers found themselves pinned down where they landed, shot to pieces on the beach itself or cowering in what cover they could find beneath the sea wall. In the end, individuals' heroism got the attackers moving away from the beaches and a little inland. Gold by contrast was relatively easy for the British 50th Infantry Division, and so was Juno for the 3rd Canadian. But at both, and even more at Sword, where the 3rd Infantry Division and the Commandos went ashore, the defenders came out of their shelters to fight as the armada approached the shore. The attackers therefore faced a storm of fire as their landing craft grounded and they crossed the beaches, as well as hand-to-hand fighting in the built-up areas immediately beyond them. But from the beginning they felt themselves in control and on the offensive, as the men at Omaha did not.

*   *   *

By nightfall on D-Day, the Allies were ashore. At Utah beach, the seaborne attack had joined up with the men of the airborne divisions in a penetration 8 miles deep. At Omaha, by contrast, the Americans were holding on by their fingernails. The attackers at Gold and Juno had linked up in a 15-mile-wide lodgement that reached inland almost to Bayeux, and the men from Sword had reached the British airborne attackers on the other side of the Orne. But between Juno and Sword there was a gap; and into this gap advanced the inevitable German counter-attack.

Throughout both world wars the determination of German counter-attacks earned fear and respect. Now the men of 21st Panzer Division struck out towards the sea. It was a newly formed division, which like all the German units within range had been heavily pounded from air and sea that day. It was under-equipped, with only a hundred tanks, but it was attacking Canadian units that had only just got ashore. The attackers advanced with cautious deliberation. The Canadians rebuffed them and the attackers withdrew to lick their wounds, in a way few German units had ever done before. In doing so they missed the opportunity to get onto the Allies' beaches before they could create an effective lodgement. 'They will get the thrashing of their lives,' Hitler had forecast. 'I am convinced that when the time comes it will be a huge relief, just like Dieppe.'[10] Instead, when the time came the men of 21st Panzer failed to thrust home their counter-attack with the determination that friends and foes had come to expect of the German army.

There were other gaps in the Allied positions, between Omaha and Utah at Carentan, and between Omaha and the British right flank at Gold. The price of the long and costly hold-up beneath the sea wall at Omaha could have been a high one. But here, in the west, the Germans had little mobile strength. To get tanks there under constant attack from the air would take time, and long before the Germans had succeeded in gathering their forces the Allies had linked their lodgements together and begun to penetrate inland. By Day 3 their land forces were solidly established; by Day 5 fighters were operating from airstrips within the bridgehead. The logistic achievement was enormous. 'During the first six days of the operation,' Eisenhower

PETER UNWIN

recorded, '326,547 men, 54,186 vehicles and 104,428 tons of stores were brought ashore over the beaches.'[11]

Alanbrooke, paying a first visit to the bridgehead, saw how it was done. On the way across the Channel:

> we continually passed convoys of landing craft, minesweepers, bits of floating breakwater . . . being towed out, parts of the floating piers . . . etc . . . About 11 am we approached the French coast and the scene was beyond description. Everywhere the sea was covered with ships of all shapes and sizes, and a scene of continuous activity . . . It was a wonderful moment to find myself re-entering France almost exactly 4 years after being thrown out . . .[12]

So the invaders, their way made straight by naval and air bombardment, their right arm strengthened by the supplies pouring in to support them, had punched their way through Hitler's Atlantic Wall far more easily than the Allied planners had feared. They faced much greater difficulty as they moved inland. In the east, the British could make little progress towards Caen. Yet the planners had laid down that the forces landing on Juno and Sword beaches should seize the city in the first assault. It was a big place, only 10 miles from the beaches, and in Allied hands it would anchor the left flank of their whole position in Normandy. But as long as the Germans held it, it blocked any Allied advance to the east, towards Paris and Germany. They hung on tenaciously, and went on holding it against bombardment from the sea, against bombardment from the air and against constant land attack. The Allies laid Caen waste, dropping a greater weight of bombs there than Bomber Command had unloaded over Hamburg; but it was weeks before they could occupy the ruins. Today Caen is a fine, but characterless, modern city, showing no direct evidence of wartime bombardment, and no trace at all of what once was William the Conqueror's capital of Normandy.

Further west, also, the Allies made slow progress. While they could flatten the fortifications of the Atlantic Wall from the air, here they faced much more formidable and ancient obstacles. Ten centuries of intensive agriculture had chopped northern Normandy into fields the size of pocket handkerchiefs. They were divided by thick hedges on banks steep enough to stop a tank and so iron-hard and matted that they defied the Allies' bulldozers. The roads that penetrated this *bocage* country were narrow, sunk deep between banks and hedges, in which a tank or truck was at the mercy of close-range ambush. Everything favoured the defence, nothing favoured armoured attack, or even strike aircraft. Here, as in Caen, the Germans could stand and fight on equal terms.

Then came the great Channel storm. Eighteen months earlier, Hitler had said to his generals, 'If only they would land half a million men, and then foul weather and storms cut them off in the rear. Then everything would be all right.'[13] Now he had his storm, one of the fiercest summer storms the Channel had seen for half a century. Eisenhower's luck with the weather, so bravely tested on 6 June, had turned against him. The storm caught some elements of the Mulberry harbours in transit to Normandy. It battered ships at sea and landing craft inshore. It broke through some of the Mulberry breakwaters that were already in place and swept away its floating wharves. The steady flow of supplies on which the armies depended was interrupted. Everything depended now not on infantrymen and tank troopers but on engineers, pioneers, transport companies. They did not allow even the worst of the weather to break the flow completely. Determination and ingenuity maintained a trickle of supplies, and then, as wind and waves gradually subsided, the flood was re-established.

Inland, a bitter infantryman's slogging match continued. Junior officers' casualty rates reached First World War levels and the old British fears of being caught up in another war of attrition in the fields of France seemed justified. But the Allies' numbers went on increasing, till they outweighed their opponents on land, as they had all along outweighed them in the air. Hitler still suspected that the Normandy assault was a mere feint and that the real attack was still to come across the Straits of Dover. He demanded that his men in Normandy fight and die where they stood, and stubbornly refused to commit to the battle the fifteen strong divisions of the 15th Army stationed north of the Seine. When German reinforcements did move forward, Allied aircraft pounded every road into Normandy. Finally, the German resistance collapsed and the Americans broke out in the west, captured Cherbourg, and flooded into Brittany.

The American marches that followed, plunging deep into France before swinging round in a great right hook behind the Germans still stubbornly defending their positions in front of the British and Canadians, take us too far from our Channel story. So does the British and Canadian advance, through Caen and on towards Falaise, to close the gap between them and the Americans far away to the south. So does the heroism of the Polish 1st Armoured Division, blocking the German escape, or the French 2nd Armoured Division's liberation of Paris. So for that matter does the Germans' achievement in getting so many of their men through the Falaise gap and out of the Allies' trap.

There are other consequences of the victory in Normandy that do stay close to the Channel coast. The first is the American seizure of Cherbourg on 26 June and the work of the engineers in getting that great port, so comprehensively laid waste by its German garrison, back to work as the Allies' main cross-Channel artery after the loss of so much of the Mulberry harbours in the great storm. A second is the advance up the Channel coast of 21st Army Group. The British and Canadians stormed across the lower Seine, across the lower Somme, up through Picardy, the Pas-de-Calais and Flanders, all the way to Brussels and the very gates of Ostend. It was an advance that took them 200 miles from the Seine to the Scheldt, in a march to compare with the German charge from the Ardennes to the Channel four years earlier.

The advance of 21st Army Group had a more serious purpose than breaking records, even than liberating Belgium. It was to capture and reopen the Channel ports, and above all Antwerp and the mouth of the Scheldt, and to destroy the bases in northern France from which the V1 flying bomb assault on southern England had been waged. The great short-range bombardment of London and southern England, with which Hitler still hoped to snatch victory from the jaws of defeat, had begun on 13 June, a week after D-Day. Now, in early September, the Canadians captured the blockhouse at Éperlecques and other V1 bases.

It took longer to capture Boulogne, Calais and Dunkirk, longer still to clear the Scheldt and put Antwerp back to work as the Allies' principal port on the continent.

There are still a few more stories to be told about the French Channel coast in the summer of 1944. They are no more than footnotes to history, but they are footnotes worth remembering.

Hitler's determination that no German units should give ground anywhere meant that pockets of resistance remained along the Channel coast long after the real fighting had moved on. At Cherbourg, the most important point of all, the German commander fought a desperate six-day fight, then destroyed all the port facilities and reported to Rommel, 'Further sacrifice cannot alter anything.' The reply came back, 'You will continue to fight until the last cartridge in accordance with the orders of the Führer.' [14] He decided for himself that the time for heroics was over and surrendered the ruins of the port to the Americans.

But elsewhere German commanders, perhaps younger or more foolish than he, continued to resist. One German garrison cut off on the French coast defied everything the Allies could throw at them. Eventually a young British officer, William Douglas-Home, who later became a successful popular playwright, invited a court-martial when he refused to press ahead with an attack which he believed was militarily unnecessary and which he feared would cost too many French inhabitants their lives. And on the little island of Cézembre, only two miles off St Malo, a German lieutenant with a garrison of 300 men held out against air attack for a month before thirst compelled him to surrender.

Even in March 1945, by which time Allied armies were deep inside Germany, the German garrison in the Channel Islands remained unbowed. Left far behind by events, its officers decided to get back into history. They launched a commando raid on Granville on the coast of Normandy, killed American and British soldiers and French civilians, released German prisoners-of-war, and took prisoners of their own back to the islands with them. In the words of an American post-mortem, as long as he stayed ashore on the continent the enemy took 'complete control of the Granville area'. Had his object been 'that of conquest, he was the conqueror'.[15]

Bad as the cause they served may have been, ordinary Germans resisted a great cross-Channel assault with gallant desperation. Their deeds deserve to be remembered beside those of the victors.

CHAPTER 18

TODAY AND TOMORROW

Towns and cities on both sides of the Channel emerged devastated from the war, but the French ones wore the deeper scars. Portsmouth, Plymouth and Southampton had been battered from the air, and Dover by long-range artillery as well. But the German bombers of 1940 and 1941 had been toys by comparison with the four-engined Allied monsters that came after them, and V1s and V2s did more moral than material damage in southern England. No English city had undergone the artillery assault that preceded a land attack. None had suffered like Caen. British travellers encountered in northern France a level of destruction quite different from anything they had seen at home.

They found poverty too, and with it deprivation and squalor. It had been a Victorian article of faith that 'the French are a dirty people'. Between the wars, Noël Coward pronounced that 'there's something fishy about the French', and English travellers found French lavatories revolting or hilarious, according to temperament. Now post-war conditions added a new dimension to their disgust. And as France resumed the game of its domestic politics, producing a multiplicity of parties and ten changes of government a year, the absurdities of the Gallic political system were added to a catalogue of reasons for kindly Anglo-Saxon contempt.

The British, in contrast, had come out of the war among the

victorious Big Three. Theirs was the only nation that had fought unoccupied from the first day of the war to its last. Now, when they went back to France for a first continental holiday, the Bank of England let them take only £75 with them, yet they travelled with the arrogance of Milord on the Grand Tour. The war had given them a fine conceit of themselves and they carried it into the late 1940s. When they crossed the Channel they saw themselves leaving a confident, victorious nation to go slumming among excitable, down-at-heel foreigners.

Yet the Channel neighbours still had much in common. Both had been financially ruined by war, yet with Germany destroyed they thought of themselves as the only serious nations in western Europe. Both faced similar tasks of post-war reconstruction. Each ruled a zone of occupation in Germany and a sector of Berlin. In March 1947 they signed a bilateral defensive alliance and two years later they joined NATO together. Gradually economic recovery in France and continuing economic hardships in Britain brought their relative living standards more closely together. Elizabeth David reminded the British of the glories of French cuisine. Paris's New Look reminded them of French glamour. Meanwhile, in Britain food rationing persisted into the 1950s. The British grew a shade less patronising, the French a degree less resentful.

Old rivalries and dislikes seemed eternal, however, and new ones came to reinforce them. To French memories of English Goddams and Waterloo had been added resentment of Dunkirk, the fighter squadrons withheld, and the attack on France's fleet. Now the French, not a people to entertain an inferiority complex lightly, balked at the continuing arrogance of 'les Anglo-Saxons'. The British were unmoved, for they remembered French military incompetence and worse in 1940, and Vichy's accommodation with the Germans. Both recalled the cross-purposes of de Gaulle's uneasy alliance with Winston Churchill, as well as their triumphs together. In 1956, at Suez, the two countries involved themselves together in an abortive attack upon an Egyptian leader, Colonel Nasser, whom they saw as a new Hitler. But at the same time they started down divergent roads to the future of Europe, with France a founder member of the European Economic Community while Britain remained a suspicious outsider. There would be no more war in the Channel, but it remained a political, economic, social and cultural dividing line.

In both countries everyday conditions of life went on improving, and every improvement had its effect on the Channel coasts and on traffic between them. More and more Englishmen took their cars to the continent, watching anxiously from the dockside as the cranes swept them up into the air and lowered them into the ferry's hold. The cult of the sun lured holiday makers further afield, to Tuscany or the Riviera or package holidays in Spain, and resorts on both sides of the Channel suffered. But they still had their regular visitors, and growing prosperity offered more people the chance of a holiday than ever before. So Brighton and Eastbourne, the French and Belgian resorts and the new holiday camps attracted families who ten years earlier would have thought themselves lucky to enjoy a day out at the seaside.

Cross-Channel travel became a mass industry for the first time. Dover, Folkestone and Newhaven all offered ferry services to France. British Rail ferries competed with the French railway, SNCF, and with a private company, Townsend Thoresen. Their pre-war ships still predominated, some of them displaying their Dunkirk evacuation battle honours. By today's standards they were small, though the train ferries conveyed through railway coaches with sleeping passengers to the continent. Others held a couple of hundred passengers and a score of cars. Drive-on, drive-off was still to come, and so were the joys of on-board shopping.

Competition appeared. You could drive down through the Kentish lanes and find on the airfield at Lydd strange, twin-engined, high-winged aeroplanes that at a price would buzz you and three cars across the Channel to Le Touquet with a dozen fellow passengers. In 1955 came the invention of the hovercraft, and four years later, on the fiftieth anniversary of Louis Blériot's first flight from Calais to Dover, the first hovercraft crossing of the Channel. By the 1970s these noisy, crab-like machines offered a fast and, all too often, unusually nauseating means of getting to the other side of the Channel. They whizzed their passengers in thirty-five minutes from Dover to Calais or from Calais to Pegwell Bay, where Hengist, Horsa and St Augustine had all set foot on English soil before them.

The Lydd Channel-hoppers died the death, but for a time the hovercraft seemed to flourish. Yet like so many post-war British inventions it never quite fulfilled the hopes its enthusiasts invested in it. The ordinary ferries continued to dominate the cross-Channel market, with their loads of school parties, lorry drivers, day excursionists and soldiers of the British Army of the Rhine on their way home on leave from Germany. Air travel went on growing, but the Channel ferries remained an essential element of business and pleasure travel. The old ships were steadily replaced by new ones that were bigger, faster and more sophisticated. Fast catamarans joined the fleets. Duty-free shipboard shopping became a part of the continental holiday ritual. And by the late 1950s minds were starting to turn yet again to the idea of a Channel Tunnel.

The waters of the English Channel were alive with traffic more imposing than the ferries serving the crossing between the island and the continent. The Straits of Dover were still the most important approach to northern Europe's inland seas, and as ports like Rotterdam and Antwerp recovered their importance, the volume of shipping passing through them from the Channel to the North Sea increased. For years the Straits had remained unregulated by anything more than the immemorial customs of the sea, but eventually Channel rules of the road were introduced. They applied to traffic far away in the west in the mouth of the Channel and, more important, in its very throat. Regulations prescribed inshore traffic zones on both sides of the Channel for fishing boats, pleasure craft and pottering coasters. In mid-Channel a safety divide was established, which in the Straits coincided with the median line, and two lanes for through traffic. Eastbound and westbound, ships were routed to keep to the right, their positions and headings carefully monitored from traffic control centres in Dover and on Cap Gris Nez.

In principle, shipping crossing the Straits gives way to ships passing through. Through these crowded waters, which handle 500 shipping movements daily, tankers and container ships move at a steady omnipotent speed. Lesser vessels are wise to beware. And real problems arise at night, in foul weather or poor visibility, above all at the point where the ferries to the continent cross the paths of the big merchant ships en route to the North Sea and the Channel. Tides and currents complicate the story. Occasional accidents demonstrate that, like the flight paths into the world's great airports, the Straits of Dover are a disaster waiting to happen, kept at bay only by radar, the vigilance of officers of the watch and the constant attention of the traffic supervisors ashore.

For two decades after the war, the transatlantic liners still made their regular imperious mark on the life of the Channel. Southampton remained the great English liner port, Le Havre the French; and the Southampton liners usually called at Cherbourg also on their way out and home. In the post-war years the great names were *Queen Mary*, *Queen Elizabeth*, *France* and *United States*, and in the 1960s *Queen Elizabeth 2* entered the lists. These great ships still brought a taste of glamour and sense of importance to the Channel that merchantmen and ferries could not. But with the growth of aviation their days were numbered. Now only cruise liners bring style to Southampton and Le Havre, and it is a meretricious glamour after the excitements of the old liner sailings to New York, with their attendant tugs, boat trains, sentimental well-wishers and bands playing 'Auld Lang Syne' upon the quay.

The impact of the Royal Navy on the Channel scene has also declined. A trip round Portsmouth Harbour passes frigates and destroyers, submarines across the water, even an aircraft carrier. Behind them are moored the symbols of Britain's naval history when it played on a more ample stage: Nelson's flagship *Victory* and, not far away, the mid-nineteenth-century ironclad *Warrior*. Quite often there are visiting NATO warships to be seen too, moored where in 1956 a British frogman disappeared in the near vicinity of a Soviet cruiser, the pride of the Red Fleet. She had brought Khrushchev and Bulganin on a state visit to

Britain, and the requirements of espionage and diplomacy got at terrible cross-purposes. The frogman, who was probably murdered by Russian frogmen, came close to wrecking a summit conference. True to the Bulldog Drummond ethos of the time, he was known to his friends as 'Buster', but his name was Commander Crabb.

Once in the last twenty years the navy put on a show in the Channel in something approaching the old style. In a mad forty-eight hours in 1982, the South Atlantic Task Force was made ready for war. On 5 April the carriers *Hermes* and *Invincible*, with their attendant destroyers and frigates, their Harrier jets and their cheering crews, sailed away from Portsmouth to recover the Falkland Islands. Families, fellow seamen and well-wishers lined the Southsea waterfront as they sailed away down the Solent. In three months they were back, chastened by the casualties of real war, but bringing victory back from the other end of the earth.

Now there is a recessional air about the navy in the Channel. Its true capital ships, the nuclear submarines, are far away. Portsmouth is unlikely to see another task force sail away to war with quite the swagger that went into its Falklands campaign, and there will never be another display of patriotic might to compare with the one laid on by the Royal Navy in the Solent to mark Queen Victoria's Jubilee. Today's sailors still raise merry hell on a run ashore, but there is about them rather less of the supreme self-confidence that the navy brought to the Channel when its ships sailed out from Portsmouth and Plymouth to rule the ocean waves.

The Channel's little ships are less vulnerable to the ebb and flow of history. Its fishermen go about their business in their old lugubrious way. At dozens of little French and British fishing harbours, inshore fishermen still sell crab and lobster fresh off their boats on the beach. At a few places like St Vaast-la-Hougue, Channel fishing can be inspected on a different, positively industrial scale. But even these big, ocean-going craft have their troubles, with pollution, poachers, conservation quotas and Common Fisheries Policy added to the perennial difficulties and dangers of the sea. At times there are squabbles with foreign rivals, sometimes between British and French fishermen, more often with the Spanish, and the navies' fishery protection ships move in to inspect net sizes, seize catches and restore order. But all the fishing fleets, whatever their home ports, face the same problem of declining stocks and the need to restrict catches if a piscine balance is ever to be restored to the narrow seas.

The atmosphere among the small-boat sailors is more ebullient. They have built on the foundations laid down by R. T. McMullen, and their craft pack the Channel's harbours, estuaries and quiet backwaters. Turn any corner beside the Channel and you can find yourself confronted with forests of masts against the sky and the sounds of water slapping against hulls, halyards rattling in the wind. When the sailing boats of the Channel go to sea together they resemble nothing more than great flocks and sharp flights of seabirds, and when they gather in the Solent for Cowes Week they cover the surface of the sea with a dreamcoat of multi-coloured canvas. More usually, they sail alone, as solitary sailors embark on gentle coastal cruises or, more boldly, on cross-Channel passages. Their numbers increase and multiply, and the cost and difficulty of renting a mooring increase with them.

These are mostly fairweather sailors; but there are thousands of serious seamen among them. They take to heart the advice McMullen constantly reiterated: prepare for the worst the elements can throw at you. Even in high summer you cannot entirely trust the Channel, for it can turn foul, even vicious, in a few hours. For a description of what a really serious Channel storm can do to you, even in a powerful cruising yacht, turn to Adlard Coles's *Heavy Weather Sailing*:

One man forward broke his wrist and was washed overboard. The dinghy, two lifebelts and the electric flare went over the side at the same time. One of the light alloy stanchions had snapped off like a carrot. The doghouse window frame was cracked on one side and water poured through the ventilators, which were submerged. One man in the cockpit was thrown over the main boom . . . 5 ft above the cockpit floor and the other two were under water, but personal lifelines saved them from going overboard.[1]

Such were the joys of pleasure sailing if you were caught in the mouth of the Solent between Selsey and the Isle of Wight in the great storm of July 1956.

Even in fair weather, hazard attends Channel sailing. You can be overwhelmed by a ferry, swamped by a fast-moving Seacat or run down by one of the leviathans for which the Straits of Dover are a commercial motorway. A tyro sailor who had set his heart on sailing his 16-foot dinghy to France describes his strategy for avoiding sudden death in the big-ship zones out in mid-Channel. 'They probably can't see you,' a beginner's guide had warned him, 'usually can't stop in time to keep from running you down, and might not know if they did.'[2] He goes to sea with trepidation. Out in mid-Channel, however, he finds the problem less daunting than it seemed on paper: 'This was less like crossing a motorway... and more like crossing a desert railway. Empty silence, then a flurry of hurtling wagons, then empty silence.' There was time and room to avoid the collision that would have swept him and his boat to perdition. All the same, it was chastening to remember that a ship moving at 25 knots 'would change from a dot on the horizon to a churning giant in only ten minutes'.

In the nineteenth century, royal and military reaction between them put an end to efforts to build a Channel tunnel. Over the next hundred years the idea repeatedly came back into favour and was repeatedly rejected, on practical, financial and particularly military grounds. Distinguished officers produced absurd, almost hysterical strategic objections, which Little Englanders supported with existential, even metaphysical arguments about the nature of insularity. In a vain effort to accommodate them the French promised to put the approach to the tunnel at their end on a seaside viaduct, which the Royal Navy could easily destroy if things ever came to war; but not even that, least Gallic of concessions, could win round the British doubters.

Yet in the First World War a Channel tunnel would have made the supply of the British Expeditionary Force easier to sustain; and in 1940 it would have got the Expeditionary Force away with less loss than at Dunkirk. In either war it would have required military ineptitude on a monumental scale to allow the tunnel to fall into the hands of an invader. So over the decades the old, military argument against anything so dangerous as a tunnel faded away. In the 1950s the project was launched yet again, and this time far-distant events came to play their part. In 1956, the directors of the Suez Canal Company lost their canal to Egyptian nationalisation. They decided to invest in a Channel tunnel instead. That proposal fell to financial objections, abetted by those who still believed on metaphysical grounds that Britain must remain an island. But by the 1980s, minds were beginning to turn once again to the old dream, and this time only financial considerations stood in the way. At last, in 1989, the work that had been stopped in the 1890s was resumed, and in December 1990 French and British tunnellers joined hands beneath the Channel. In May 1994 Queen Elizabeth II took a train through the tunnel to join President Mitterrand in the great celebrations which declared the cross-Channel fixed link open.

It is, as all the world knows, a rail link, used equally by freight trains, through passenger expresses and shuttle services between the French and British terminals. It runs for 31 miles, 23 of them under water, plunging 150 feet below the seabed in a continuous belt of grey chalk that links England's geology to the continent's. It cost £12 billion and took 13,000 men to create it, and the vast boring machines they used cut through three times as much rubble as could be accommodated in the great pyramid of Cheops. In the year 2000 alone it carried 2.8 million cars, 1.1 million trucks, 80,000 coaches and 7.1 million passengers between Britain and the continent. Some day something more ambitious may become possible – perhaps a drive-through tunnel for electrically powered motor vehicles. For the moment it is good news that the present tunnel is paying its way, if scarcely living up to the financial hopes of its first investors.

The tunnel itself makes no physical impact on the outside world, the two terminals no more than two extensive marshalling yards. Yet at the proposal and planning stage the bored tunnel concept which was finally adopted faced competition from other schemes that would have seriously changed the Channel landscape. One bidder, Euroroute, proposed to create two artificial islands 5 miles offshore, linked to one another and the mainland by a combination of bridges and tunnels. Another, Eurobridge, wanted to sling a tube across the Channel, suspended high above the water from two giant towers. Either scheme would have faced meteorological challenges and interfered with sea traffic in a way that the bored tunnel does not. Whether driving our own cars to the continent would change the cross-Channel psychological relationship is anyone's guess. In another half century the time may come for links more ambitious than the Chunnel and give us the chance to find out.

As it is, the existence of a fixed link has already affected the nature of the Channel, and the relationship of Britain to the continent. The ferry companies have so far survived the commercial competition from the tunnel, just as they have cushioned the impact of the end of duty-free sales within the European Union. The business of the Channel ports has not been laid waste by the building of the tunnel, though the municipality of Dieppe is administering first-aid to the docks at Newhaven to keep them and their own town in cross-Channel business. The old fears for the security of the island have been shown up for the nonsense they always were. Cross-Channel investment flourishes, with more and more French-owned businesses setting up in the towns of Kent and Sussex, and British retailers a prominent presence in the purpose-built shopping centres of the French Channel ports. Only in one poignant way has the tunnel produced the invasion that its opponents always feared. Refugees from Kosovo, Afghanistan and Congo gather at the Sangatte tunnel terminal and take terrible risks to smuggle themselves aboard a train. They are driven by the hope that when it breaks surface behind Sandgate on the other side of the Channel they will find a new and better life in England. For them at least the Channel marks a real difference.

Even before the coming of the tunnel, the growth of cross-Channel traffic was already driving the ferry companies to new investment. The size of their ships grew as the threat of the tunnel increased and drive-on-drive-off became the norm. It persisted even after the open car decks that it required contributed to tragedy. In March 1987 the Townsend Thoresen *Herald of Free Enterprise* went to sea with her bow doors open and capsized a mile outside the harbour at Zeebrugge, with the loss of 200 lives. It was a terrible reminder that, however often a ship puts to sea, carelessness can bring disaster, and even the ship's name mocked private-sector triumphalism.

But the disaster did not stop the steady year-on-year increase of passenger and freight traffic. The ferry companies bought yet bigger and faster ships, still with the open decks below, and above them with the shopping and eating opportunities that ensure that their passengers need never see the sea. Fast catamarans have been introduced too, to supplement or replace the hovercraft services. Calais and Dover have modernised and extended their port facilities, Calais' spreading amply along the shore towards Gravelines where the Armada's fugitives went aground, Dover's jammed in below the cliffs on which the Britons stood and shook their spears at Julius Caesar.

The completion of the European Single Market brought a further stimulus to cross-Channel traffic. The most important effect was the steady increase in heavy freight traffic between Britain and the continent. Shipboard duty-free sales were abolished, but there were still plenty of Britons prepared to take a trip to France or Belgium and bring back alcohol and tobacco bought at continental prices. Their doings – sometimes their misdeeds – attracted more attention than more serious cross-Channel commerce. Single Market or no, immigration and customs still faced problems, which seemed to grow with every passing year. One was the smuggling of illegal drugs, concealed in a container truck or slipped into the country on a dark night from a yacht or fishing boat. Another was the terrorist threat from an innocent-looking ship bringing a floating bomb into a sleeping port. A third, and the most poignant, was the smuggling of illegal immigrants into Britain. From time to time bewildered Bangladeshis or Afghans are found by the roadside in Kent or Sussex, abandoned there by the syndicates that have smuggled them across the Channel. Other illegal immigrants are found concealed amid the loads of container trucks. And on one tragic occasion, a container was opened on its arrival in Dover from the Netherlands and disgorged a cargo of corpses, all that was left of a party of young Chinese men and women in search of a better life, who had died a terrible death of asphyxiation on the way.

Here, for the moment, ends the long and tangled history of the English Channel. The two countries that have talked, glared, traded and fought across it are united in a European Union and a European Single Market. They do more business together than ever in their troubled past, but still in separate currencies, the French in the new-fangled euro, the British in their proud though precarious pound. For French companies, Britain is scarcely a foreign market. The same is true of British companies and their French customers. The tunnel provides a reliable fixed link between Britain and the continent. The ferries are equally reliable, carrying more tonnage and as many people. Cross-Channel travel is a commonplace of life for millions of people. The British now go to France for their hip replacements, and the French come to language schools in Eastbourne and Brighton to learn the English language.

Yet Britain and France are in another way as distinct from one another as ever. Language remains an obstacle, despite the efforts of ordinary French men and women and more and more English people to overcome it. So do historical memories, and everyday ways of conducting oneself in society. The Channel remains what it has always been, dividing line, obstacle, thoroughfare between European nations and avenue linking Europe with the wider world.

What lies beyond the horizon? We move from present into future, and facts and evidence give way to downright guesswork.

The first issue is the future of the nation state, and particularly France and Britain. Will they survive for long in the new century as entities recognisable today? Will they succumb to popular anomie, to globalisation? Will the growth of regions erode state boundaries? Will Britain and France find themselves dissolved within the 'ever closer union of the peoples of Europe' to which the Treaty of Rome commits them?

Never say never; but I guess that Britain and France will be with us for decades yet, at least for the five that take us to the middle of the twenty-first century. They have given up many of the attributes of the nation state, but their peoples retain a strong sense of themselves as French and British citizens, different from other peoples. They have bound themselves into communities, alliances and international organisations that they could never have imagined, let alone joined, a century ago. Both are active members of the United Nations, permanent members of the Security Council. Their soldiers already wear the United Nations' blue berets as often as their own, and both countries will get still further involved in international efforts to give shape to twenty-first-century international society. But when all that is said and done, Frenchness and Britishness remains as the first and most significant characteristic of most of the two countries' peoples, a sense of nationhood still largely measured by differences from others.

The European Union complicates matters. Without it, Britain and France could be simply British and French, keeping each other at arm's length as they used to do. But both are committed to the European Union, if in different ways, recognising that it brings them more gain than loss. France will go on defining Europe as a reflection of French ways and British talk of leaving the Union will turn out to be just talk. France, proudly French as it is, has already given up the control of its frontiers to one European grouping and its franc to another. I guess that Britain will do the same with its coasts and currency within a decade.

Between them the free movement of peoples, the European Single Market and the euro will go on altering the nature of society, economics and business in both countries, in ways that steadily change things for the better, if at the price of the occasional hairy moment of social or economic crisis. Both countries will go on changing to meet the circumstances of a changing world. Britain is wholly committed to NATO, France an Alliance member with many a reservation about the way it works in practice. If NATO survives, both will remain involved in its doings. At the same time the two countries are building an identifiably European military capacity, one says within NATO, the other says close to but distinct from it. I guess that between them the French, the British and the other Europeans will carry this process considerably further, till in the end they have created something approaching the European army, which present-day political wisdom claims to be inconceivable.

One reason for that, and for many other changes that are ahead, lies across the Atlantic. Over the next ten years or so, Britain and France are likely to find more and more reason to dissent from the actions of a solipsistic and increasingly dangerous United States. When they do, they will turn with greater fervour to the development of a bigger, more powerful, more closely integrated European Union. The sceptical in Britain and France will say that such integration threatens their own precious national characteristics. Others, less sceptical, will see in it some hedge against the overpowering dynamism of American politics, economics and society. I guess that over time the sceptics will lose that particular argument. In consequence the Atlantic will get wider and the Channel narrower.

Neither Britain nor France will want to cut itself off from the wider world. So the United Nations and other global organisations will enrol both countries in efforts to do more good, or at least less harm, to all those millions on the fringes of international society. They will be more open to people from other continents. One of the consequences will be more immigration, more cross-Channel movement, and more squabbles about immigrants and refugees. At the end of the line I guess that there will be yet more dark faces on the streets of London and Paris, more new Frenchmen and new Britons. The Channel never kept new tribes, new races, new religions, new influences out of Britain. It will not start to do so now.

Environmental threats too will render irrelevant the Channel's old role as a natural demarcation line between different worlds. Already English and French mothers are taking unprecedented pains to slosh suntan cream on their babies on French and English beaches. If the world's sea level rises, so will the level of the Channel, indiscriminately threatening both French and English seaside resorts. So too with the world economy: it ebbs and flows with all the unstoppable power of the tides, and no single country, not even a Britain that remained resolute to keep the pound and reject the euro, would be unaffected by its tempo. Terrorists, drug dealers and drug customers, demonstrators against globalisation, genetic engineers, all these too ignore frontiers. They all diminish the importance of national identities, undermine the differences between states. Each of them reduces the significance of the Channel.

Yet millennia of history are not to be undone overnight. We have seen the British and the French defining themselves for the best part of 500 years by cross-Channel differences and, even as wartime Allies, finding as much to quarrel about as to agree on. From birth to death, the archetypal Englishman and Frenchman still continue to lead very different lives. Language, diet, dress, interests, all mark them down as English or French. They are content with that, and inertia keeps them so, content to do today what they did yesterday, and glad to do tomorrow what they did today.

But beside these archetypal millions are other British and French men and women who lead lives increasingly similar to lives being led on the other side of the Channel. They more and more define themselves by job or age or social class, by intellectual interest or sexual inclination, by company or trade union commitment, rather than by the old badges of nationality and language. The everyday lives of such people erode national identities quite as much as government action or international agreements; yet they are still far from having eliminated them altogether.

So the significance of the Channel will go on changing. It will remain both a barrier and a bridge between Britain and the continent. It will remain a seawater highway from the oceans into the heart of Europe. It will simultaneously link and separate countries which remain very different from one another but which gradually grow more alike.

In political and military terms the future of the Channel looks like being less interesting and dramatic than its past. But it will remain an intrinsically important part of the lives of the two countries that border on it. Millions of travellers – holidaymakers and businessmen, school-children and teachers, soldiers and academics, politicians and bureaucrats – will go back and forth across it. Its waters will go on mattering to seamen, fishermen, small-boat sailors and beachcombers, its beaches delighting generation after generation of the bucket-and-spade brigade.

It will go on delighting the poets too as it delighted Matthew Arnold. In 'Calais Sands', he cast his mind back to the historical Channel:

> A thousand knights have rein'd their steeds
> To watch this line of sand-hills run,
> along the never-silent strait,
> To Calais glittering in the sun.

He also looked across the water:

> Yet now my glance but once hath roved
> O'er Calais and its famous plain;
> To English cliffs my gaze is turn'd.
> O'er the blue strait mine eyes I strain.

Arnold set a greater poem on the other side of the straits that separate England and France. He ended 'Dover Beach' with a cry of pain at the decline of faith, seeing a world:

> Swept with confused alarms of struggle and flight,
> Where ignorant armies clash by night.

But he found comfort in the beauty of the Channel:

> The sea is calm tonight
> The tide is full, the moon lies fair
> Upon the straits; on the French coast the light
> Gleams and is gone; the cliffs of England stand
> Glimmering and vast, out in the tranquil bay.

But there is power in the Channel, as well as beauty and comfort, and in the end it is the power that dominates. When the winds blow in from the west, the waves pound against the cliffs and the currents suck millions of tons of sand from one shore and deposit them on another, the Channel reminds mortal men and women of its power. It was there before them, it will be there after them. Meanwhile, it lets them use it as it has always done. In the story of the use that human beings have made of its waters, of its harbours and of its ever-changing moods, we have the history of the English Channel.

ENDNOTES

Prologue

1 Cited in Mackesy, *The War for America*, page 192.
2 Sellar and Yeatman, *1066 and All That*, page 11.

Chapter 1

1 There are two good examples in Davies, *The Isles*, page 2, and Williamson, *The English Channel*, page 18.
2 Denys Brunsdon, cited in the *Independent*, 4 December 2001.
3 Julius Caesar, *The Civil War*, pages 62–3.
4 Julius Caesar, *The Conquest of Gaul*, page 77.
5 Ibid., page 79.
6 Ibid., page 80.
7 Ibid.
8 Ibid.
9 Ibid., page 97.
10 Ibid., page 98.
11 Ibid., pages 98–9.
12 Ibid., page 99.
13 Ibid., page 100.
14 Ibid., page 101.
15 Ibid., page 105.
16 Ibid., page 109.
17 Ibid., page 110.
18 Tacitus, *The Agricola*, page 64.
19 Schama, *A History of Britain*, page 29.

20 For a useful map, see Williamson, *The English Channel*, pages 46–7.

21 Schama, *A History of Britain*, page 36.

22 Ibid., page 40.

23 King (ed.), *Baedae; Opera Historica*, Vol. I, page 59.

Chapter 2

1   Stenton, *Anglo-Saxon England*, page 1.

2   Swanton (ed.), *The Anglo-Saxon Chronicle*, page 13.

3   Scott Moncrieff (ed.), *Beowulf*, page 14.

4   King (ed.), *Baedae: Opera Historica*, Vol. 1, page 71.

5   Schama, *A History of Britain*, page 44.

6   Swanton (ed.), *Anglo-Saxon Chronicle*, page 15.

7   Gildas, *De Excidio Britanniae*, cited in Schama, *A History of Britain*, page 44.

8   Davies, *The Isles*, page 139.

9   King (ed.), *Baedae: Opera Historica*, Vol. 1, pages 77–9.

10 Ibid., Vol. 2, page 75–7.

11 Cited in Lacey and Danziger, *The Year 1000*, page 60.

12 Swanton (ed.), *Anglo-Saxon Chronicle*, page 22.

13 Julius Caesar, *The Conquest of Gaul*, page 111.

14 Cited in Lacey and Danziger, *The Year 1000*, page 32.

15 Schama, *A History of Britain*, page 64.

16 Swanton (ed.), *The Anglo-Saxon Chronicle*, page 91.

17 Ibid., page 54.

18 Ibid., page 63.

19 Cited in Magnusson and Forman, *Viking: Hammer of the North*, page 22.

20 Swanton (ed.), *The Anglo-Saxon Chronicle*, page 65.

21 Cited in Lacey and Danziger, *The Year 1000*, pages 77–8.

22 Swanton (ed.), *The Anglo-Saxon Chronicle*, page 90.

23 Ibid., pages 77–9.

24 Ibid., page 132.

25 Ibid., page 158.

26 Davies, *The Isles*, page 236.

27 Swanton (ed.), *The Anglo-Saxon Chronicle*, page 196.

28 Ibid., page 199.

29 Douglas (ed.), *English Historical Documents*, Vol. II, page 224.

30 Swanton (ed.), *The Anglo-Saxon Chronicle*, page 199.

31 Douglas (ed.), *English Historical Documents*, Vol. II, page 229.

Chapter 3

1 Swanton (ed.), *The Anglo-Saxon Chronicle*, page 209.

2 Ibid., page 212.

3 Ibid., pages 213–14.

4 Ibid., page 238.

5 Ibid., pages 257–8.

6 Ibid., page 258.

7 Ibid., page 219.

8 Ibid., page 237.

9 Cited in Ward, *Brittany and Normandy*, pages 135–6.

10 Swanton (ed.), *The Anglo-Saxon Chronicle*, page 249.

11 Douglas (ed.), *English Historical Documents*, Vol. II, page 297.

12 Feiling, *A History of England*, page 117.

13 Swanton (ed.), *The Anglo-Saxon Chronicle*, page 268.

14 Schama, *A History of Britain*, page 121.

15 Arnold-Baker, *The Companion to British History*, pages 629–30.

16 Attwater, *The Penguin Dictionary of Saints*, page 317.

17 Cited in ibid.

18 Ibid., pages 317–18.

19 Schama, *A History of Britain*, page 164.

Chapter 4

1 Cited in Burne, *The Crécy War*, page 54.

2 Ibid., page 55.

3 Froissart, *Chronicles*, page 54.

4 Ibid., page 56.

5 Cited in Burne, *The Crécy War*, page 214.

6 Froissart, *Chronicles*, page 59.

7 Cited in Brentnall, *The Cinque Ports*, pages 155–6.

8 Shakespeare, *Henry V*, Act IV, Scene 1.

9 Keegan, *The Face of Battle*, page 79.

10 Cited in Ward, *Brittany and Normandy*, page 86.

11 Burne, *The Agincourt War*, page 267.

12 Froissart, *Chronicles*, page 273.

Chapter 5

1 Davies, *The Isles*, page 378.

2 Cited in Brentnall, *The Cinque Ports*, page 249.

3 Schama, *A History of Britain*, page 292.

4 Cited in Pollard, *Tudor Tracts*, pages 4, 5.

5 Cited in Rule, *The Mary Rose*, page 25.

6 Sir Peter Carew, cited in Rule, ibid., page 37.

7 Cited in *The Mary Rose*, The Mary Rose Trust, page 3.

8 Cited in Holinshed, *Chronicles*, page 137.

9 Cited in Pollard, *Tudor Tracts*, page 290.

10 Davies, *The Isles*, page 397.

11 Ibid., page 434.

Chapter 6

1 Rowse, *The Expansion of Elizabethan England*, page 240.

2 Waugh, *Edmund Campion*, page 55.

3 Cited in ibid., page 203.

4 Cited in Longmate, *Defending the Island*, Pimlico edn, page 431.

5 Mattingly, *The Defeat of the Spanish Armada*, page 17.

6 Cited in ibid., page 17.

7 Cited in Rowse, *The Expansion of Elizabethan England*, page 246.

8 Cited in Mattingly, *The Defeat of the Spanish Armada*, page 190.

9 They are tabulated in Appendix I in Martin and Parker, *The Spanish Armada*.

10 Mattingly, *The Defeat of the Spanish Armada*, page 293.

11 Cited in ibid., page 304.

12 Martin and Parker, *The Spanish Armada*, page 3.

13 Cited in Pollard, *Tudor Tracts*, pages 485–6.

14 Cited in Mattingly, *The Defeat of the Spanish Armada*, page 315.

15 Cited in Rowse, *The England of Elizabeth*, page 14.

16 Shakespeare, *Richard II*, Act II, Scene 1.

17 Bacon, *Of the True Greatness of Kingdoms, Etc*, in Whateley (ed.), *Bacon's Essays*, page 291.

Chapter 7

1 Recorded in Mencken (ed.), *A New Dictionary of Quotations on Historical Principles*, page 840.

2 Cited in Buchan, *Oliver Cromwell*, page 422.

3 Latham (ed.), *The Shorter Pepys*, page 34.

4 Ibid., page 40.

5 Ibid., page 53.

6 Ibid., page 626.

7 Ibid., page 785.

8 Ibid., page 788.

9 Ibid., page 1023.

10 Morris (ed.), *The Illustrated Journeys of Celia Fiennes*, pages 122–9.

11 Ibid., pages 69, 71, 73 and 197.

12 Ibid., pages 206–7.

13 Williamson, *The English Channel*, page 260.

14 Belloc, *The Cruise of the Nona*, pages 180, 181.

15 Cited in Williamson, *The English Channel*, page 335.

Chapter 8

1 John Ireland, *Hogarth Illustrated*, cited in Shesgreen (ed.), *Engravings by Hogarth*, page 72.

2 Cited in Shesgreen, ibid., pages xxvii–xxviii.

3 Defoe, *A Tour Through the Whole Island of Great Britain*, page 57.

4 Morris (ed.), *The Illustrated Journeys of Celia Fiennes*, page 202.

5 Voltaire, *History of the War of 1741*, page 1.

6 Defoe, *A Tour Through the Whole Island of Great Britain*, pages 56–7.

7 Cited in Johnson, *The Offshore Islanders*, page 248.

8 Defoe, *A Tour Through the Whole Island of Great Britain*, page 52.

Chapter 9

1 Cited in Guttman, *Defiance at Sea*, page 19.
2 Cited in ibid., page 22.
3 Rodger, *The Wooden World*, page 31.
4 Both engravings are reproduced in Shesgreen, *Engravings by Hogarth*, Plates 90, 91.
5 Boswell, *London Journal*, page 74.
6 Cited in Mackesy, *The War for America*, page 196.

Chapter 10

1 Cited in Schama, *Citizens*, page 320.
2 Macdonell, *Napoleon and His Marshals*, pages 27–28.
3 Cited in Longford, *The Years of the Sword*, page 83.
4 Cited in Oman, *Nelson*, page 470.
5 Cited in ibid., page 475.
6 Mahan, *The Life of Nelson: The Embodiment of the Sea Power of Great Britain*, page 521.
7 Cited in ibid., pages 521–2.
8 Macdonell, *Napoleon and His Marshals*, page 85.
9 Ibid.
10 Mahan, *The Influence of Sea Power upon the French Revolution and Empire 1793–1812.*, Vol. 2, page 118.
11 Macdonell, *Napoleon and His Marshals*, page 101.
12 Victor Hugo, *The Battle of Waterloo*, cited in Strawson, *The Duke and the Emperor*, pages 229–30.
13 Cited in Rose, *Life of Napoleon*, Vol. I, page 523.

Chapter 11

1 Pevsner, *The Buildings of England: Hampshire*, page 350.
2 Guedalla, *The Second Empire*, page 95.
3 Cobbett, *Rural Rides*, cited in Trevelyan, *Illustrated English Social History*, Vol. IV, page 28.
4 Hueffer, *The Cinque Ports*, page 45.

5 A story in Julian Barnes's collection *Cross Channel* describes the impact on French sensibilities of the English navvies who drove a railway line through the Normandy uplands to the coast.

6 McMullen, *Down Channel*, page 185.

7 Ibid., page 45.

8 Ibid., page 216.

9 Cited in Longford, *Pillar of State*, page 458.

10 Cited in Longmate, *Island Fortress*, page 353.

11 Ibid., page 356.

12 Blériot, in *Eyewitness to History*, ed. John Carey; cited in website: www.ourworld.compuserve.com/homepages/OLDNEWS/bleriot.htm

13 Belloc, *The Cruise of the Nona*, page 240.

14 Ibid., page 150.

Chapter 12

1 Cited in Longmate, *Island Fortress*, page 415.

2 Cited in Gilbert, *First World War*, page 35.

3 2nd Lt Jack Girling, cited in Macdonald, *Voices and Images of the Great War*, page 89.

4 Lt Crosse, 2nd Battalion Oxford and Buckinghamshire Light Infantry, cited in ibid., page 15.

5 *The Times*, 25 August 1914, cited in Macdonald, *Voices and Images of the Great War*, page 20.

6 Cited in Keegan, *The First World War*, page 38.

7 Brown, *The Imperial War Museum Book of the Western Front*, page xix.

8 CSM Sidney Chaplin, 4th Battalion, Gloucestershire Regiment, cited in Macdonald, *Voices and Images of the Great War*, page 93.

9 Graves, *Goodbye to All That*, page 132.

10 Sassoon, *Memoirs of an Infantry Officer*, page 128.

11 Private Notley, cited in Allison and Fairley, *The Monocled Mutineer*, page 60.

12 Private Reg Lawrence, 3rs South African Infantry Battalion, cited in Macdonald, *Voices and Images of the Great War*, page 219.

13 CSM John Gray, Gordon Highlanders, cited in Allison and Fairley, *The Monocled Mutineer*, page 59.

14 Sassoon, *Memoirs of an Infantry Officer*, page 88.

15 Sapper E. Davidson, RE, cited in Macdonald, *Voices and Images of the Great War*, page 180.

16 Sassoon, *Memoirs of an Infantry Officer*, page 90.

17 Lewis, *Sagittarius Rising*, page 92.

18 Cited in Halpern, *A Naval History of World War I*, page 346.

19 Capt. C. M. Slack, 4th Battalion, East Yorkshire Regiment, cited in Macdonald, *Voices and Images of the Great War*, page 268.

20 Cited in Keegan, *The First World War*, page 430.

21 Cited in Gilbert, *First World War*, page 409.

22 Private H. J. Haynes, 2nd/6th Battalion, Royal Warwickshire Regiment, cited in Macdonald, *Voices and Images of the Great War*, page 267.

23 Cited in Gilbert, *First World War*, page 409.

24 Macdonald, *To the Last Man, Spring 1918*, page 143.

25 Cited in Keegan, *The First World War*, page 435.

26 Cited in Gilbert, *First World War*, page 414.

Chapter 13

1 For this and later quotations from Belloc, *The Voyage of the Nona*, see pages 102, 141, 142, 143, 144, 231, 239.

2 Greene, *Brighton Rock*, page 6.

3 Ibid., page 62.

4 Waugh, *Men at Arms*, page 197.

5 Cited in Smith, *Channel Crossing*, page 18.

Chapter 14

1 Alanbrooke, *War Diaries 1939–1945*, page 4.

2 Cited in Davies, *The Isles*, page 750.

3 Alanbrooke, *War Diaries 1939–1945*, page 37.

4 Ibid., page 59.

5 Colville, *The Fringes of Power*, page 131.

6 Ibid., page 133.

7 Cited in Jenkins, *Churchill*, page 594.

8 Colville, *The Fringes of Power*, page 137.

9 Cited in Gilbert, *Second World War*, page 73.

10 Cited in Lord, *The Miracle of Dunkirk*, page 47.

11 Colville, *The Fringes of Power*, page 213.

12 Cited in Warner, *The Battle of France*, page 166.

13 Ibid., page 170.

14 Cited in Nicolson, *Alex*, page 142.

15 Cited in Gilbert, *Second World War*, page 90.

16 Cited in ibid., page 92.

17 Alanbrooke, *War Diaries 1939–1945*, page 74.

18 Jenkins, *Churchill*, page 619.

19 Colville, *The Fringes of Power*, page 161.

Chapter 15

1 Colville, *The Fringes of Power*, page 134.

2 Cited in Hough and Richards, *The Battle of Britain*, page 90.

3 Cited in Gilbert, *Second World War*, page 104.

4 Cited in Ray, *The Battle of Britain*, page 29.

5 Cited in Saunders, *Channel Defences*, page 101.

6 Cited in Colville, *The Fringes of Power*, page 212.

7 Cited in Parker, *The Battle of Britain*, pages 182–3.

8 Cited in Hough and Richards, *The Battle of Britain*, page 154.

9 Cited in Gilbert, *Second World War*, page 122.

10 Alanbrooke, *War Diaries 1939–1945*, page 107.

11 Cited in Colville, *The Fringes of Power*, pages 146–7.

12 Hough and Richards, *The Battle of Britain*, page 135.

Chapter 16

1 Alanbrooke, *War Diaries 1939–1945*, page 138.

2 Cited in Longmate, *Island Fortress*, page 527.

3 Cited in Bouchard, *The Channel Dash Forecast*; www.datasync.com/
   ~bouchard/rich/channel_dash.htm

4 Alanbrooke, *War Diaries 1939–1945*, page 229.

5 Cited in Keegan, *Six Armies in Normandy*, page 121.

6 Alanbrooke, *War Diaries 1939–1945*, page 257.

7 Cited in Ziegler, *Mountbatten*, page 189.

8 Cited in ibid., page 190.

9 Cited in Gilbert, *Second World War*, page 354.

10 Cited in Ziegler, *Mountbatten*, page 186.

11 Jenkins, *Churchill*, page 746.

Chapter 17

1 Cited in Keegan, *Six Armies in Normandy*, page 53.

2 Ibid., page 19.

3 Alanbrooke, *War Diaries 1939–1945*, page 246.

4 Cited in Keegan, *Six Armies in Normandy*, page 65.

5 Ibid., page 14.

6 Eisenhower, *D-Day to VE Day: General Eisenhower's Report 1944-45*, page 71.

7 Ibid., pages 74–75.

8 Colville, *The Fringes of Power*, page 492.

9 Keegan, *Six Armies in Normandy*, page 81.

10 Cited in ibid., page 143.

11 Eisenhower, *D-Day to VE Day: General Eisenhower's Report 1944-45*, page 91.

12 Alanbrooke, *War Diaries 1939–1945*, page 556–7.

13 Cited in Keegan, *Six Armies in Normandy*, page 143.

14 Cited in ibid., page 160.

15 Cited in Gilbert, *Second World War*, page 649.

Chapter 18

1 Coles, *Heavy Weather Sailing*, page 131.

2 Smith, *Channel Crossing*, page 220.

BIBLIOGRAPHY

The story of the English Channel embraces much of English, French and European history. A comprehensive bibliography would be impracticably bulky, and the books listed here do no more than provide sidelights on particular aspects of the Channel's history.

Lord Alanbrooke, *War Diaries 1939-1945*, Phoenix, London, 2001

William Allison and John Fairley, *The Monocled Mutineer*, Quartet, London, 1979

Matthew Arnold, *Poems*, Macmillan, London, 1877

Charles Arnold-Baker, *The Companion to British History*, Longcross Press, Tunbridge Wells, 1996

Donald Attwater, *The Penguin Dictionary of Saints*, Penguin, London, 1965

C N Barclay, *Battle 1066*, Dent, London, 1966

Julian Barnes, *Cross Channel*, Picador, London, 1997

Venerable Bede (J E King ed.), *Bede: Opera Historica*, Heinemann, London, 1930

Hilaire Belloc, *The Cruise of the Nona*, Constable, London, 1925

James Boswell, *London Journal*, Reprint Society, London, 1952

Margaret Brentnall, *The Cinque Ports and Romney Marsh*, Gifford, London, 1980

Malcolm Brown, *The Imperial War Museum Book of the Western Front*, Macmillan, London, 1993

John Buchan, *Oliver Cromwell*, Reprint Society, London, 1941

Alfred H Burne, *The Crécy War*, Wordsworth, London, 1999

Alfred H Burne, *The Agincourt War*, Wordsworth, London, 1999

Julius Caesar, *The Civil War*, Penguin, London, 1967

Julius Caesar, *The Conquest of Gaul*, Penguin, London, 1951

Richard Cobb, *The French and Their Revolution*, Murray, London, 1998

K Adlard Coles, *Heavy Weather Sailing*, Adlard Coles, London, 1967

William Cobbett, *Rural Rides*, London, 1830

Linda Colley, *Britons: Forging the Nation, 1707-1837*, Pimlico, London, 1992

John Colville, *The Fringes of Power*, Hodder & Stoughton, London, 1985

Barry Cunliffe, *Facing the Ocean*, Oxford University Press, Oxford, 2001

Barry Cunliffe, *The Extraordinary Voyage of Pytheas the Greek*, Penguin, London, 2001

Barry Cunliffe, *Fishbourne: A Guide to the Site*, Sussex Archaeological Society, Chichester, 1977

Norman Davies, *Europe*, Oxford University Press, Oxford, 1996

Norman Davies, *The Isles*, Macmillan, London, 2000

David C Douglas, *English Historical Documents*, Eyre & Spotiswode, London, 1953

Bernard Dumpleton, *The Story of the Paddle Steamer*, Venton, Melksham, 1973

Dwight D Eisenhower, *D Day to VE Day: General Eisenhower's Report 1944–45*, HMSO, London, 2000

Keith Feiling, *A History of England*, Macmillan, London, 1951

John Froissart, *Chronicles*, Routledge, London, 1891

P N Furbank and W R Owens (eds.), *Daniel Defoe: A Tour Through the Whole Island of Great Britain*, Yale University Press, New Haven, 1991

Charles E Gibson, *The Story of the Ship*, Abelard–Schuman, London, 1958

Martin Gilbert, *First World War*, Weidenfeld & Nicholson, London, 1994

Martin Gilbert, *Second World War*, Fontana, London, 1989

Robert Graves, *Goodbye to All That*, Folio Society, London, 1981

Graham Greene, *Brighton Rock*, Penguin, London, 1954

Philip Guedalla, *The Second Empire*, Hodder & Stoughton, London, 1922

Jon Guttman, *Defiance at Sea*, Cassell, London, 2002

Paul G Halpern, *A Naval History of World War I*, University College London, London, 1994

Peter Hawes and Mark Holloway, *Hengistbury Head Archaeology Trail*, Bournemouth Leisure & Tourism, Bournemouth, 1994

Raphael Holinshed, *Chronicles*, London, 1808

Richard Hough and Denis Richards, *The Battle of Britain*, Penguin, London, 2001

Ford Madox Hueffer, *The Cinque Ports*, Blackwood, Edinburgh, 1900

Geoff Hutchinson, *The Battle of Hastings, 1066: A Brief History*, Hutchinson, Hastings, 1998

Roy Jenkins, *Churchill*, Macmillan, London, 2000

Paul Johnson, *A History of the English People*, Phoenix, London, 1995

John Keegan, *The Face of Battle*, Vintage, New York, 1977

John Keegan, *The First World War*, Random Century, London, 1998

John Keegan, *Six Armies in Normandy*, Pimlico, London, 1992

Charles Kingsley, *The Poems of Charles Kingsley*, Dent, London, 1927

Rudyard Kipling, *The Works of Rudyard Kipling*, Wordsworth, Ware, 1994

Robert Latham (ed.), *The Shorter Pepys*, London, 1985

Robert Lacey and Danny Danziger, *The Year 1000*, Abacus, London, 1999

Yves Lecouturier, *The Beaches of the D-Day Landings*, Editions Ouest-France, Rennes, 1999

Cecil Lewis, *Sagittarius Rising*, Folio Society, London, 1936

Elizabeth Longford, *Wellington: the Years of the Sword*, Panther, London, 1971

Elizabeth Longford, *Wellington: Pillar of State*, Panther, London, 1975

Norman Longmate, *Defending the Island* and *Island Fortress*, Pimlico, London, 2001

Walter Lord, *The Miracle of Dunkirk*, Wordsworth, London, 1998

Lyn Macdonald, *1914–1918: Voices and Images of the Great War*, Penguin, London, 1988

Lyn Macdonald, *To the Last Man: Spring 1918*, Viking, London, 1998

A G Macdonell, *Napoleon and his Marshals*, Macmillan, London, 1950

Piers Mackesy, *The War for America*, Longmans, London, 1964

Magnus Magnusson and Werner Forman, *Viking: Hammer of the North*, Orbis, London, 1979

A T Mahan, *The Influence of Sea Power upon the French Revolution and Empire, 1793-1812*, Sampson Low, London, 1893

A T Mahan, *The Life of Nelson: The Embodiment of the Sea Power of Great Britain*, Sampson Low, London, 1899

Colin Martin and Geoffrey Parker, *The Spanish Armada*, Mandolin, Manchester, 1999

Garrett Mattingly, *The Defeat of the Spanish Armada*, Pimlico, London, 2000

R T McMullen, *Down Channel*, Hart-Davis, London, 1949

Christopher Morris (ed.), *The Illustrated Journeys of Celia Fiennes*, Michael Joseph, London, 1982

James Morris, *Pax Britannica*, Faber, London, 1968

Nigel Nicolson, *Alex*, Pan, London, 1976

Carola Oman, *Nelson*, Reprint Society, London, 1950

Matthew Parker, *The Battle of Britain*, Headline, London, 2000

A Temple Patterson, *Southampton*, Macmillan, London, 1970

Nikolaus Pevsner, *The Buildings of England: Hampshire*, Penguin, London, 1967

A F Pollard, *Tudor Tracts 1532-88*, Longmans, London, 1903

John Pollock, *Harold Rex*, Bosham, 1996

John Ray, *The Battle of Britain*, Cassell, London, 2000

Jasper Ridley, *A Brief History of the Tudor Age*, Robinson, London, 2002

N A M Rodger, *The Wooden World*, Collins, London, 1986

J H Rose, *Life of Napoleon I*, Bell, London, 1904

A L Rowse, *The England of Elizabeth*, Macmillan, London, 1951

A L Rowse, *The Expansion of Elizabethan England*, Macmillan, London, 1955

Margaret Rule, *The Mary Rose*, Conway, London, 1982

Mogens Rud, *The Bayeux Tapestry and the Battle of Hastings, 1066*, Christian Eilers, Copenhagen, 1988

Cornelius Ryan, *The Longest Day*, Wordsworth, New York, 1999

Siegfried Sassoon, *Memoirs of an Infantry Officer*, Faber, London, 1930

Andrew Saunders, *Channel Defences*, Batsford, London, 1997

Simon Schama, *A History of Britain*, BBC Books, London, 2001

Simon Schama, *Citizens: A Chronicle of the French Revolution*, Viking, London, 1989

C K Scott Moncrieff (tr.), *Beowulf*, Chapman & Hall, London, 1921

Peter Sedgley, *Wings Over the Solent*, Red Funnel Ferries, Southampton

W C Sellar and R J Yeatman, *1066 and All That*, Methuen, London, 1930

Sean Shesgreen, *Engravings by Hogarth*, Dover, New York, 1973

Jack Simmons, *The Victorian Railway*, Thames & Hudson, London, 1991

Humphrey Slater and Correlli Barnett, *The Channel Tunnel*, Wingate, London, 1958

Sebastian Smith, *Channel Crossing*, Hamish Hamilton, London, 2001

Frank Stenton, *Anglo-Saxon England*, Oxford University Press, Oxford, 1943

John Strawson, *The Duke and The Emperor*, Constable, London, 1994

Michael Swanton (ed.), *The Anglo-Saxon Chronicle*, Dent, London, 1996

Tacitus, *The Agricola*, Penguin, London, 1948

Voltaire, *History of the War of 1741*, Nourse, London, 1756

Greg Ward, *Brittany and Normandy*, Rough Guides, London, 1999

Philip Warner, *The Battle of France*, Simon & Schuster, London, 1990

Kathy Watson, *The Crossing*, Headline, London, 2000

Evelyn Waugh, *Edmund Campion*, Longmans, London, 1935

Evelyn Waugh, *Men at Arms*, Penguin, London, 1976

Richard Whateley (ed.), *Bacon's Essays*, Parker, London, 1857

L G Wickham Legg (ed.), *Select Documents of the French Revolution*, Oxford University Press, Oxford, 1905

J A Williamson, *The English Channel*, Collins, London, 1959

Philip Ziegler, *Mountbatten*, Fontana, London, 1986

INDEX

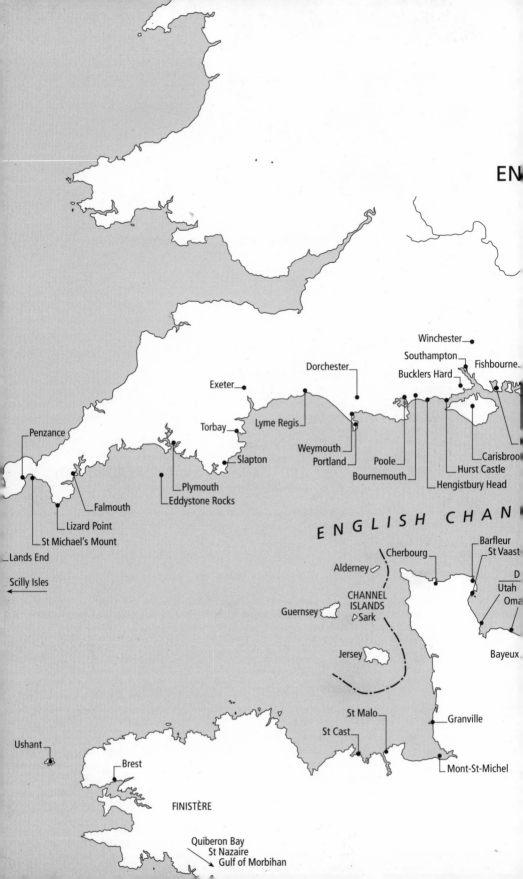

ENGLISH CHANNEL map

Winchester

Southampton
Bucklers Hard
Fishbourne

Dorchester

Exeter

Torbay
Lyme Regis

Weymouth
Portland
Poole
Carisbrook

Penzance
Slapton
Bournemouth
Hurst Castle

Plymouth
Hengistbury Head

Falmouth
Eddystone Rocks

Lizard Point

St Michael's Mount

Lands End

Scilly Isles

ENGLISH CHAN

Cherbourg
Barfleur
St Vaast

Alderney

D
Utah
Oma

CHANNEL
ISLANDS
Guernsey
Sark
Jersey

Bayeux

St Malo
Granville

St Cast

Ushant
Brest
Mont-St-Michel

FINISTÈRE

Quiberon Bay
St Nazaire
Gulf of Morbihan